Nineteenth-Century Major Lives and Letters

Series Editor: Marilyn Gaull

This series presents original biographical, critical, and scholarly studies of literary works and public figures in Great Britain, North America, and continental Europe during the nineteenth century. The volumes in *Nineteenth-Century Major Lives and Letters* evoke the energies, achievements, contributions, cultural traditions, and individuals who reflected and generated them during the Romantic and Victorian periods. The topics: critical, textual, and historical scholarship, literary and book history, biography, cultural and comparative studies, critical theory, art, architecture, science, politics, religion, music, language, philosophy, aesthetics, law, publication, translation, domestic and public life, popular culture, and anything that influenced, impinges upon, expresses, or contributes to an understanding of the authors, works, and events of the nineteenth century. The authors consist of political figures, artists, scientists, and cultural icons including William Blake, Thomas Hardy, Charles Darwin, William Wordsworth, William Butler Yeats, Samuel Taylor Coleridge, and their contemporaries.

The series editor is Marilyn Gaull, PhD (Indiana University), FEA. She has taught at William and Mary, Temple University, New York University, and is Research Professor at the Editorial Institute at Boston University. She is the founder and editor of *The Wordsworth Circle* and the author of *English Romanticism: The Human Context*, and editions, essays, and reviews in journals. She lectures internationally on British Romanticism, folklore, and narrative theory, intellectual history, publishing procedures, and history of science.

PUBLISHED BY PALGRAVE MACMILLAN:

Shelley's German Afterlives, by Susanne Schmid
Coleridge, the Bible, and Religion, by Jeffrey W. Barbeau
Romantic Literature, Race, and Colonial Encounter, by Peter J. Kitson
Byron, edited by Cheryl A. Wilson
Romantic Migrations, by Michael Wiley
The Long and Winding Road from Blake to the Beatles, by Matthew Schneider
British Periodicals and Romantic Identity, by Mark Schoenfield
Women Writers and Nineteenth-Century Medievalism, by Clare Broome Saunders
British Victorian Women's Periodicals, by Kathryn Ledbetter
Romantic Diasporas, by Toby R. Benis
Romantic Literary Families, by Scott Krawczyk
Victorian Christmas in Print, by Tara Moore
Culinary Aesthetics and Practices in Nineteenth-Century American Literature, edited by Monika Elbert and Marie Drews
Reading Popular Culture in Victorian Print, by Alberto Gabriele
Romanticism and the Object, edited by Larry H. Peer
Poetics en passant, by Anne Jamison
From Song to Print, by Terence Allan Hoagwood
Gothic Romanticism, by Tom Duggett
Victorian Medicine and Social Reform, by Louise Penner
Populism, Gender, and Sympathy in the Romantic Novel, by James P. Carson
Byron and the Rhetoric of Italian Nationalism, by Arnold Anthony Schmidt
Poetry and Public Discourse in Nineteenth-Century America, by Shira Wolosky
The Discourses of Food in Nineteenth-Century British Fiction, by Annette Cozzi

Romanticism and Pleasure, edited by Thomas H. Schmid and Michelle Faubert
Royal Romances, by Kristin Flieger Samuelian
Trauma, Transcendence, and Trust, by Thomas J. Brennan, S.J.
The Business of Literary Circles in Nineteenth-Century America, by David Dowling
Popular Medievalism in Romantic-Era Britain, by Clare A. Simmons
Beyond Romantic Ecocriticism, by Ashton Nichols
The Poetry of Mary Robinson, by Daniel Robinson
Romanticism and the City, edited by Larry H. Peer
Coleridge and the Daemonic Imagination, by Gregory Leadbetter
Dante and Italy in British Romanticism, edited by Frederick Burwick and Paul Douglass
Jewish Representation in British Literature 1780–1840, by Michael Scrivener
Romantic Dharma, by Mark S. Lussier
Robert Southey, by Stuart Andrews
Playing to the Crowd, by Frederick Burwick
The Regions of Sara Coleridge's Thought, by Peter Swaab
John Thelwall in the Wordsworth Circle, by Judith Thompson
Wordsworth and Coleridge, by Peter Larkin
Turning Points in Natural Theology from Bacon to Darwin, by Stuart Peterfreund
Sublime Coleridge, by Murray J. Evans
Longing to Belong, by Sarah Juliette Sasson
British Literary Salons of the Late Eighteenth and Early Nineteenth Centuries, by
    Susanne Schmid
Coleridge's Experimental Poetics, by J. C. C. Mays
Emily Dickinson's Rich Conversation, by Richard E. Brantley
Sara Coleridge, by Jeffrey W. Barbeau
Staging Romantic Chameleons and Imposters, by William D. Brewer
John Thelwall, edited by Judith Thompson
Other British Voices, by Timothy Whelan
Louisa Stuart Costello, by Clare Broome Saunders
Romantic Poetry and Literary Coteries, by Tim Fulford

Romantic Poetry and Literary Coteries
The Dialect of the Tribe

Tim Fulford

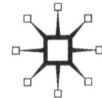
First published in 2015 by
PALGRAVE MACMILLAN®
in the United States—a division of St. Martin's Press LLC,
175 Fifth Avenue, New York, NY 10010.

Where this book is distributed in the UK, Europe and the rest of the world,
this is by Palgrave Macmillan, a division of Macmillan Publishers Limited,
registered in England, company number 785998, of Houndmills,
Basingstoke, Hampshire RG21 6XS.

Palgrave Macmillan is the global academic imprint of the above companies
and has companies and representatives throughout the world.

Palgrave® and Macmillan® are registered trademarks in the United States,
the United Kingdom, Europe and other countries.

ISBN: 978–1–137–53396–8

Library of Congress Cataloging-in-Publication Data

Fulford, Tim, 1962–
    Romantic poetry and literary coteries : the dialect of the
tribe / Tim Fulford.
        pages cm.—(Nineteenth-century major lives and letters)
    Summary: "How does Romantic poetry read if seen as the product of
social authorship—the group language of coteries of writers, editors,
publishers and critics—rather than as a series of verbal icons—original
lyrics and romances composed by individual geniuses? Romantic Poetry
and Literary Coteries explores Romanticism as a discourse characterized
by tropes and forms that were jointly produced by literary circles –
writing communities – in self-conscious opposition to prevailing social
and political values and in deliberate differentiation from the normal
practices of contemporary print culture. Among the tropes examined
are allusion and borrowing; among the forms discussed are blank-verse
effusions, political squibs, magazine essays, millenarian prophecies,
long-form notebook verse, illustrated tour poems and prose journals.
Coteries considered comprize the Southey/Coleridge circle, including
Bowles, Cottle, Cowper, Lamb, Lloyd, Robinson and Wordsworth; the
Bloomfield circle, including Capel Lofft and Thomas Hood; the Clare
circle, including Byron, Cowper, William Knight and John Taylor; the
Cockneys, including Richard Brothers, William Bryan, De Quincey, Hood,
Leigh Hunt, Robert Mudie, Patmore"—Provided by publisher.
    Includes bibliographical references and index.
    ISBN 978–1–137–53396–8 (hardback)
    1. English poetry—19th century—History and criticism.
2. Romanticism—England. 3. Literature and society—England—
History—19th century. 4. Poets, English—19th century. I. Title.
PR590.F86 2015
821'.709145—dc23   2015006813

A catalogue record of the book is available from the British Library.

Design by Newgen Knowledge Works (P) Ltd., Chennai, India.

First edition: August 2015

10 9 8 7 6 5 4 3 2 1

Contents

Acknowledgments   vii

List of Abbreviations   ix

Introduction   1

Part I   "A Sect of Poets": The Dialect of Friendship in Southey, Coleridge, and Their Circles

1   The Politicization of Allusion in Early Romanticism: Mary Robinson and the Bristol Poets   23

2   Brothers in Lore: Fraternity and Priority in *Thalaba*, "Christabel," and "Kubla Khan"   63

3   Signifying Nothing: Coleridge's Visions of 1816— Anti-allusion and the Poetic Fragment   79

4   Positioning *The Missionary*: Poetic Circles and the Development of Colonial Romance   99

Part II   The "Rural Tribe": Laboring-Class Poets and the Tradition

5   The Production of a Poet: Robert Bloomfield, His Patrons, and His Publishers   131

6   Iamb Yet What Iamb: Allusion and Delusion in John Clare's Asylum Poems   165

Part III   The Lingo of Londoners: The "Cockney School"

7   Romanticism Lite: Talking, Walking, and Name-Dropping in the Cockney Essay   189

8 Allusions of Grandeur: Prophetic Authority and
   the Romantic City   213

Notes   233
Index   255

Acknowledgments

My thanks to all those who have helped shape this book, notably Kerri Andrews, Stuart Andrews, Sally Bushell, Carol Bolton, Julia S. Carlson, Paul Cheshire, Jeff Cox, Ashley Cross, David Fairer, Marilyn Gaull, John Goodridge, Lynne Hapgood, Ian Haywood, David Higgins, Simon Kovesi, Greg Kucich, Peter Larkin, Lucy Newlyn, Morton D. Paley, Dahlia Porter, Lynda Pratt, Matthew Sangster, David Vallins, Alan Vardy, and Joshua Wilner. Some chapters were derived in part from the following articles: "The Electrifying Mrs. Robinson," *Women's Writing*, 9 (2002), 23–36 (part of chapter 1); "Coleridge's Sequel to *Thalaba* and Robert Southey's Prequel to *Christabel*," *Coleridge, Romanticism and the Orient: Cultural Negotiations*, ed. David Vallins, Kaz Oishi, and Seamus Perry (London: Bloomsbury, 2013), pp. 55–70 (part of chapter 2); "Coleridge's Visions of 1816: the Political Unconscious and the Poetic Fragment," *Romanticism and Victorianism on the Net*, 61 (April 2012) (part of chapter 3); "British Romantics and Native Americans: The Araucanians of Chile," *Studies in Romanticism*, 47 (2008), 225–52 (part of chapter 4); "To 'crown with glory the romantick scene': Robert Bloomfield's 'To Immagination' and the Discourse of Romanticism," *Romanticism*, 15 (2009), 181–200 (part of chapter 5); "Bloomfield in His Letters: The Social World of a London Shoemaker Turned Suffolk Poet," in *Robert Bloomfield: The Inestimable Blessing of Letters*, ed. John Goodridge and Bridget Keegan, *Romantic Circles Praxis* (January 2012) (part of chapters 5 and 7); "Personating Poets on the Page: John Clare in His Asylum Notebooks," *John Clare Society Journal*, 32 (2013), 27–48 (part of chapter 6); "Talking, Walking, and Working: The Cockney Clerk, the Suburban Ramble, and the Invention of Leisure," *Essays in Romanticism*, 18 (2011), 75–95 (part of chapter 7); "Babylon and Jerusalem on the Old Kent Road," in *Romanticism and the City*, ed. Larry Peer (New York: Palgrave Macmillan, 2011), pp. 241–59 (part of chapter 8).

ABBREVIATIONS

Banks of Wye	*The Banks of Wye*, ed. Tim Fulford, (Romantic Circles Online Edition). *http://www.rc.umd.edu/editions/wye*
BL	*The Letters of Robert Bloomfield and His Circle*, ed. Tim Fulford and Lynda Pratt, (Romantic Circles Online Edition). http://www.rc.umd.edu/editions/bloomfield_letters/
ByPW	*The Complete Poetical Works*, ed. Jerome J. McGann and Barry Weller, 7 vols. (Oxford: Oxford University Press, 1991)
CBL	S. T. Coleridge, *Biographia Literaria*, ed. James Engell and W. Jackson Bate, 2 vols. (London and Princeton: Princeton University Press, 1983)
Christabel	S. T. Coleridge, *Christabel, Kubla Khan, the Pains of Sleep* (London, 1816).
CL	*Collected Letters of Samuel Taylor Coleridge*, ed. E. L. Griggs, 6 vols. (London: Oxford University Press, 1956–1971)
CN	*Collected Notebooks of Samuel Taylor Coleridge*, ed. Kathleen Coburn, 5 vols. (London and Princeton: Princeton University Press, 1957–2002)
Cowper	*The Poems of William Cowper*, ed. John D. Baird and Charles Ryskamp, 3 vols. (Oxford: Oxford University Press, 1980)
CPW	S. T. Coleridge, *Poetical Works*, ed. J. C. C. Mays, 6 vols. (London and Princeton: Princeton University Press, 2001)
DeQ	*The Works of Thomas De Quincey*, gen. ed. Grevel Lindop, 21 vols. (London: Pickering and Chatto, 1999–2002)
EOT	S. T. Coleridge, *Essays on His Times*, ed. David V. Erdman, 3 vols. (London and Princeton: Princeton University Press, 1978)

Excursion	*The Excursion*, ed. Sally Bushell, James A. Butler, and Michael C. Jaye (Ithaca and London: Cornell University Press, 2007)
Friend	S. T. Coleridge, *The Friend*, ed. Barbara E. Rooke, 2 vols. (London and Princeton: Princeton University Press, 1969)
Jerusalem	William Blake, *Jerusalem.* blakearchive.org
Lects 1808–19	S. T. Coleridge, *Lectures on Literature 1808–19*, ed. R. A. Foakes, 2 vols. (London and Princeton: Princeton University Press, 1987)
LS	S. T. Coleridge, *Lay Sermons*, ed. R. J. White (London and Princeton: Princeton University Press, 1972)
MRW	*The Works of Mary Robinson*, gen. ed. William D. Brewer, 8 vols. (London: Pickering and Chatto, 2009)
Prelude	William Wordsworth, *The Prelude: The Four Texts (1798, 1799, 1805, 1850)* (Harmondsworth, UK: Penguin, 1995)
SiR	*Studies in Romanticism*
SL	*The Collected Letters of Robert Southey*, gen. eds. Lynda Pratt, Tim Fulford, and Ian Packer (Romantic Circles Online Edition, 2009–) http://www.rc.umd. edu/editions/southey_letters/
Songs	William Blake, *Songs of Innocence and Experience.* blakearchive,org
SPW	*Robert Southey. Poetical Works 1793–1810*, gen. ed. Lynda Pratt, 5 vols. (London: Pickering and Chatto, 2004)
Task	William Cowper, *The Task and Selected Other Poems*, ed. James Sambrook (London and New York: Longman, 1994)
WL	*The Letters of William and Dorothy Wordsworth. I. The Early Years: 1787–1805*, ed. Ernest de Selincourt, rev. Chester L. Shaver (Oxford, 1967) (EY); *The Middle Years, 1806–17*, 2nd ed., ed. E. de Selincourt, rev. Mary Moorman (Oxford, 1969) (MY); *The Later Years*, 2nd ed., ed. Ernest de Selincourt, rev. Alan G. Hill (Oxford: Oxford University Press, 1978) (LY)
WLB	Wordsworth, *Lyrical Ballads and Other Poems 1797–1800*, ed. James Butler and Karen Green (Ithaca and London: Cornell University Press, 1992)

INTRODUCTION

A sect of poets, that has established itself in this country within these ten or twelve years
> —Francis Jeffrey, review of Southey,
> *Thalaba the Destroyer* in
> *The Edinburgh Review*,
> 1 (1803), 63

Few, amid the rural-tribe, have time
To number syllables or play with rhyme
> —George Crabbe, *The Village* (1783),
> lines 25–26

That perverse singularity of judgement which haunts the tribe of poets
> —*Blackwood's Edinburgh Magazine*,
> 10 (August–December 1821), 184,
> on Southey

The real objects of his admiration are the Coterie of Hampstead
> —J. G. Lockhart, "On the Cockney School of Poetry,"
> *Blackwood's Edinburgh Magazine*, 2 (October 1817),
> 38–40, on Leigh Hunt

I have two related aims in *The Dialect of the Tribe*: first, to explore the formative role played in the production of Romanticism by coteries that comprised not only writers but also editors, patrons, booksellers, and critics; second, to understand the significance of the trope that was the hallmark of coterie style—allusion. The coteries I examine overlapped temporally and spatially; they even shared some of their members. Together they forged and reforged a literary language built on new, as well as traditional, uses of allusion.

Romantic coteries were intense friendship groups in which a new poetic language was forged in common, often collaboratively, and usually, at least initially, in private. They involved men and women and they acted as circles of production and consumption as well as composition. Poetry was criticized, edited, transcribed, circulated, performed, heard, and read within the group. It was also made public by the group—in joint recitations, collaborative collections, group anthologies, and house magazines and newspapers. Once made public, the poetry led the group to be defined by its critics—sometimes more tightly than by the poets themselves. "Sect," "gang," and "tribe" were names given by reviewers who recognized that the new poets challenged established taste because their language originated in lower-class speech communities. "Tribe" implied that the poets shared the values and beliefs of the American Indians: they were uncouth, uncivilized, savage. It is this class and racial condescension that T. S. Eliot picked up in his declaration that the poet's task is to "purify the dialect of the tribe." His remark has, for all its implicit distaste, something in common with Wordsworth's argument, in the Preface to *Lyrical Ballads*, that the poet makes "a selection of the real language of men" "purified indeed from . . . its real defects" (WLB, pp. 741, 744). The Preface was viewed as the manifesto of a radical coterie, a "sect of poets": its derivation of poetic language from common speech led conservative critics to brand Wordsworth, Coleridge, Southey, Lamb, and Lloyd as being perversely and politically déclassé. They had mired themselves in lower-class slang and patois but they did not purify it; rather, it tainted them—they were collectively identifiable because they took on the linguistic patterns of uneducated cultural groups—and, in that sense, were tribal.

While Crabbe and *Blackwood's* called laboring-class and Lake writers "tribes," Francis Jeffrey popularized "sect" as the collective noun. The new poetry, it was implied, smacked of the cult phraseology of religious enthusiasts as well as the uncouth terms of savages. It was a collective dialect, a self-reinforcing discourse that dragged traditional literary language into lower-class venues: the chapel and the sweat lodge. To conservative arbiters of taste such as Jeffrey, it was both new and dangerous, and it needed purification from its class affiliations, its social leveling, and its political radicalism. Jeffrey blamed its appearance on Southey, Coleridge, Wordsworth, and their friends. It is this coterie on which I focus first. By the 1960s and 1970s, it was renamed "the Wordsworth circle" and praised rather than blamed— praised in part because it was often reduced to the Wordsworth/ Coleridge axis; other members whose writings did not fit the models of imaginative and symbolic language that critics idealized were relegated to the background.[1] Although those models were challenged in the 1990s, it has taken longer to restore to view the work of the neglected members. Here, developing the work of several recent

scholars,[2] I continue the process of restoration—framing it as a West Country coterie comprising a series of overlapping and shifting partnerships[3] in which—as well as Coleridge and Wordsworth—Southey, De Quincey, Bowles, Mary Robinson, and Charles Lloyd all played parts. Later, in the Lakes, part of this coterie was reconstituted, featuring Southey as strongly as Coleridge and Wordsworth.

The second and third coteries I discuss are those assembled by so-called peasant poets, Crabbe's "rural tribe": Robert Bloomfield and John Clare. These coteries intersected with each other (Clare being an admirer of Bloomfield, who acted as his mentor), and with the kind of poetry the West Country and Lakes coteries had fashioned.

The fourth is the "Cockney school," billed at the time as an urban successor to the "tribe of poets" in the Lakes. The Cockneys were branded as a lower-middle-class coterie who brought onto the page the cant lingo of London tradesmen: they smacked of the shop. Here again I aim to change our understanding of the group—so well discussed by Jeffrey Cox, Greg Kucich, and Gregory Dart[4]—by focusing on some of its less central members—Bloomfield and "cockney Clare"[5] among them—and by emphasizing its ambivalent relationships to the rural poetry of the Lake poets on the one hand, and, on the other, to the Cockney culture common among artisans and tradesmen. Discussing Lamb as well as Thomas Hood and P. G. Patmore, I suggest that in the Cockney coterie the Romantic sublimity fashioned in West Country and Lakes poetry in opposition to London was replayed in the petit bourgeois form of the confessional essay, with a self-reflexive awareness of indebtedness that was overwritten by conscious display of difference. Romanticism, it follows, emerges from my discussions as a dialogue between, on the one hand, provincial and rural groupings and, on the other, their metropolitan followers. Its hallmarks—imagination, sublimity, and confession—were jointly forged by a group of university poets in reaction against London culture and later reforged by circles of laboring and middle-class writers who wrote from that London culture. Yet the country and the city were not simply in opposition, for the discourse of each was inflected by the other: writers such as Bloomfield, Clare, and Leigh Hunt had a foot in both camps. Romanticism was a conflicted response, of both fascination and repulsion, to the commercial and consumerist culture that centered on London. Its trajectory was shaped by spatial, temporal, and class differences, but above all by group identity—by the shared writing and reading practices of literary coteries.

WRITING COMMUNITIES

What is revealed by examining Romanticism as a discourse made and remade in coteries? In what follows I replace emphasis on the solitary author—the sublime egotist Wordsworth and damaged archangel Coleridge—or even on an expanded roster of individual writers—with a social history of literary production in groups. Thus, I analyze poetry in relation to the conditions in which composition, publishing, and reading took place—conditions affected by a culture undergoing a series of rapid transformations that altered the status and role of authors. It was, as Coleridge and Southey put it, an "age of personality" (*Friend*, II, 286–87): one in which a capitalized publishing market served an expanded reading public and scores of new newspapers, journals and magazines traded in the personal—whether by hostile reviews that attacked an author's private character, or by gossip about literary celebrities.[6] The formerly private became public, and writers experienced unprecedented pressures: their self-belief and self-possession, their ability to make a living and to earn reputation, was placed in doubt. As Jon Klancher,[7] Lee Erickson,[8] and Andrew Franta[9] have shown, literary value was put into competition with commercial value as never before. Some were able to bridge the two: among writers who excelled in traditional "high" cultural forms of poetry there were new opportunities of profit and renown for those who learned to trade on their authorial personae. Byron, for instance, earned money and fame from his creation of a poetic persona that seemed to offer access to intimate details of his life.[10] Coleridge, on the other hand, regarded contemporary print culture with suspicion because its commercialization of publication replaced traditional relationships between author, patron, bookseller, and reader with a monetarized relationship between a writer and a distant public whose purchases were guided by reviewers and magazine journalists.

If publication became commercialized, it also became politicized to a new extent. The dramatic acceleration of capitalism altered both living conditions and cultural values. The interrelated rise of imperialism and the manufacturing system, and of consumerism and commodity fetishism, left many people in Britain and the colonies exploited, alienated and disorientated. The resultant political campaigns for reform, fuelled by the example of the French Revolution, triggered a fractious contest for cultural and political authority. Reformers were countered by repressive laws that made direct criticism of the established political and religious order highly dangerous. Campaigners were also resisted by an anti-Jacobin press that attacked radicals' characters, leaving the public sphere personalized as well as politically polarized.[11]

It was under pressure from this politicization, which they traced to London, that young intellectuals banded together in the provinces to support each other's writing and to find ways of gaining access to print. The problems and opportunities presented by a commercialized and politicized public sphere created a group identity, labeled as such by critics and adopted by the writers themselves. Nor was the group confined to writers: editors and publishers were also important in creating the new literary coterie—and indeed some members of the group performed all three roles.[12] At least in the early years of the "Jacobin crew"[13] based in Bristol and Somerset, to be an author was, it appeared, to be part of a group that jointly generated and published text—sometimes even printing that text too. It follows, then, that a figure such as Southey—poet, anthologist, editor, publicist, collaborator—was more significant in shaping the group language than the relatively marginal Wordsworth. The "Bristol sound" was sometimes so much a collaborative production that to speak of a text having one author became meaningless: produced and reproduced for different occasions, it existed in different versions as the work of different combinations of creators (as Jack Stillinger[14] has shown of a number of poems attributed variously to Coleridge, Southey, and Wordsworth singly and in combination[15]).

Investigating Romantic poetry as the product of what Margaret Ezell has called "social authorship"[16] alters our understanding of its creation, production, and consumption—and also changes the picture of the producers involved. If it brings Southey to the fore, it also reminds us that the Bristol circle and Lake sects included women, at times at least—though their participation was not necessarily on an equal basis. In *The Dialect of the Tribe*, I explore the uneasy but nevertheless highly productive inclusion of Mary Robinson in a circle of Bristol writers; I develop recent work by Lucy Newlyn[17] and Susan Wolfson[18] in which the "separate spheres" produced by the critical separation of men's and women's writing are replaced by new tracings of literary relationships that, at their closest, involved a process of shared composition that was mutually formative for both the male and female writer involved. Wolfson has found in the Wordsworths' relationship a new model in which Romantic writing emerges from a constitutive interaction that brings an author into being not as a subject but as an intersubject.[19] And even where the relationship was less close than the Wordsworths', several scholars have found evidence of mutual redefinition. Ashley Cross, for example, has revealed how

Southey and Mary Robinson, though they never met, each came into their own as poets as their work converged in a poetic dialogue conducted in the columns of a newspaper.[20]

Wordsworth's poems provide one example of partnership in action at the center of a literary circle. As Sally Bushell[21] has shown, Wordsworth's household was a poetry workshop, linked to a wider circle that included Southey, Scott, and Coleridge.[22] A poem typically began orally with William and Dorothy walking and talking and then William turning conversation into verse, muttering the measures as he paced back and forth. These measures were moved onto paper by the scriptorial labor of William's female relatives, who might then read aloud what they had written down, whereupon it would be revised, sometimes orally, sometimes directly on the manuscript, and then written out again. Sent to be printed in Bristol and London, the text would be prepared for publication by a friend employed to negotiate with the booksellers and make alterations as it went through the press (for *Lyrical Ballads* this role was played by the coterie member Humphry Davy—chemist, poet, and philosopher). A result of Bushell's work is that we understand even so apparently autonomous and individual an "author" as the "William Wordsworth" credited on the title page of *Lyrical Ballads* (1800/1802) and *Poems in Two Volumes* (1807) as a singular identity for a writing community without which the man William Wordsworth could not move his verse from his mind and his tongue onto the page. Here, I examine similar, though shorter lived, writing workshops formed by Southey and Coleridge, by Bloomfield, his friends and bookseller, and by Clare and his asylum keeper William Knight.

COTERIE LANGUAGE

A social history of the production of Romanticism shows it being generated in partnerships, collaborations, and workshops, being revised and edited by coterie members, and being issued in homemade collections (Coleridge's 1796 sonnets and *The Friend*; Bloomfield's tour poem and sketchbook *The Banks of Wye*, for example). But what does it reveal about Romantic form and style? Here, I offer a series of analyses that aim to reveal, by teasing out the intricate threads that relate one text to another, the ways in which historical pressures were refracted in particular uses of literary tropes that marked and, in part, constituted a common style. These tropes are allusion[23]—modulating, when less self-advertising and declarative,[24] into borrowing,[25] and echo[26]—phrasings that are shared by many members without clearly belonging to one originator, collectively forming a dialect.[27]

In an era in which poetry competed as never before in a professionalized and commercialized literary market, poets displayed their credentials by playfully alluding to and borrowing from the work of popular respected forebears—bolstering their cultural authority by placing themselves "among the English poets";[28] they also referenced each other's words, or published words mutually generated, badging their togetherness and marking their difference from other print genres with which they competed for notice: there was strength in (poetic) numbers. Drawing upon others' words was, then, the flexible resource of writers facing a market that placed the role and identity of the author in doubt; it played a strategic socio-poetic part in fashioning new poetic languages and in redefining the cultural figure of the poet. If it generated an intimate dialogue with fellow poets of past and present, if it obliquely invoked allies, it did so in proportion to the hostility of poets' receptions. Allusion and borrowing characterized a language of intimacy—sometimes, of love—forged in adversity and in response to the babble of publicity. They also, on occasion, featured in a language of critique used to indicate a new-found difference from a collaborator[29] and a language of hate used to attack enemies whom it was too dangerous to criticize directly.[30] Appearing throughout their work, allusions, borrowings, and echoes were fundamental to the Romantic poets' modus operandi[31]—more prevalent and longer lived, if less immediately striking, than the rustic language and confessional effusions for which they were also renowned—essential in welding literary coteries together.

CHAPTERS AND THEMES

In examining coterie language in relation to various kinds of public discourse, *The Dialect of the Tribe* takes its cue from the New Historicist work begun in the 1980s. I am, however, more interested than many critics of that time in the ways in which this discourse intersected with events in writers' private lives. Indeed, the mediation of public events and narratives into poetic style and form via the poet's pressing personal concerns is the process I attempt to unravel in each of the chapters. Formalism, that is, benefits from historicism when the micro-historical, including the biographical, is combined with the study of the large scale. In the 1790s, for example, one of the formative aspects of the Southey/Coleridge coterie was a diagnosis, derived from Cowper, of commercial capitalism as a disease, one effect of which was the dehumanizing exploitation of the poor and power-less at home and abroad. It was as anti-metropolitan, anti-mercantile, anti-imperialist poets that the Bristol coterie forged a common identity. The attack on commodification was seminal, and persisted in the coterie's work long after it abandoned revolutionary politics, not least because, in a commercialized print culture, authors experienced their own commodification: they found their private lives becoming enactments of a process that they had become poets by attacking. Commodification, in sum, was an originary and long-lived spur of the coterie language of the period: if it predated the revolutionary politics that are usually seen as foundational for Romanticism, it also continued to shape its terms. As I show, it determined the public careers—and broke the identities—of laboring-class poets, whose dependence on literary coteries was a fragile defense against their exploitation by the market, which packaged them for commercial success, only later to drop them.

The exploitation of laborer poets was, Bloomfield and Clare knew, a small matter in comparison with the exploitation of laborers who did not write. Still worse was the exploitation of native peoples under colonialism. I explore responses to this colonialist form of commodification in several chapters, arguing that the Bristol coterie drew together as Robinson and Southey, in particular, created fictional indigenous voices that were far more oppositional and troublingly ambiguous than can be explained by accounts of Orientalism as a process whereby the West projects onto the East a fantasyland of its own making. Adding to debates begun by Edward Said, and nuanced by Nigel Leask, Javed Majeed, Saree Makdisi,[32] I show not only that anti-imperialism was formative of Romantic poetry in the Bristol coterie but also that this Bristol verse was, in turn, formative of a later pro-colonialist and evangelizing poetry practiced by Southey, Bowles, and their followers and set in America. One coterie language engendered another, giving a set of poets the power to generate common terms to address changed historical and geographical circumstances. The pro-missionary, avowedly Christianizing group of poets that coalesced around Southey and William Lisle Bowles in the 1810s found its common voice by adapting the antireligious Orientalism of the 1790s' coterie.

In chapter 1, I examine the 1790s' coterie in detail, exploring the historical reasons for its gradual formation as a group of writers, editors, and publishers united by a shared language in which allusion and borrowing featured in particular ways. 1795 was a crucial year: it was then that the government passed laws targeting the radical campaigners who, in the wake of the French Revolution, had protested against the culture of consumption and its degradation of the laboring classes. Speaking and writing against government policy now risked imprisonment; reformers found their private characters smeared by anti-Jacobin writers and caricaturists. In response, the Bristol radicals began jointly to develop a verse style—what we now call early Romanticism—characterized by both oblique allusions to public figures (and political issues) and supportive allusions to each other (and each other's writings). At its center were Coleridge and Southey. The latter, especially, had a formative role and one of my aims (building on the work of Curran, Butler, and Pratt[33]) is his rehabilitation as a more significant player in Romanticism's genesis than Wordsworth. Within this coterie, allusion to and borrowing from each other's writing had a socio-literary function: by mutual reference the poets developed shared ways of phrasing and favored topoi; by playing on these, new poems could be extrapolated from existing ones, and the group's poetic idiom extended.[34] It was by these figures that, as Felicity James has remarked, the partners put into practice an "ideal of friendship and sympathetic feeling" that lay at the very center of their "creative and social identity."[35] Likewise, David Fairer, in the course of his illuminating restoration of Lamb and Lloyd to the center of the circle, has written that "friendship was for them inseparable from a process of poetic nurturing"; "Poetic organisation," it follows, "is the medium through which friendship operates."[36] It was by echo, borrowing, and allusion that they interacted, collaborated, and imitated each other, generating common themes, honing a shared style, and experimenting with new genres.

There were others members too, less discussed, whose effect upon the group dynamic I want to restore to view. Two of these were older authors whose work the Bristolians revered and jointly imitated (indeed this mutual reverence was one of the bonds between them)—William Cowper and William Lisle Bowles. Another was a later entrant whose career hitherto made her an embodiment of the issues that were discussed in Cowper's poetry—Mary Robinson. Robinson's participation in the coterie from its London circumference, I argue, reorientated her authorial self and that of Coleridge and Southey. It turned all three, in poetic dialogues and when editing and anthologizing, toward a radical poetry whose radicalism was as much about dramatizing the exploitation of women and of native people by the commodifying capitalism that they associated with the commercial capitalism of "Cockney"[37] London as it was about enthusiasm for the French Revolution. This poetry was identified as the product of a Bristol coterie, even when it appeared in a London newspaper—it was explicitly a provincial challenge to the commercial capital (and Robinson had been born and raised in Bristol). Its central publication was not *Lyrical Ballads* (1798); nor was Coleridge's partnership with Wordsworth its dominant relationship. The multiple partnerships of Southey, Coleridge, and Robinson with each other and with Cottle set its agenda, which featured in Robinson's *Lyrical Tales* (1800) but most strongly of all in the *Annual Anthology* that Southey edited in 1799 and 1800. This collection, published by Cottle, featured verses by Robinson, Southey, Coleridge, Cottle, Lovell, Davy, and other Bristolians and invoked the memory of Chatterton. Among the poems included were "Fire, Famine and Slaughter," "This Lime-Tree Bower My Prison," "The Haunted Beach," "The Battle of Blenheim." My discussion aims to demonstrate the collection's crucial role in defining the originary locality, language, and concerns of what we now call Romanticism.

Within the intense sociability that characterized Romantic coteries, antisocial pressures were always present. Personality clashes and literary differences were inflected by public criticism, political reaction, and commercial failure. Coleridge's personal insecurity and neediness—the very characteristics that caused him to create coteries—made him especially sensitive to these pressures, and led him to destroy what he had created. When coterie language became so established that it was subjected to public attack, Coleridge felt constrained rather than supported by it, and tended to repudiate it, only to revise it in a new direction. He then attempted to draw others into the revisionary process, reconstituting the coterie with some of its original members and some new ones. Self-differentiation from a language of sociability was, in other words, a central process of that language's renewal: it was on the tension between a group and an individual that it depended—so long as that tension could be productively accommodated. In chapter 2, I turn to a moment in which a productive accommodation was achieved, and a destroyed coterie remodeled, producing a period of intense co-creativity, only for self-differentiation gradually to overwhelm the renewed partnership. I examine a little-studied Somerset episode that allows us to see two of the quintessential Romantic poems—*Thalaba the Destroyer* and "Kubla Khan"—as collaborative products of the West Country coterie. As is well-known, the intensity of the Pantisocracy project broke into acrimony in 1795. Patched up, Coleridge and Southey's relationship brought forth further collaboration and joint publication, only to break down again in 1797 when Southey thought his verse parodied by Coleridge as the latter, differentiating himself from Lamb and Lloyd, satirized the sweet simplicity of their joint style. Coleridge then brought the Wordsworths into the Bristol coterie, recentering it on Nether Stowey, Somerset, until the trip to Germany in autumn 1798, where the three took different paths. Having returned to Stowey without the Wordsworths in summer 1799, Coleridge found himself apart from all his recent, close collaborators. The circle was broken. In August, however, the estranged Southey arrived in Stowey and repaired their breach. The poets then worked alongside each other at the same table, drafting a coauthored poem, "Mohammed." Their unfinished individual texts, "Kubla Khan," "Christabel," and *Thalaba the Destroyer* were modified by this period of joint authorship and its fallout: each borrowed from the other as each poet developed the other's language in and as his own. The borrowings vary: some lie below the immediately visible surface—they were used, perhaps unconsciously, as phrases prompting revision. Other borrowings were highlighted. These were employed first to pay tribute to the friend's writing sponsoring one's own and later to indicate a point of departure, since, after their intense collaboration of 1799, in 1800 and 1801 each poet began to define himself in apposition (if not opposition) to the other.[38] The result was the reworking of two of the cardinal texts of Romantic Orientalism, "Kubla Khan" and *Thalaba*, which finally reached published form reshaped by manuscript revisions evidencing mutual influence but also growing difference. This process of revision was of considerable significance to literary history, since "Kubla Khan" and *Thalaba* set the agenda for poetic portrayals of the east throughout the nineteenth century.

In the 1790s, Coleridge had been one of the writers to make the confessional a feature of his new poetry. In chapter 3, I examine a poem of 1803 that was prompted by another moment of self-differentiation in which a group language, and coterie identity, was reworked, as Coleridge again moved away from the Wordsworths and turned toward Southey. Composed after a tense separation from William and Dorothy on a tour of Scotland, "The Pains of Sleep" was first transcribed in a letter urging Southey to come to live alongside Coleridge in Keswick. It was a product of a crisis experienced when the Lake District coterie that Coleridge shared with the Wordsworths had broken down; it was part of a strategy for reconstituting that circle with Coleridge's oldest collaborator of all. It had, that is, a coterie function that mattered more than publication (it did not reach print for a further 13 years). *A cri de coeur* seeking his friends' succor and asserting his proficiency at the confessional poetry that Wordsworth had mastered, "The Pains of Sleep" was a coterie poem, related to the "Dejection" manuscripts and the "Immortality Ode." When, in 1816, Coleridge did publish it, it became a test case for the issues surrounding publication of the confessional verse that was an innovation of the circle. I look at the poem in its 1816 context, arguing that Coleridge uses a strategy of anti-allusion, rather than confession, in order to publicize the personal in terms less candid than they appear. The poem gestures toward the confessional but does not actually confess; it alludes to deeds and texts, as refracted in Coleridge's dreams, but does not detail them. It hints, but it is impossible to discover exactly to what it hints: thus it maintains a *cordon sanitaire* between the personal and the political, shielding the reader and perhaps Coleridge himself from the implications of his past involvement in a Jacobin coterie. In this respect, I suggest, it is an epitome of the genres in which, after 1815, Coleridge placed his writing when publishing it—the Romantic fragment—the allegoric vision—the reverie—the dream—the psychological curiosity. All are structured by anti-allusion: they are truncated, veiled, unrealized because they invoke larger texts and contexts that Coleridge keeps hidden. These include the relationships with the Wordsworths and with Southey that had led to composition. However, when we restore those larger texts and contexts to sight with the resources of modern scholarship (an ability not possessed by Coleridge's contemporaries), and understand what was being invoked, then anti-allusion appears as a return of the repressed—a metamorphosed trace of anxieties that Coleridge could neither confront face-to-face nor forget. Anti-allusion, like the dreamwork to which it often refers, is the displaced form of Coleridge's political unconscious, a mark of his inability either to ignore or detail his transit from a leader of a Jacobin circle of poets in the 1790s to an isolated and anti-Jacobin prose writer in the 18 teens. His idealization of the poetic fragment—"Kubla Khan" and "Christabel"—is a related aspect of the same inability. Coleridge does not silence his past so much as summon it as an absence by publishing works that bespeak their severance from that past.

Chapter 4 returns to the less guilty, more straightforward use of allusion and borrowing to cement poetic partnerships and to develop political poetry that features in chapters 1 and 2. It argues that one of the most popular genres of the Romantic era, the colonial romance that brought Scott and Byron fame and fortune, had a source in the relationship between the Coleridge/Southey circle and its mentor, Bowles. In the 1790s, Coleridge and Southey developed their anti-capitalist, anti-imperialist poetry by borrowing from Bowles's lyrics about Indians—uncommodified rustics, noble savages. They alluded to Bowles's verse in gratitude and admiration even as they gave it a sharper political edge. By the 1810s, however, the relationship had reversed: Bowles now, for the first time, turned to a long narrative poem. *The Missionary*, a historical romance with topical relevance about the colonial conquest of Chile, borrowed from Southey's *Thalaba* and *Madoc* (1805). Bowles sought help from his former disciples: Southey, now Bowles's equal rather than acolyte, gave advice; Coleridge helped Bowles correct his text. *The Missionary* was a late offshoot of a circle of which Bowles, invoked by allusion, had been a founding father. It continued what Southey had begun—the creative modification of that circle's 1790s poetry into a new genre responding to the new political circumstances in which European war was precipitating liberation struggles in the East and in Spanish America. Displacing contemporary imperial politics into historical narrative, Bowles alluded to Coleridge's conversation poems and echoed Wordsworth's lyrical ballads, as well as borrowed form and phrase from the Indian songs Southey had written in dialogue with his own. These allusions were visible marks of an emulative modification of his own writing in the light of his onetime disciples'. They reveal a how a poetic circle becomes a spiral—how new genres emerge from the mutual, revisionary development of each other's work by poets who admire and trust one another. *The Missionary* turned out to be a germinal text: it gave its admirer Byron a model for the colonial romances with which he made his name.

In part 2, I take a different social and geographical perspective on the issues of country versus city, and of poetic language and class, that featured in part 1. I turn my attention to two writers who were connected both to the rural world idealized by the Bristol, Stowey, and Lakes coteries and to the commercial London that manufactured and marketed products. Robert Bloomfield was a London artisan who made shoes in a garret—a Cockney by location and occupation and in his connections to London artisan writers including Thomas Hardy, the revolutionary; as a child, however, he had been a farmhand in rural Suffolk. John Clare, Bloomfield's admirer, had also been a farm laborer as a youth; as an adult he visited London and participated in the circle of Cockney writers associated with the *London Magazine*. As authors, both men were hybrids—of both the country and the city. But, what was it to be a laboring-class poet who wrote of the countryside but was produced, packaged, and published in the metropolis—a bucolic Cockney? In what ways was the poetry of the West Country and Lakes coteries a model or a problem? What kinds of literary circle enabled composition and publication, and what tensions beset them? What were the relationships with higher-class literary circles—with Wordsworth and Southey, on the one hand, and the essayists of the Cockney school on the other? In chapter 5, I discuss Bloomfield as a more prominent rural poet by far in the first decade of the nineteenth century than Wordsworth. His *Farmer's Boy* sold over 100,000 copies; the follow-up, *Rural Tales*, was scarcely less popular. He struggled, however, to complete two poems that attempted to occupy the ground that Wordsworth and his circle had staked out. An ode to imagination and a poem on the river Wye emulated "Tintern Abbey," not least because Bloomfield needed to create himself as an author—a writer whose subjectivity was sensitive and powerful enough to justify demanding readers' attention over a long poem that aimed at the lofty aesthetics of the sublime and the picturesque. Wordsworth was a model, as were Gilpin and Gray; successful completion depended, however, on overcoming disadvantages that none of these models faced. As a laborer and artisan, few of Bloomfield's social peers were able to provide literary companionship; fewer still were able to assist in bringing manuscripts into print. Gaining access to publication and fashioning himself as an author involved a partnership with a patron—Capel Lofft—from a different class, of a different educational upbringing and with different cultural expectations. Social inequality made the partnership insecure.[39] Bloomfield, like his admirer Clare, came to resent the interference of the local gentleman whose support had first helped him dedicate himself to writing.

Economic changes in the book market further plagued the relationship, for they produced tension between patrons and booksellers. Bloomfield's popularity encouraged booksellers to view their ledgers, rather than the "taste" of gentlemen patrons, as the arbiters of literary value. He was a commercial commodity, rather than the product of private upper-class investment in the "lower orders"—yet the patron whose benefactions had helped launch his career did not see matters that way and made compliance with his editorial intervention the price of continued support. This insistence in turn jeopardized Bloomfield's growing relationship with his publisher,[40] a relationship that itself proved vulnerable to market fluctuations, however sustaining it was personally.

In these difficult circumstances, the confident self-assertion as an author that Wordsworth, buoyed by the West Country circle, achieved in "Tintern" was a forlorn hope for Bloomfield. Allusion functioned as a way of asserting his standing among the English poets. Rather than an assumption of privilege, it was an act of resistance, an invocation of the great poets that bolstered the "peasant" poet's authority and placed him in company that was not attempting to use his words for profit. It was beset by anxiety, however, because laboring-class writers had to justify, against class prejudice, their claim to be worthy inheritors of tradition whereas literary gentleman could presume upon their fitness by virtue of their education and their social authority. The resistance and the anxiety are registered in Bloomfield's allusive "Ode to Immagination"—a poem modeled on eighteenth-century poets—which he abandoned after his patron altered its versification. He turned, instead, to a use of private allusion—in-jokes and knowing references—to maintain and renew a coterie of gentlewomen readers and friends who were free of designs upon him and his writings. This friendship group renewed his writing: the poetry he published under its influence was marked by the informal chattiness that stemmed from the group's shared experience. His confidence boosted by intelligent women's attentiveness, he was able to turn in-jokes outward and shape a public landscape poetry that plays comically with past poets' rhymes and rhythms. Allusive and innovative, this nature poetry was Augustanism revised as was only possible for a poet able to survey, in retrospect, the entirety of Augustan verse—a poet with the radically different perspective of a laborer. Hudibrastic, colloquial, touristic, it represents landscape by reworking Pope, Dyer, Darwin—the neoclassical tradition—in the chatty terms of Samuel Butler. A vibrant contribution to the romanticization of one of Romanticism's natal territories—the Wye valley—Bloomfield's poetry meditates on time, memory, and nature in a way that suggests a resistance to Wordsworth's self-centering lyricism at Tintern Abbey, for Bloomfield's allusions reveal him not as the lone focal point of the valley's "sense sublime" but as one of a company of poets, artists, and tourists who have been inspired there. In this sense, he is closer to Coleridge in "This Lime-Tree Bower"—a fellow rural poet whose poetry proceeds by acknowledging its dependence on a group of friends and writers.

For laboring-class writers, coteries were always vulnerable to class difference from within, as well as condescension from without. Bloomfield's literary circle was more fragile than Coleridge's, even if just as vital to his art. When the woman at the circle's center died young, Bloomfield lost much of the confidence needed to bring long works to publication. He had little literary support within the social circles of his own class to carry him over the destructive withdrawal of other patrons and the commercial collapse of his publisher,[41] and was forced to leave London, and its literary market, for the obscurity of a rural village, where Southey tried to rally financial support among his own literary circle.

Marketed in class terms as the "village minstrel,"[42] John Clare was a successor to Bloomfield as a publishing phenomenon—an embodiment of the Wordsworthian rustic who not only spoke the "best part of language" (WLB, p. 744) but also turned it into poetry. But the published Clare was no solitary rural genius: he appeared in print, as did Wordsworth, via a metropolitan production team that took his poems from mind to manuscript to publication. Clare's publisher John Taylor, as Jonathan Bate[43] has shown, worked in detail on his texts, suggesting revisions, introducing punctuation, selecting poems until a publishable collection was reached. He did not impose this editing upon Clare but operated through dialogue; he also introduced the poet to the circle of authors and illustrators that worked for his *London Magazine*—a community that gave Clare confidence in his vocation. When Taylor was driven out of the market and to the verge of madness by the publishing slump after 1825, Clare found this vocation almost impossible to pursue and his identity began to fragment. In chapter 6, I show how he reconstituted it, *de profundis*, by virtue of a literary coterie, real and imaginary, that he forged in Northampton lunatic asylum. Taylor's part of editor, sponsor, and "publisher" was played by the steward William Knight; visitors provided an audience; Coleridge, Cowper, and Byron were summoned as textual voices as Clare marshaled a writing community—virtual rather than real—around himself. This community centered on Cowper: just as Cowper inhabited Coleridge's poetic voice in "Frost at Midnight," he also appeared in Clare's. For Clare, however, borrowing and allusion were figures of desperation, means of sustaining his identity as a poet (his identity *in toto*) in a madhouse "babel" that threatened to entangle his words in a perplexity of meaningless tongues. The "mad" Clare forged an imaginary partnership with the "lunatic" Cowper, filling notebooks with poems written as if he *were* Cowper—effectively affirming his identity as poet by personating another. He did the same thing with Byron and with the poet-prophet of the Book of Revelation, creating a dramatic dialogue between their poetic voices and visions, as inhabited by him. In this context, borrowing compensated for lunatic babble and poetic isolation by forging a scripted partnership. While this tactic demonstrates the importance of literary community to Clare's writerly self—he needed others to echo, borrow from, and allude to in order to be himself as an author—it also shows him producing, in manuscript, carefully structured literary works that aspire to be coherent wholes.

Mixing verse and prose, Clare's notebooks substitute for the poetry collections that partnership with Taylor had once put into print but are in some respects more innovative and searching than those collections: they are as much a crafted, varied, long-form articulation of Romantic selfhood as Wordsworth's *Prelude* and Coleridge's notebooks.

Part 3 turns again to London, as the commercial and consumerist center of which Coleridge, Southey, Robinson, and Wordsworth were so suspicious, and to the metropolitan circle of writers grouped around Leigh Hunt—the group of which Clare was a visiting member. My focus is on two aspects of Cockneyism that, I hope, change our perspective on it: one is its membership—I explore, as Cockney writings (i.e., as texts of lower- and middle-class London artisans and tradesmen), the letters of Bloomfield and the prophecies of millenarians. Another is its revisionary style: I explore the Cockneys' redefinition of the West Country school's use of allusion to name-check friends and collaborators in published works, so as to affirm sociability and speak from a group. It was this allusiveness that first earned them the label of a "Cockney school" (itself an allusion to the "Lake school").

The redefinition of name-dropping—or of hinting at names—was a matter of genre. Writing essays for the popular periodical market, the Cockney circle teased readers with a little celebrity gossip, proffering tidbits from the private lives of literary characters. A reader had only to be sufficiently in the know to convert "Mr. C—" to "Coleridge" to feel included in the social world of celebrated geniuses. In essays, letters, and light verse, the Cockneys took the Southey/Coleridge circle's name-dropping to a more intimate level. They did so to fuel a desire that was characteristic of the new mass-market media age in which newspapers, journals, and magazines spread information with unprecedented speed—a desire for what Coleridge disparagingly called "literary and political gossiping" (CBL, I, 41). Embracing the gossipy, they offered the readers of this commodified writing an image of uncommodified sociability on the model of the suburban ramble of a group of friends—a convivial Sunday escape from city to a country inn, rather than the solitary sublime of Wordsworth crossing the Alps in his epic "poem on the growth of my own mind." Walking and writing of themselves as walking companions, the Cockneys helped invent leisure in its modern form: the office worker's weekend stroll in the country and the magazine essays that describe that stroll remain popular cultural forms today; rambling and reading about rambling have become defining habits of the English middle classes (are, indeed, parts of a multimillion pound "leisure industry"). Essayistic prose, rambling in form as well as content, was, then, a quintessential Cockney genre in whose wake we are still following. The darker side of this bourgeois Romanticism, however, was that the miniaturization of what Wordsworth and Coleridge had celebrated as pedestrian liberty occurred because the Cockneys, and their readers, were tied to drudgery in the urban workplace six days a week. Lamb and Bloomfield sounded a note of desperation in seizing on walking as a rationed antidote to a depressing round of mental stress and physical confinement in the office: they were among the earliest to articulate the angst in the soul of that figure of modernity—the functionary, the bureaucrat, the clerk.

My final chapter is a nexus of many of the discussions threaded through *The Dialect of the Tribe*. It examines the interrelations between city and country, rural and Cockney coteries; it takes forward my analysis of the magazine essay; and, returning to the subject with which I began, it discusses allusive coteries in the radical politics of the 1790s. I investigate the flowering of apocalyptic prophecy in 1790s London as a literalization of allusion: Cockney artisans and tradesmen became visionaries who viewed their ability to apply biblical phrases to modern times not as evidence of their figurative prowess, but of a real fulfillment of prophecy—evidence of the imminent destruction of the city and its remaking as an earthly millennium. They did so, I argue, not just because the French Revolution seemed to them to presage the Last Days but also because London's commodifiying and consuming culture left them not only poor but also unable to make sense of their lives: as Wordsworth and Blake both saw, the new London alienated people from themselves as well as exploited them. Prophecy let Cockneys—the artisan classes of the capital—make sense of it all: thus, commercial London bred an allusive response that refused to accept its allusiveness.

It was the failure of the apocalypse to arrive that discredited the prophets and highlighted the figurality of their discourse. By 1815, it was no longer possible in London to win a popular following as a prophet promising that the capital would be transformed into a millennial city. Prophecy was evidently figural. As such, however, it lived on, transferred and transformed, in the literary visions of another member of the *London Magazine* coterie who happened to be a former member of the Lakes coterie too: Thomas De Quincey. In the *Confessions of an English Opium Eater*, De Quincey imagined London as Babylon and located the New Jerusalem in the Lake District as described by Wordsworth. This siting, I argue, depended on alluding

to Wordsworth's unpublished poetry—making De Quincey an urban
Aaron to a rural Moses. But De Quincey's borrowing was inflected
by guilt that he betrayed Wordsworth's nature prophecy in his own,
secondhand, Cockney version of it; it was also shaped by his resentment of Wordsworth's rejection of his discipleship. The result was a
self-destructive, belated Romanticism that endorsed literary figurality
as the discourse of redemptive prophecy, but insisted that redemption would occur in the poetry of the rural coterie that De Quincey
alluded to, and in the countryside—not in the city and the allusive
prose of the Cockney essayists in which De Quincey situated himself. In effect, figurality was crystallized as an issue as a result of the
friction between various allusive responses to a historical situation,
and to geographical locations and the coteries centered on them. The
heavy use of tropes became a chief characteristic of a "literature" that
De Quincey now defined, for the first time, in opposition to factual
kinds of writing. "English literature" was brought to birth in his allusive prose as a discourse "of power"—its power residing in a figurality
of which allusiveness was an essential element. Poetry was the highest
kind of literature, and Wordsworth the greatest kind of poet, not only
figurative but also self-conscious of what was at stake in figurality
(and thus a prophet). But this self-conscious figurality—this redemptive power of literature—could only operate on propitious ground—
in the country coterie of like-minded poets rather than in the urban
isolation of commodified proletarians. De Quincey's allusions made
the Romantic city irredeemably fallen and the countryside, as articulated in lyric verse, the site of spiritual regeneration—a geography
that would become, over the next 150 years, more and more powerful
in British culture and in "English literature." In the beginning was
the Word-sworth.

PART I

"A SECT OF POETS": THE DIALECT OF FRIENDSHIP IN SOUTHEY, COLERIDGE, AND THEIR CIRCLES

CHAPTER 1

THE POLITICIZATION OF ALLUSION IN EARLY ROMANTICISM: MARY ROBINSON AND THE BRISTOL POETS

The Bristol coterie came into being as young writers, recoiling from the culture of conspicuous consumption and political repression they associated with London, formed themselves into a group united by its common diagnosis of that culture as the expression of a commodifying capitalism. They used allusion both to forge a common language—a dialect—and to satirize that culture obliquely when direct attack became dangerous. They made it their common task to show that its hidden cost was the reduction of value to material possession—a reduction that not only corrupted the consumer but also exploited the producer, who was himself reduced to a commodity.[1] In this respect Britons had become, Coleridge remarked (anticipating Marx), "Fetich worshippers."[2]

Fashioning a common language by tracing commodity fetishism to the mercantile and imperialist capitalism of the London elites, the Bristol poets also exposed its dissemination across the country and the globe. In doing so they carried on a distinct 1780s current of political criticism into the 1790s, where it flowed in a larger river: the French Revolution radicalized politics; after the execution of the king and queen and the Terror, it also provoked a government backlash in Britain that had material effects on Jacobin campaigners, and on the language they used, whether in speeches, articles, novels, or poems. From 1794, political dissent became criminalized and satirical

allusion became politicized to an unprecedented degree. The republican orator John Thelwall, for instance, was tried for treason, partly on the basis that an informer had overheard him make an allusion: "Mr. Thelwall took a pot of porter and blowing off the head, said—'This is the Way I would serve kings.'"[3] Witnesses in his defense claimed that Thelwall had said "tyrants" rather than "kings": on the interpretation of the specificity of his figure, the verdict depended. Thelwall was acquitted, because the jury could not be persuaded that to imagine a monarch's death amounted to an intention to cause it. Nevertheless, direct criticism was now clearly highly dangerous, and allusion scarcely less so:[4] political criticism had, henceforth, to adopt an oblique figurality allowing its import to be understood but preventing that import from being proved. The literal, the direct, and the easily decoded had to give way to the joke, the innuendo, the historical example. These forms of allusion became marked features of a political poetry that had to adapt in order to survive government repression—a strategy of radical poets gagged by law. Brought together by this repression and by their invention of an obliquely allusive discourse to counter it, the Bristol poets expressed mutual admiration by alluding to each other, and to each other's writing. Thus, allusion had a double use— to carry on political critique on one hand, and to assert solidarity on the other. It forged the dialect of the new poets, becoming a badge of their existence as a circle united in private friendship and in public challenge to established authority in the political—but also the aesthetic—spheres. Established authority, on its part, paid writers and artists to discredit the radical poets, both by direct satire of their work and by allusions to their private lives—innuendos. This second kind of allusion, a reactionary weapon in a literary culture polarized by political enmity, blurred, without explicitly breaching, the boundary of acceptable public discourse: it smeared an opponent's character, rather than disprove his arguments, but did so by hints and nudges rather than statements of fact.

One of the chief issues over which radical poets fashioned a joint challenge to authority was slavery—the reduction of people to things, in Coleridge's analysis, in pursuit of profit from the production of inessential but fashionable commodities—sugar, coffee—"bartering freedom and the poor man's life / For gold, as at a market!" ("Fears in Solitude," lines 63–64; CPW, I, i, 471). The slave trade was financed and organized from Liverpool and Bristol, as well as London, and it was in campaigning against it in Bristol that Coleridge and Southey, alluding to each other's words—as well as to fellow Bristol poets Hannah More and Ann Yearsley and Bristol publisher-poet Joseph

Cottle—aligned themselves as a new generation of anti-metropolitan, anti-imperialist, anti-capitalist writers. Their Bristol-issued publications constituted a provincial, dissenting critique of mercantilism from one of mercantilism's main centers, just as Blake's self-published, home-printed works did from London. (In a poem published by Cottle, Coleridge wrote of a "Bristowa" "son of Commerce" with a "thirst of idle gold"[5]). These publications, in their mode of production as well as in their form and content, stood against an increasingly capitalized book market controlled from the metropolis that, Wordsworth complained, had reduced literature to: "frantic novels, sickly and stupid German Tragedies, and deluges of idle and extravagant stories in verse"—fashionable commodities to be consumed at speed and then trashed (WLB, p. 747).

One poet often neglected when the Bristol circle is discussed was Mary Robinson. A satellite member based in London, Robinson was nevertheless crucial to its continued existence, after Coleridge's disruptive self-differentiation from its common language in 1797. The coterie was eventually remodeled to include her, and as such was, in ways not always noted by critics, inflected by her example and her verse. Robinson, in fact, refocused its concerns, for she was uniquely qualified to voice an attack on commodity fetishism and its effect on people at home and in the empire. She had grown up in Bristol, daughter of a merchant adventurer who had left his family to live with his American mistress after a failed scheme to establish a whale fishery, exploiting Inuit labor, in an area of Labrador recently wrested from French control. In the early 1780s she had become London's most celebrated fashion icon—famous for her beauty and her scandalous lifestyle as a kept mistress, and a courtesan. Constantly in the newspapers and magazines, she knew, firsthand, the commodifying effects of conspicuous consumption and the print culture that fostered it, having both exploited and been exploited by this culture. By the 1790s, crippled by illness, dropped by her aristocratic "protectors," Robinson had reinvented herself as a poet, novelist, and feminist critic of the commodification of women. In this chapter, I shall examine the part she played in shaping early Romanticism, as both the object and practitioner of allusions that signposted and cemented the literary partnerships she entered with the Bristol poets, at first Coleridge and then increasingly Southey. Southey was a vital figure, both as a poet to whose work she alluded, and as the organizer of joint publications for the partnerships that he, Robinson, and Coleridge forged. His *Annual Anthology* (1799/1800) was a foundational collection of the new generation's poetry, as significant as *Lyrical Ballads*.

Raree Shows, Print Culture, and the Commodification of the Body

The culture of conspicuous consumerism that the young writers joined in criticizing was epitomized by a capital city that marketed and displayed products and bodies. London, in their diagnosis, was a huge "raree show." If the annual Bartholomew Fair was the epitome of this Cockney culture, vulgar displays were also found in London's gardens, taverns, and shopping streets. The young Wordsworth, fresh from the country, encountered "troops of wild beasts, birds and beasts / Of every nature, from all climes convened" (*Prelude*, 1805, VII, 244–47). Brought from the new colonial territories, Indian jugglers swallowed swords, while Mohawks performed the war whoop. The famous brothel keeper, Charlotte Hayes, advertised a live spectacle featuring "a dozen beautiful Nymphs, unsullied and untainted…who breathe health and nature and who will perform the celebrated rites of Venus, as practised at Tahiti."[6] After watching the nymphs dance, the paying voyeurs were invited to join in. In London's great exhibition, beautiful women, like savage warriors, were commodified bodies on show and for sale. Wordsworth summed up his disgust at the city with a phrase that perceptively linked shopping and sex: "Getting and spending we lay waste our powers."[7] In a perverted matrix of desire, passion became acquisition: the purchase of things, including people reduced to things, was what turned people on—an onanistic displacement of loving coition. London was a place where everything was turned into a titillating commercial performance—its value reduced to its price (*Prelude*, 1805, VII, 236, 190). To Wordsworth, the metropolitan culture was that of a vulgar, commodified class of artisans and clerks—Cockney mechanics whose debased values corrupted the nation at large: he spoke of all Britons, and not just Londoners, when he wrote "We have given our hearts away, a sordid boon!"[8]

In opposing poetry to a society given over to consumerism and to commercial spectacle, Wordsworth took his cue from William Cowper. In *Task*, Cowper diagnosed these as new trends, as vices spread across the nation by the expansion of commercial print—the newspapers that, from the 1780s, began to proliferate in the provinces as well as the capital, spreading gossip and thus bringing to birth the celebrity culture in which we are still living. If, as Benedict Anderson has argued,[9] newspaper reading promoted a communal experience of vicarious participation that fostered a sense of nationhood, nevertheless this community was divided—since many who recognized themselves as part of the newspaper-reading public were disgusted by the vicariousness it promoted and resisted being part of a national public shaped by that means. Cowper saw his own newspaper reading as an addictive habit that was dizzying but also desensitizing, finding that he consumed real people's lives from a distance without gaining the moral insights that, in literature, made fictional characters revelatory of truths about human nature. In *Task* (1785) he wrote:

> There forests of no-meaning spread the page
> In which all comprehension wanders lost;
> While fields of pleasantry amuse us there,
> With merry descants on a nation's woes.
> The rest appears a wilderness of strange
> But gay confusion, roses for the cheeks
> And lilies for the brows of faded age,
> Teeth for the toothless, ringlets for the bald,
> Heav'n, earth, and ocean plunder'd of their sweets,
> Nectareous essences, Olympian dews,
> Sermons and city feasts and fav'rite airs,
> Aetherial journies, submarine exploits,
> And Katterfelto with his hair on end
> At his own wonders, wond'ring for his bread.

(Task, IV, 74–87; Cowper, II, 188–89)

Here, Cowper replicates in verse the disorientating effects of reading the London paper's mixture of news, gossip, and advertisements for patent medicines and forthcoming shows. He makes the self-promoting catchphrase of the itinerant mountebank Katterfelto,—"wonders, wonders"—into a hyperbolic exclamation that collapses into the profit motive that underlies it: the travelling showman is punningly "wond'ring for his bread." This pun picks up the earlier use of "wandering" to describe the effect of the profit-driven sensationalism of the newspaper on the reader, who is led astray amid a jumble of stories, advertisements, and announcements that leaves him unable to sort the relative values of the different forms of print that the page carries.[10]

Among the advertisements were notices of the latest spectacle to be viewed for a price. Thus, the newspapers promoted and participated in a culture of mobility in which people were treated as goods to be transported for the entertainment of mass publics: if the "hunter Indian" was on London's streets, it was because he had been brought there to be viewed as a spectacle, whether in the flesh or through the medium of print. The newspaper reader was at one end of a chain that began, in Cherokee villages and on Polynesian islands, with army officers and naval captains who transported Indians to London where they cut deals with publicans and showmen to exhibit them for a profit. Also on show, and discussed in the papers, were the mistresses and courtesans who catered to the sexual desires of rich men: they paraded, in fashionable dress, in Hyde Park and Vauxhall Gardens; in Covent Garden and Drury Lane, meanwhile, walked their Cockney imitators—the street prostitutes who, wearing the cast-off dresses of wealthy ladies, were often hard to distinguish from respectable women. The markers of class and indicators of propriety were, in commercial London, subverted.

Mary Robinson was, from 1780 to 1783, the most fashionable courtesan in the city. Her open appearance among the most power-ful men in the land meant she was constantly in the news—her love of fashionable gowns and expensive jewels described, her appearance dwelt upon in lavish detail. She was both a purchaser of luxury com-modities and herself a purchased commodity—a symbol to satirists of a culture of spectacle that placed appearance and glitter before substance and achievement and that endangered the country because it threatened to corrupt those who admired it from afar through the medium of print. The satirists used Robinson to suggest that beneath the expensive frocks and newly bought jewels, it was the sexual dis-play of the body that fashionable London existed for and sought to make endlessly new: she was but another "raree show."

If satire was destructive of Robinson's credibility, it was also for-mative of her self-representation: Robinson's experience of being the object of critique, a visual commodity emblematic of a fleshly com-modity, made her into a resourceful manipulator of her own com-modity status.[11] As Michael Gamer and Terry Robinson have shown, Robinson successfully staged a version of herself—at first in the the-ater, later via portraits, appearances, and the newspaper press—as a celebrity.[12] Unlike other courtesans, Robinson saw that print culture was the key to her public image, and that her public image—rather than her personal reputation among a select group of aristocratic men as a satisfying lover—was vital to her position. Her credit depended on her circulation in the form of images and type.[13] That she maintained it for so long reveals that she swiftly understood that she must manip-ulate her commodification by print successfully enough to counter the allusions that aimed to strip her of her glamour and reveal her as a whore—to reduce her to a commodified body. Thus, she established a partnership with the journalists Henry and Mary Bate: the advantage was mutual; she kept herself in the public eye; they sold copies of their new paper *The Morning Herald* by securing exclusive details of her engagements, affairs, and outings. The Bates also stressed Robinson's accomplishments, presenting her as a wit as well as a beauty—more than just a beautiful body. But it was the emphasis on her lavish outfits that stimulated most interest: it was probably stories about her dress that inspired Cowper to complain about newspapers spreading a new obsession with fashion from town to country. He wrote in 1784, when Robinson had recently been receiving saturation coverage, of shepherdesses who emulated society beauties:

> The rural lass
> Whom once her virgin modesty and grace,
> Her artless manners and her neat attire
> So dignified, that she was hardly less
> Than the fair shepherdess of old romance,
> Is seen no more. The character is lost.
> Her head adorn'd with lappets pinn'd aloft
> And ribbands streaming gay, superbly raised
> And magnified beyond all human size,
> Indebted to some smart wig-weavers hand
> For more than half the tresses it sustains;
> Her elbows ruffled, and her tott'ring form
> Ill propp'd upon French heels; she might be deemed
> (But that the basket dangling on her arm
> Interprets her more truely) of a rank
> Too proud for dairy-work or sale of eggs.

> (*Task*, IV, 534–49; Cowper, II, 200–1)

Here, Cowper yearns for a pastoral innocence that can be sustained only so long as rural areas remain beyond the circulation of commodities—and of the newspapers that breed the desire for commodities. Wordsworth would later adopt a similar position. Robinson, on the other hand, assumed no position outside that circulation— either she must manipulate her commodification or be commodified by pressmen hostile to her: when she dressed as a shepherdess it was knowingly, in a sophisticated allusion to the naive rural charm that she knew men found cute. Meanwhile, if real shepherdesses dressed like fashionable ladies, it was because they had motives that Cowper could not understand: living humdrum lives dominated by the demands of work and by the traditional social mores of the village, they envied the freedom, independence, and excitement represented by Robinson. They might not want to risk copying her sex life (though reading about it offered vicarious escape from their own circumscribed positions as daughters, wives, mothers) but they did want to imitate her dress.

Robinson's partnerships with painters and pressmen had, by 1783, established her as a new phenomenon—almost, in today's terms, a brand. They had given her considerable power over her own image, and over her own life, albeit both were precarious, being vulnerable to the public's appetite for novelty as much as to satire (which was, after all, a backhanded tribute to her fame). But the following year, her credit gave out: she became ill; her aristocratic protectors withdrew; tradesmen called in their bills despite her celebrity; she was declared bankrupt and her possessions sold at auction. Nevertheless, the partnerships stood her in good stead when a paralysis gradually overtook her and her days at the center of the *haut ton* ended. When she turned to writing, she was able to use old alliances with the press to publicize her novels; she had also had rich experience of the presentation of the private self in public to turn to her own use. Robinson, in fact, refashioned herself to function in the literary milieu just as she previously had when an actress and a courtesan. Her poetry also developed from her fashion sense—or rather, fashion strategy: she remade herself in writing time and again as she once had through her clothes. This flexibility served her well when her first poetic publications were newspaper and journal pieces, written under pseudonyms, which carried on a flirtatious verse correspondence with the Della Cruscan poets. She put her experience of manipulating newspaper reports to literary use: publishing in the Della Cruscans' favored outlets, mimicking their hallmark modes of address and subject matter, alluding to their poems in hers, she rapidly learned their erotics of sociability[14] and became a corresponding partner, rather than an aspiring acolyte, of their central figure, Robert Merry. Allusion to their poems, in effect, led her to a voice that was her own yet part of a coterie style: she became a deliberately effusive and emotive poet of sensibility.

Robinson's participation in the Della Cruscan circle made her, once more, an object of mockery by conservative critics. If satirists had used her to target politicians in the early 1780s, they now made her the object of vicious personal innuendo. That they did so reveals that they identified her publications as being more dangerous in their tendency than her career as a celebrity courtesan had been. It also indicates the extent to which public discourse had been transformed in an era of postrevolutionary anti-Jacobinism. Convulsed by alarmism about the likelihood of revolution, the discourse of loyalism, often financed by government, made allusions to private life part of its currency. In Robinson's case, Tory satirists who resented her feminism and her exposure of the venal hypocrisy of the governing class homed in on her body. They treated her disablement as just punishment for her past participation in a culture that had marketed her sexuality. In 1791, William Gifford, a Tory opponent of Whiggism and Jacobinism, hinted that her paralysis had been brought on by an abortion, performed to let the courtesan continue her trade. Comparing her verse to the song "Light o' Love," Gifford alluded to *Much Ado about Nothing* (III, iv) where that song is called a tune "that goes without a burden," suggesting that it lacked depth without a bass line—but also punningly implying Robinson had rid herself of the burden of the baby she had been carrying.[15] The allusion also mobilized Beatrice's bawdy banter about the cuckolding of husbands; it thus reminded readers who knew their Shakespeare that Robinson had been, throughout her time as a kept mistress, a married woman. Pleased with its own multiple allusiveness—or abusiveness—Gifford's reference, like those of his master, Pope, conceitedly enacted the argument it existed to defend—that poetry ought to remain what it had traditionally been, the preserve of an educated, witty, male elite. Robinson's disability was both textual and sexual, poetic justice for her promiscuity in literature and life, and Gifford, policing gender roles, was determined to rub in that justice all over again. He told her with gleeful viciousness to "forget her state and move on crutches towards the grave."[16] After Robinson's death, he added a note revealing that it was as much her political as her poetical writing that had provoked his attack: "This wretched woman," he wrote, "in the wane of her beauty fell into merited poverty, exchanged poetry for politics, and wrote abusive trash against the government at the rate of two guineas a week."[17]

RADICAL ALLUSION

Robinson's writing, as Gifford saw, became progressively more radical through the 1790s. In the process, it became more allusive—and differently allusive. If in 1791 allusion was personalized and pointed in a fractious political culture, by the middle of the decade it had become a matter of life and death. As I showed above, the 1794 treason trials made allusion a capital issue: the prosecution of radicals hinged on whether an expression could be construed as a means of imagining the king's death. The following year, the Seditious Meetings and Assemblies Act made it illegal for a venue to host lectures on "any supposed public grievance, or any matters relating to the Laws, Constitution, Government, or Policy of these kingdoms."[18] Direct statements of republicanism, and direct criticisms of the monarch or ministers, risked arrest and trial. Easily construed allusions also did. Critics of the government had henceforth to tread very carefully, and so had recourse to obliquity. Oblique allusions that were understood but could not be proved to refer to present circumstances became central features of radical discourse. Thelwall, after his acquittal on treason charges, turned to the classical past, offering in 1795 lectures on ancient Rome about which Henry Crabb Robinson wrote "He certainly possesses great address in producing through the medium of another country the very spirit of our own Institutions which it might be dangerous openly to publish."[19] The tactic was ingenious: talking about Caesar and the Roman empire, Thelwall could be scathing about current affairs without ever mentioning them.[20] The lectures were popular: their defiance of the censorship laws, in E. P. Thompson's words, was "a national event."[21] Unable to prosecute Thelwall, local Tories frequently had his public meetings broken up by mobs.

In Bristol, Southey and Coleridge followed Thelwall's allusive strategy, Coleridge having been forced by the new laws to discontinue his lectures on contemporary politics. From March to April 1795, Southey gave a course of lectures, with Coleridge's assistance, that were ostensibly "unconnected with—at least not *immediately* relative to—the politics of the Day" (CL, I, 155). He used historical subjects to provide analogies with the present times: "Teaching what is right by showing what is wrong" (SL 125, March 21, 1795). Southey's audience was republican; he included apostrophes to "Paine, hireless Priest of Liberty!" (SL 126, May 9, 1795) but avoided direct attack on the king and ministers, discussing instead the Roman Empire, the "Manner and Irruptions of the Northern nations" and the "American War."[22] Coleridge published the lecture on the northern nations in *The Watchman* in 1796, his journal that took for its motto a phrase uttered by Jesus exhorting Jews to give up sin and follow him, rather than doubt him and seek his death, "That All may know the Truth, and that the Truth may make us free." In a letter, Coleridge reported with glee the power that this allusion gave his discourse. A Tory responded to it by declaring "'A *Seditious* beginning!' . . .—. 'Sir!' said Mr. Fellowes—'the motto is quoted from another Author'—'Poo! quoth the Aristocrat—what Odds is it whether he wrote it himself or quoted it from any *other seditious Dog*?' 'Please' (replied Mr. F.) 'to look into the 32nd Chapter of St. John, and you will find, Sir! that that *seditious Dog* was—JESUS CHRIST!'" (CL, I, 179–80). The radical gospel, echoing in Coleridge's words, gave him the moral authority to call on political enemies to join him, a liberator like

Jesus. Revolution was the Bible; freedom a matter of renouncing the sin of political lies. Allusion stumped Church and King supporters, undermining their claims that God and religion were on the side of the established order, and that they were civilized and the Jacobins ignorant: Coleridge called the Tory's cry of sedition another proof "among thousands that Aristocrats do not read their Bible."

Oblique allusion also became Robinson's method in her last, radical phase—a hallmark of her new, Jacobin literary company. Robinson's source text, however, was not the Bible but the cant language of aristocrats and their hangers-on. As a former kept mistress of such men, she was uniquely placed among the Jacobins to allude in this way. As before, Robinson's move to a new discourse was prompted by her entry into a new literary circle. In 1796 the Della Cruscan, Merry, himself a radical in politics, introduced her into the still more radical William Godwin, and her writing also became progressively more radical as she associated with Godwin's circle. The satirical allusions of *Walsingham* were followed by the feminist polemic of *A Letter to the Women of England* (1799), a work shaped by acquaintance with Mary Wollstonecraft. Citing the *Vindication of the Rights of Woman*, Robinson condemned the libertinism that tolerated male and punished female infidelity and treated women as consumable bodies to be cast off when their physical attraction waned. Again, she undermined the claims of the Whig leadership to offer any alternative to the exploitative social mores of ruling classes. She alluded to the Prince of Wales as an example: "He is still the lordly reveller; the master of his pleasures; the tolerated breaker of his oath." Women, "under similar circumstances," had to "endure neglect, infidelity and scorn."[23] The justice of this charge was of little avail when made by Robinson, for it only reminded readers of her past success in putting her own married body on show for a price. Even as a radical writer, then, Robinson had to renegotiate the commodification of her body, a commodification she had once exploited for money and fame. In *A Letter* she achieved this renegotiation by learning from Wollstonecraft to reject not just the conduct of high society but also the gendered aesthetics that underpinned the social assumptions of that society. She was led, that is, in a more analytical direction than hitherto, probing the ideology that made gender roles seem natural and challenging the personal allusions, the innuendos, that smeared those who did not play those roles with propriety. Robinson distilled Wollstonecraft's analysis,[24] but also added to it the vehemence that stemmed from her own experience as a woman whom high society had encouraged—seduced—into making herself its plaything. She extended one of

Wollstonecraft's polemical comparisons: women were like slaves, albeit willing slaves—they wore "glittering shackles," mental and physical, because they were taught to want to fit themselves to societal norms that prescribed that they must be beautiful, feeble, and helpless. The physical shackling of black slaves in the sugar islands was, it followed, the logical extreme of what happened to women in Britain: it achieved by force a commodification of people that was produced at home by ideology. Robinson had made the connection implicitly in her 1796 novel *Angelina*, condemning the plantation landowner Sir Edward Clarendon for treating both his slaves and his daughter as marketable property.[25]

A SATELLITE MEMBER: ROBINSON AND THE POETRY OF THE BRISTOL COTERIE

To both Coleridge and Southey, personal allusions of the kind suffered by Robinson were symptoms of "an age of personality" (*Friend*, II, 286–87). They showed that cultural life had descended, in the repressive atmosphere generated by Pitt's Tory government, to unmanly abuse of private character. Attacks of Gifford's kind might shelter behind the implicit form of allusion, but were nevertheless ungentlemanly, violating the code of honor on which public discourse had depended. Coleridge himself was abused, not by name but by allusion, in Gifford's *Beauties of The Anti Jacobin* as a deserter of wife and children because his political writing challenged the establishment's pro-war, antireform policies at home, in Europe, and in the colonies.[26] This was an astute, if dirty, line of attack because Coleridge's writing consistently idealized domestic affection and the loving family—including his own—as a means of throwing into relief the commodification of people in the empire that Britain had built to service its consumer society. This commodification was visible on the streets of Bristol where the wives of rich West Indies merchants took the air complete with the latest fashion accessory—an African page boy.[27] Less apparent, but discoverable in stories if, like Coleridge's friend Thomas Clarkson, one asked enough awkward questions of sailors in dockside taverns, were the bodies and minds broken on the slave ships. Coleridge and Southey, as Timothy Morton has shown,[28] came into their own as poets by connecting the violence done to black people with the genteel culture of wealthy whites: the sugar sweetening the tea that was drunk by polite ladies and gentlemen was, in their rhetoric, the blood of slaves. Consumption of a fashionable drink—a mark of gentility—became, in an horrific parody of the eucharist, a sign of vampirism (and it was Southey who incorporated vampirism into English poetry for the first time).

Reduction of genteel culture to the predatory commodification on which, beneath its dissimulations, it depended, was a powerful proto-marxist literary technique that Cowper, Coleridge, and Southey all employed. It often led in an apparently misogynist direction: fashionable women were targeted because they posed as creatures of sensibility who were horrified by cruelty yet ignored the exploitation on which their lifestyles depended. It is important to notice, moreover, that this technique did not result in a blanket condemnation of genteel ladies: the poets also suggested that fashionable femininity could be a culture that entrapped women. They picked out the "unfortunate woman," in Coleridge's words—the courtesan, the mistress, the unmarried lover—as products of this culture, deceived as much by its allure as by the promises of a particular man. Indeed that man might himself be affected by the libertine values of a culture in which a beautiful woman was a surface to be desired and, if possible, purchased on credit—possessed on the promise of marriage. Coleridge's comments on marriage aligned him with Wollstonecraft's and Robinson's critique: in 1796, he cited her *Vindication* when opposing "the philosophy of sensuality" that required women to be soft, weak, and delicate to be worthy of men's love.[29] Sensuality left women enchained, like slaves, because it deprived them of mental freedom: Coleridge made the point in "France: An Ode"—"The Sensual and the Dark rebel in vain, / Slaves by their own compulsion! In mad game / They burst their manacles and wear the name / Of Freedom, graven on a heavier chain!" (lines 85–88; CPW, I, i, 467).

By April 1798, when "France: an Ode" was published in *The Morning Post*, Coleridge and Robinson had been engaged in a literary correspondence in the newspaper's columns since the previous November, when its editor Daniel Stuart hired them both to contribute poetry and thereby lift its tone above that of its rivals, so boosting its reputation and its circulation (poetry, apparently soaring above the mundane world of commerce, thus became a commodity bought so that the paper could mask its own commodity status[30]). Robinson contributed poems until mid-1798, when illness caused her to retire: her replacement Robert Southey produced scores of pieces until he left to travel abroad at the end of 1799, whereupon Robinson returned and published over 100 contributions, many of them responding to Southey's, before her untimely death in December 1800.

The exchange begun in the *Morning Post* became the most important partnership of Robinson's poetic career: it altered not only her direction but also that of Coleridge and Southey, her interlocutors, and even of Wordsworth, who became involved in this new literary circle by proxy when Coleridge sent his verse to the paper and when Robinson, taught to admire his lyrical ballads, imitated them in her own 1800 volume *Lyrical Tales*. It was Coleridge who initiated the partnership, on December 6, 1797, with a poem that was prefaced as a response to the recently published *Walsingham*. The following day, his "To an Unfortunate Woman, Whom I Knew in the Days of Her Innocence: Composed at the Theatre" appeared. This was a piece that Coleridge had written earlier in the year but that had been excluded from his *Poems* (1797). He polished the poem and then published it alongside Robinson's work in the newspaper so that it seemed to refer to her own notoriety as a former courtesan and actress while also responding to a major theme in *Walsingham*—the social injustice of condemning a woman for her sexual reputation. It also replicated the mode of the Della Cruscan correspondence in which Robinson had previously featured, when poets personally unknown to each other had developed a literary coterie—a flirtation indeed—in the pages of a periodical. Moreover, Coleridge's poem was more Della Cruscan in diction than the conversation poems he was concurrently writing in tandem with Wordsworth: it could not but seem a tribute to Robinson's past writing that showed, by alluding to her style,[31] that her poetry made her a valued literary partner, however notorious her sexual history.

> Maiden, that with sullen brow
> Sitt'st behind those virgins gay,
> Like a scorch'd and mildew'd bough,
> Leafless 'mid the blooms of May!
> Him who lur'd thee and forsook,
> Oft I watch'd with angry gaze,
> Fearful saw his pleading look,
> Anxious heard his fervid phrase.
> Soft the glances of the Youth,
> Soft his speech, and soft his sigh;
> But no sound like simple Truth,
> But no *true* love in his eye.
> Loathing thy polluted lot,
> Hie thee, Maiden, hie thee hence!
> Seek thy weeping Mother's cot,
> With a wiser innocence.

Thou hast known deceit and folly,
Thou hast felt that Vice is woe:
With a musing melancholy
Inly arm'd, go, Maiden! go.
Mother sage of Self-dominion,
Firm thy steps, O Melancholy!
The strongest plume in Wisdom's pinion
Is the memory of past folly.
Mute the sky-lark and forlorn,
While she moults the firstling plumes,
That had skimm'd the tender corn,
Or the beanfield's odorous blooms.
Soon with renovated wing
Shall she dare a loftier flight,
Upward to the Day-Star spring,
And embathe in heavenly light.

                                   (CPW, I, i, 323)

For all the sentimentality of its portrait of maternal love and for all
the condescension of its assumption of command ("go, Maiden!
Go"), the poem ends with an allusion to the apotheosis that concludes Robinson's "Sappho and Phaon" sonnet sequence (see sonnet 44, lines 13–14). Its reference to the skylark, meanwhile, offers a
Burnsian vision[32] of a renewal that readers of the *Morning Post* would
easily have been able to relate to Robinson's renaissance as a writer—
the skylark being a symbol not just of flight from the past but also of
poetic song. Coleridge implies that by her verse Robinson sheds the
reputation that left her defined by her sexualization: she ends not as
an "unfortunate" tainted body but a soaring illuminate.

Coleridge's poem renewed a feminized strain of verse that preceded his relationship with Wordsworth and persisted beyond it. It
presented him as a man of liberated sensibility, who valued lyrical
exchange and spiritual sympathy with literary women, rather than
the possession of their bodily charms. His next contribution to the
Morning Post, "The Vision of the Maid of Orleans, a Fragment" continued this exchange. It was printed immediately before Robinson's
"The Snow Drop" in the issue of December 26. Robinson's poem,
taking advantage of the seasonal emphasis on peace and forgiveness,
used the flower as an image of herself as an abandoned, tender, crippled female:

All weak and wan, with head inclined,
Its parent breast, the drifted snow;

> It trembles while the ruthless wind
> Bends its slim form; the tempest lours,
> Its em'rald eye drops crystal show'rs
> On its cold bed below.[33]

Coleridge's "Visions" (an extract from "The Destiny of Nations") uses similar maternal and sentimental imagery to link Robinson with Joan of Arc, a paragon of female virtue and revolutionary sympathy. For instance, Joan encounters a family frozen to death as they tried to escape the sacking of their village:

> She mean time,
> Saw crowded close beneath the couverture
> A mother and her children—lifeless all,
> Yet lovely! not a lineament was marred—
> Death had put on so slumberlike a form!
> It was a piteous sight! and one, a babe,
> The crisp smile frozen on its innocent lips
> Lay on the woman's arm, it's little hand
> Smooth on her bosom. Wildly pale the maid
> Gaz'd at the living wretch...

> (lines 203–12; *Morning Post*, December 26, 1797;
> cf CPW, II, i, 289–90)

In context, Coleridge's old fragment now demonstrated his credentials as a radical man of feeling by aligning the disabled Robinson with Joan, and with the dead mother, as an innocent female who was sacrificed to the cruelty of the British aristocracy. It also showed him bringing to his own political discourse the language of sensibility for which Robinson's verse was admired, and was thus a decorous tribute to her writing. Moreover, the poem derived from his earlier collaboration with Southey, so was a product of one partnership being revived to establish another. It was in turn followed on January 3, 1798 by Coleridge's "The Apotheosis; or, the Snow-drop," replying to Robinson's snowdrop poem, and by further praise of *Walsingham* the next day.[34]

Coleridge's motives in beginning a literary exchange with Robinson have been explained variously as pity for an ill and impoverished woman poet, desire to associate himself in print with a writer much better known than he, and admiration of Robinson's technical skill as a prosodist.[35] To these I want to add two more that reveal a trajectory in the development of early Romanticism that has been obscured by too exclusive a concentration on *Lyrical Ballads*. First, Robinson was an exceptional figure and writer for reasons that made her fascinating to Coleridge. She had been friend of Wollstonecraft, and was thus a newcomer to a circle of writers of which he was a distant member; his curiosity was piqued. She had a personal history that gave her a unique perspective upon the Wollstonecraftian feminism by which he was influenced; she had a literary style through which she alluded to her past as an embodiment of the commodification produced by the culture of conspicuous consumption to which he also objected.

Second, Coleridge began his poetic relationship with Robinson just after one with Charles Lloyd and Charles Lamb had broken down. He drew her into a literary circle in compensation for their loss, for coteries were vital to him, just as they were to Southey, Robinson's other *Morning Post* correspondent. Having rejected careers in the church, and having alienated themselves by their radical politics from a young poet's traditional means of advancement—a nobleman's patronage—both men sought support by forging groups of like-minded intellectuals. Furthermore, having had their poems refused by the main London publisher of dissenting literature, Joseph Johnson, they were confirmed in making a provincial city the center of what they hoped would be a national network. Robinson had succeeded from, and still published in, London, but was born and educated in Bristol. When she, Coleridge, and Southey were unveiled as the poets of the *Morning Post*, it was as representatives of Bristol writing: "Bristol is remarkable as the birth-place of POETIC GENIUS: The names of CHATTERTON, Mrs. ROBINSON, Mr. SOUTHEY, Miss MORE, and Mrs. YEARSLEY, will prove the assertion."[36] This Bristol writing came in the 1790s to stand for opposition to aristocratic politics and mores: Coleridge and Southey were supported by local dissenting ministers opposed to the slave trade and to the religious and political establishment. These clerics mobilized their connections with Unitarians, Baptists, and Quakers in the industrial midlands: when in 1796 Coleridge went on a lecture tour to gain subscribers for his Bristol-based journal *The Watchman*, it was to dissenting congregations he was introduced and it was from dissenting businessmen that he gained financial support, in the form of an annuity from the Wedgwood brothers and a commission to mentor Charles Lloyd, the son of a Quaker banker. Coleridge then drew Lloyd into a West Country literary coterie that also included his London friend Lamb, and Southey. The young Bristol bookseller and poet Joseph Cottle had already been enthused and became a central figure, publishing their work, creating a congenial meeting place above his shop, and lending them money. A proud Bristolian, he would edit, with

Southey, and publish from Bristol, an edition of Bristol poet Thomas Chatterton. He had already backed the joint writing and lecturing that Coleridge and Southey, together with their Pantisocrat brother Robert Lovell, had produced in 1795. In 1796, he financed and distributed *The Watchman* and issued, at Coleridge's request, a collection of Coleridge's, Lamb's, Lloyd's, and Bowles's sonnets. In 1799 and 1800 he would publish *The Annual Anthology*—the Bristol-based anthology that featured poems by all of the friends, including some by himself and some by newcomer Humphry Davy. Such joint Bristolian publications helped bring the coterie into being, to define and develop its shared language, and to gain it attention. Coleridge's writing flourished—depended even—on his participation in them; they overcame the pressure of solitary authorship; they counteracted the isolation stemming from the repressive political climate; they gave legitimacy to the language he and his friends had worked out in conversation and manuscript.

Coleridge's *Poems* (1797) was allusive through and through: published by Cottle under Coleridge's name but collecting verse by Lloyd and Lamb too, it showed Coleridge as the leader of a group that was not so much a collaboration of individual authors as the expression of mutually developed writerly identity: the contributors (Cottle included, as publisher and editor) built friendship by giving and gaining support in the writing process: each partner helped develop the other's work and addressed poems to the others; all alluded to each other's poems; Coleridge, however, took the lead (not without provoking tension with Lamb).[37] Allusion, in fact, was the volume's key feature, its constant reminder of the shared agenda and mutually developed language. In a volume that celebrated the sustaining power of friendship and the healing effect of country living, allusion expressed both at once.[38] Thus, Lloyd, in his "Lines addressed to S. T. Coleridge," thanks his friend for a truth-telling affection that has taught him to gird his loins and turn away from solipsistic self-pity:

> Where from the beaten pathway to recede
> Reason had taught, Folly's fantastic weed
> To rend indignant, and the impassion'd swell
> Of Pleasure's voice (bidding the bosom dwell
> On softest themes) to scorn with deafen'd ear—
> Where I this perform'd—yet dropt a tear!
> I now shall gird me cheerily to part
> From these disarmed tempters of the heart!
> For Truth might e'en the coldest breast surprise
> Wafted in Friendship's gentle melodies.

Lloyd enacts his gratitude by making an allusion: his phrase "dropt a tear!" invokes Coleridge's 1795 "Composed While Climbing the Left Ascent of Brockley Coomb, in the County of Somerset," a landscape poem that concludes "Elm-shadow'd Fields, and prospect-bounding Sea! / Deep sighs my lonely heart: I drop the tear / Enchanting spot! O were my SARA here" (CPW, I, i, 203–4). The invocation evidences the bracing effect of Coleridge's "gentle melodies," for whereas Lloyd, anguished by the heart's temptations, had "dropt a tear" for himself, Coleridge cries for someone to share his experience of nature's beauty (Lamb uses the phrase in similar fashion in one of his contributions).[39] Lloyd's importation of Coleridge's words into his poem thus exemplifies the corrective effects of friendship, articulated in verse, and stimulated by nature, on a self too enclosed even to realize, as Coleridge realizes, that sentimentality stems from solitude. Read retrospectively back into Coleridge's poem, the allusion puts Lloyd in the position that Coleridge had wanted Sara to occupy: Lloyd becomes Coleridge's walking companion, virtually sharing the view taking and verse making, just as Coleridge, elsewhere in the 1797 volume, had depicted him in actuality:

> O then 'twere loveliest sympathy, to mark
> The berries of the half up-rooted ash
> Dripping and bright; and list the torrent's dash—
> Beneath the cypress or the yew more dark,
> Seated at ease, on some smooth mossy rock;
> In social silence now, and now t' unlock
> The treasur'd heart; arm link'd in friendly arm,
> Save if the one, his muse's witching charm
> Mutt'ring brow-bent, at unwatch'd distance lag,
> Till high o'er head his beck'ning Friend appears,
> And from the forehead of the topmost crag
> Shouts eagerly
>
> ("To C. Lloyd, on his Proposing to Domesticate
> with the Author")[40]

"Shouts eagerly" is somewhat more energetic than "Drop a tear"; the latter was a favorite phrase, it is also worth noting, of Coleridge's hero William Lisle Bowles, who uses it to identify the poet as a soul too secluded and sensitive for the bustle of the busy world. Borrowing it, the Coleridge circle also placed themselves in Bowles's line, even while critically modifying its use. What was in Bowles a sign of a sensitivity born of solitariness became an index of the need for and benefits of sociability.

Poems (1797) was, when published, the apogee of the Bristolian, early Romantic use of allusion to articulate a language of uncommodified friendship. It marked that language as an exemplification of what it described, a way of living free from the exploitation that characterized Britain's governing classes at home and abroad. Yet, only a few weeks after its appearance, Coleridge undermined its language from within by means of the very strategy on which it had depended. Tired of the clinging neediness of Lloyd, who had taken up residence with him, Coleridge increasingly chafed at the disconnection between Lloyd's unfriendly behavior and the language of friendly sincerity that he had espoused. His own preference for energetic activity rather than pining passivity also motivated him to publish, in the *Monthly Magazine* for November 1797, allusive parodies that mocked not only Lloyd's, but also Lamb's and his own poetic vocabulary. The so-called Nehemiah Higginbottom sonnets offended Lloyd and Lamb (and Southey too), not least because they used allusion ironically rather than affectionately, to ridicule rather than bolster the language of sensitive sociability that Coleridge had encouraged his friends to write for most of the previous year. "To Simplicity," for example, parades "mystic" as a cant term of little meaning used to accrue a spurious sublimity:

> And then with sonnets and with sympathy
> My dreamy bosom's mystic woes I pall

> (lines 9–10; CPW, I, i, 356–57)

Coleridge knew the word was frequently used by Lloyd ("Mystic meanings half conceiv'd invest / The simplest forms" and "many a mystic thrill"[41]). Lloyd, however, may have been echoing Coleridge himself in using the term: "mystic dance" appears in "Religious Musings," "mystic ringlets" in "Songs of the Pixies," and "mystic grove" in "On the Christening of a Friend's Child" (all in *Poems* [1797][42]). Coleridge was mocking a word that was not only a favorite motif of the group inherited from the Della Cruscans (whence Robinson also borrowed it),[43] but also epitomized the significance of allusion to it. Not surprisingly, this brought the coterie to a crisis: Lamb and Lloyd, however, attempted to continue without Coleridge when in 1798 they published their verse in a joint volume dedicated to Southey.[44]

Coleridge's self-differentiating mockery of his coterie's language was disruptive, but dynamic. By late 1798, Lamb also declared himself disenchanted with the poetry he had formerly espoused, writing of "the race of sonnet writers & complainers, Bowles's & Charlotte Smiths, & all that tribe, who can see no joys but what are past, and fill people's heads with notions of the Unsatisfying nature of Earthly comforts": he would no longer speak the dialect of their tribe.[45] In time, he would reforge his links with Coleridge, as Southey also did—but not until 1799. In 1797, however, when Coleridge began his newspaper correspondence with Robinson, the coterie in which he had functioned since 1794 seemed destroyed. He turned toward Robinson only a few weeks after the Higginbottom debacle in an effort to renew a circle that had centered upon him but that he had undone. Thus, he carried into his addresses to Robinson many of the characteristics he had developed in Bristol. They were affectionate and allusive, as his poems to Lamb and Lloyd had been; they were also Bristolian in their resistance to commercial imperatives and establishment taste, and in their appearance in the main opposition newspaper—a venue that also meant the poets had regular contact with each other and with a larger readership than they could reach by publishing books of verse under their own names.

If Coleridge saw Robinson as a fellow lyricist he could admire and a victim of libertinism he could pity, she found in him an up-and-coming poet who took her verse seriously and paid tribute to her as a writer, and who sympathized with her post-Wollstonecraft analysis of the destructive effects of consumer capitalism on those allured and abused by it. She rapidly refashioned her verse in a Coleridgean direction, using a plainer diction and portraying victims of commercial exploitation. Thus, the two poets each remodeled themselves—Coleridge modified the effusive Bristol style he had parodied in the Higginbottom sonnets, so as to engage Robinson's own effusive manner; she modified her ornamented style one in the light of his more colloquial dictions. They became visibly of the same radical camp—in politics but also in their revolutionary poetic style—and were attacked as such, alongside Southey, by the government hireling James Gillray in his brilliant caricature of radical friendship, "The New Morality." Gillray, alluding to "To a Young Ass," a Coleridge poem that extended Jacobin benevolence to an exploited beast of burden, featured Coleridge, Lamb, Lloyd, and Southey metamorphosed into animals, while Robinson's novels pour out of a "cornucopia of ignorance."

Gillray's picture was correct to link Robinson not only with Coleridge, but also with Southey. As the chief contributors of poetry to the *Morning Post*, Robinson and Southey followed in each other's verse steps, alluding to each other's poems. Indeed, this vicarious

correspondence, which perpetuated the terms, concerns, and publication modes of the Bristolians, kept the coterie in being, albeit in
displaced form. *The Morning Post* preserved Bristol-style poetry from
London, although it left both Southey and Robinson wondering
whether they would be reduced to paid hacks churning out verse, or
whether they could retain independence and avoid becoming slaves
of the commercial printing press. As Ashley Cross shows, one way
in which they negotiated this dilemma was to publish poems that
play upon their own commodity status as items to sell newspapers.
Southey's verses on gooseberry pie, and Robinson's on bringing in the
bacon, for example, were jokes on their own status as pieces cooked up
for consumption. Reducing the sonnet and the ode—genres normally
associated with lofty and impassioned topics—to celebrations of eating, they were uneasy jests about the poets' inscription, for money, in
the medium they distrusted because of its commercial values. Cross
says of this verse, "Its commodity status becomes its aesthetic."[46]

The *Annual Anthology*

It was in late 1799 that the newspaper dialogue's continuation of
the Bristol style succeeded in renewing the coterie. Coleridge, having repaired his partnership with Southey in September, came to
London in November to write political articles for the *Morning Post*.
He socialized with Godwin and with Stuart, the editor, as Robinson
also did. Coleridge then introduced Robinson to the *Lyrical Ballads*,
a collection in which the themes of their earlier correspondence—
the exploitation and suffering of women—figure large, and to the
unpublished "Kubla Khan"; impressed, she quickly began to write
new verse in response. "The Haunted Beach" was published in the
Morning Post on February 26, 1800. Soon Coleridge recommended
the poem and another, "Jasper" (its title alluding to Southey's poem
of the same name), for insertion in the second volume of the *Annual
Anthology*, which Southey was then preparing as a public statement of
the new Bristol poetry. Robinson, Coleridge told his friend, was "a
woman of undoubted Genius" (CL, I, 562–63) who "was extremely
flattered by the Idea of its being there, as she idolizes you and your
doings" (CL, I, 575–76). If this rather fulsome rhetoric was designed
to assuage any doubts Southey might have had, it also reveals how
keen Coleridge was to include Robinson in a renewed and expanded
Coleridge/Southey coterie to its and her own advantage. In fact, he
need not have worried that Southey might be reluctant to include
the new poems. In December 1799, Southey had written seeking for

the *Anthology* copies of Robinson's and Coleridge's previous verse exchange in the *Morning Post*—"Anselmo, the Hermit of the Alps," "Ode to the Snow Drop" and Coleridge's "The Apotheosis, or the Snow Drop."[47] Coleridge did not provide these copies but Southey was content to insert Robinson's new poems instead. In doing so, he added Robinson to a remodeled Bristol coterie with a reputation for radical politics: Robinson was for the first time publicly a Jacobin poet. Her poems, themselves influenced by Coleridge's, would be resituated by Southey and thus transformed from the ephemeral context of their newspaper publication into representatives of the new generation's poetry, verse intended collectively to make a mark as innovative and Bristolian.[48]

As Ashley Cross argues, the *Anthology* was a relatively new form of publication,[49] a means of giving higher status to magazine and newspaper verse by reprinting it in book form, of demonstrating the poetic standards of its editor, and of revealing the common concerns and shared language uniting a selection of poems that nevertheless exhibited considerable generic, thematic, and tonal variety. To Southey's later regret, the publication risked his and his friends' conventional reputations as poets of high-status genres (epic and ode) by mixing together poems of different kinds, serious and trivial. At the time, however, this variety was both an effort to please readers by including all aspects of Bristol poetry—humorous, occasional, as well as lofty—and an aesthetic challenge to established taste: mixing high and low, Southey engaged in a kind of editorial leveling that the *Monthly Magazine* and the *Anti-Jacobin* viewed as an attack on "literary precedence" and moral distinction.[50] The *Anthology* imposed no hierarchy; readers could find their own paths in it: it emblematized democratic choice and thus seemed Jacobinical in form as well as content, not least because the presence in it of Robinson, the former courtesan, suggested that its mixture of poems and poets was akin to sexual promiscuity. Robinson's demi mondaine reputation threatened to confirm conservatives' gibes that social and political radicalism was merely an apology for vice and immorality. Her commodified body was a ghostly presence looming behind the *Anthology* and vexing its editor, for all the publication's opposition to commodification.

"The Haunted Beach" and "Jasper" were not in themselves controversial poems; they became so when anthologized. The former reveals Robinson alluding to Coleridge's new ballads: she borrows from his "Rime of the Ancyent Marinere" the sea setting, the vivid color imagery, the internal rhymes, the motif of a guilty sailor supernaturally doomed to repeat his penance, as well as certain characteristic phrases. Derived from an incident she had witnessed in 1788, when a battered corpse was washed up and left unburied on Brighton beach, "The Haunted Beach" suggests that the poetic treatment of ordinary bodily lives that she encountered in *Lyrical Ballads*, and especially in Coleridge's supernatural contributions to that volume, gave her a new mode in which she could articulate the experience of the common people. But Robinson was no mere copyist; she adapted, rather than adopted, the form of Coleridge's nautical ballad, creating what he praised as an "absolutely original Stanza,"[51] which intertwined lines of different metrical balance with an intricate and unusual rhyme scheme:

> The Spectre-*band*, his messmates brave
>   Sunk in the yawning ocean!
> While to the mast, he lash'd him fast,
>   And brav'd the storm's commotion!
> The *winter* Moon upon the sand
>   A silv'ry carpet made,
> And mark'd the sailor reach the land—
> And mark'd *his* Murderer wash his hand,
> Where the green billows play'd.[52]

The last three lines of the stanza derive their macabre Gothic from *Macbeth* obsessively washing his hands to remove Duncan's blood and declaring "Will all great Neptune's ocean wash this blood / Clean from my hand? No, this my hand will rather / The multitudinous seas incarnadine, / Making the green one red" (II, ii). This verbal allusion overlays the allusions to "The Ancyent Marinere" that persist throughout; its effect, moreover, is enhanced by the prosody. Robinson's rhyme scheme suspends the expected resolution, protracting the verse by introducing a couplet that, conclusive though its rhyme might normally be, is itself superseded. Suspending the reader's expectations of narrative sequence was, of course, vital to Coleridge's own supernatural poetry, and in appreciating Robinson's music Coleridge paid tribute to an ability that he understood to be more than merely technical. It was, he thought, through control of meter and rhyme that poetry could make readers suspend their disbelief in the supernatural.

The 1800 *Anthology* has been unjustifiably underestimated by critics.[53] Coleridge thought highly enough of it to collect there for the first time some of his most innovative and original poems: "This Lime-Tree Bower my Prison," with its allusion to "gentle-hearted Charles" Lamb, and "Lewti," another piece originating from shared writing (it had begun as Wordsworth's poem) badged the anthology as a public discourse emerging from private friendship, an expression of radical solidarity by a new group of poets coming into print together. Thus Robinson's "Haunted Beach," a balladic tale of natural/supernatural retribution to be visited upon men who exploit their fellow humans, was echoed by the supernatural "The Raven" and a poem that also alluded to Shakespeare's *Macbeth*—"Fire, Famine and Slaughter."

First published in *The Morning Post* on December 8, 1798, "Fire, Famine and Slaughter" was a fierce example of oblique allusiveness. In its context in the *Anthology*, it is a Bristolian work, its manipulation of the language of *Macbeth* resembling Robinson's. Indeed, placed in proximity to "The Haunted Beach," it seemed to allude to her allusion to Shakespeare's play, for it too invoked specters and witches to arraign the guilt of contemporary figures—chiefly Prime Minister William Pitt. A grim parody of the spell uttered by the weird sisters, it does not name names: nowhere is "Pitt" mentioned, though it's stated that "letters four do form his name." But neither does it depend solely on innuendo—on the sneering allusion to the private character of a public figure that Coleridge saw as a disreputable tactic of the anti-Jacobin writers. Rather, Coleridge uses a series of satiric substitutions to attack Pitt for his war policy: invoking Macbeth, he associates him with Hecate, god of the witches and chief instigator of evil; calling up *Paradise Lost*, he links him with Death, creature of "carnage, prey innumerable" (X, 268); punning on Revelation (20.1), he relates him to "the bottomless pit" and the four horsemen of the apocalypse.

BOTH.
Who bade you do't?

SLAUGHTER.
The same! the same!
Letters four do form his name.
He let me loose, and cry'd Halloo!
To him alone the praise is due.

FAMINE.
Thanks, Sister!, thanks! the men have bled,
Their wives and their children faint for bread.
I stood in a swampy field of battle;
With Bones and Sculls I made a rattle,
To frighten the wolf and the carrion crow,
And the homeless dog—but they would not go:
So off I flew, for how could I bear

To see them gorge their dainty fare.
I heard a groan, and a peevish squall,
And thro' the chink of a cottage wall—
Can you guess what I saw there?

BOTH.
Whisper it, Sister! in our ear.

FAMINE.
A baby beat its dying mother,
I had starv'd the one, and was starving the other!

(lines 24–41; *Annual Anthology*,
2 [1800], p. 233)

The poem was a lasting popular success as a Jacobin satire because its form and voice were new: Coleridge's allusive parody of Shakespeare and the Bible produced a macabre comedy that was both grotesquely funny and deadly serious. It owed its existence, however, to the very repression intended to stamp out radical attacks on the government: the combination of allusion to past poets and to present politicians was an innovative response to the laws that made direct critique of ministerial policy—especially the war with France—highly dangerous. It made, in fact, a virtue of this situation; it showed allusive poetry coming into its political own because it could laugh readers into making moral links between apparently unconnected words and discourses—Pitt and Hecate, witchcraft and statecraft, poetry and politics.

"Fire, Famine and Slaughter" was itself echoed by Southey's "The Battle of Blenheim," a political ballad that also worked by allusion. Ostensibly about the French war of 1704, it treated the past as a figure for the present campaign in France. Like Coleridge, Southey mobilizes irony by exposing the horrors of killing in the words of a narrator who appears to justify, or even approve of them:

With fire and sword the country round
    Was wasted far and wide,
And many a childing mother then,
    And new-born infant died.
But things like that, you know, must be
At every famous victory.

They say it was a shocking sight
    After the field was won;

For many thousand bodies here
    Lay rotting in the sun;
But things like that you know must be
After a famous victory.

Great praise the Duke of Marlbro' won,
    And our good Prince Eugene.—
Why, 'twas a very wicked thing!
    Said little Wilhelmine.
Nay—nay—my little girl, quoth he,
It was a famous victory.

And everybody praised the Duke
    Who such a fight did win.
But what good came of it at last?—
    Quoth little Peterkin.
Why that I cannot tell, said he,
But 'twas a famous victory.

(lines 43–68; Annual Anthology,
2 [1800], pp. 36–37)

If Southey shares the sardonic humor and macabre imagery of "Fire, Famine and Slaughter," he also invokes the form and diction of the "Ancyent Marinere." His ballad echoes Coleridge's ballad, for it too takes the form of a confession—a man of experience telling a story to an innocent. It borrows Coleridge's words, transferring to a political context the mariner's description of a thousand rotting bodies:

And a million million slimy things
Liv'd on—and so did I.

I look'd upon the rotting Sea,
And drew my eyes away;
I look'd upon the eldritch deck,
And there the dead men lay.

(lines 230–35; CPW, I, i, 390)

Southey also draws upon the mariner's admission of guilt, "I had done a wicked thing": the allusions strive to politicize his narrator's voice of experience, lending the tale he tells the innocent children a tinge of uncanny horror. Meanwhile the refrain "'twas a famous victory" becomes increasingly hollow with each repetition: progressively ironized, it alludes to the gap between the patriotic rhetoric surrounding and the actual achievement of the contemporary Duke of York, who, unlike the Duke of Marlborough, had signally failed to win any famous victories when commanding an anti-French invasion in Flanders in 1794. At the Battle of Turcoine, York had dithered, never bringing all his troops into action, resulting in an ignominious defeat in which an infantry regiment was wiped out.

The aim of the poem's allusiveness, like that of "Fire, Famine and Slaughter" was thus to show that the ideology of glory that justified imperialist war served the consumption of the poor by the powerful. In these two poems, and in "The Raven," Southey and Coleridge established the Jacobin agenda that is promulgated by the *Anthology*: mobilizing critical voices from the past, referencing each other, a group of poets displays mutual influence, affirms solidarity, and celebrates friendship as a counter example to a government defined by its commodification and destruction of ordinary citizens at home and in the forests and plantations of the colonies.

It was not only Southey's and Coleridge's verse that gave the volume its anticapitalist agenda. The poem that Southey selected to immediately precede Robinson's "The Haunted Beach" also attacked the commercial exploitation of the poor. "An Elegy Written in a London Church Yard" begins as a parody that contrasts the rustic innocence celebrated by Gray with squalor and vice of the Cockney poor. But it becomes increasingly sympathetic and radical as it progresses, concluding that the capital's petty criminals and prostitutes are no more vicious than the avaricious stockbrokers: all are traders.

> Nor you, ye prudes, in envious spleen delight
> When hapless maidens err, by love betray'd:
> Did ye not want the attractions to incite,
> Yourselves might prove the victims ye upbraid.
> […]
>
> Perhaps within this cheerless spot is laid
> Some youth once mur'd in squalid city jails;
> Hands that the merry bag-pipe sweetly play'd,
> Or rak'd the streets in search of rusty nails.
>
> But commerce never with her ample range,
> Rich with gay spoils, their avarice provok'd;
> They never learn'd to barter at Exchange;
> No city feast for them with dainties smok'd.

(lines 21–40, 45–52; pp. 248–49)

By dwelling on prostitutes and fallen women, the "Elegy" cannot but appear allusive to the previous life of the author of the next contribution. Robinson's "Haunted Beach" is thus framed in terms of her biography—as if Southey, editing the volume, wanted to justify the inclusion of so scandalous a woman by showing her former profession to be an example of the metropolitan commodification of people to which his Bristol collection was opposed. Whether Robinson welcomed this contextualization we do not know: on the face of it, however well-meaning it was intended to be, it nonetheless made it difficult for the poetic products of her mind to stand apart from the reputation of her body. Robinson's position was, Susan Luther claims, an extreme form of the difficulty faced by many women poets in the period: how to "claim her erotic and lyrical power without having to deny their contiguity so as to escape being once more (negatively) defined as her flesh."[54]

Lingering definition by her flesh is not, however, the only contextualization of Robinson in the *Anthology*. Before the "Elegy" appears a poem by the Rev. C. H. Sherive that associates her with a Bristolian Parnassus. "On leaving Bristol Wells" makes the hilly city the inspiring home ground of poets cut off in their prime, their delicate sensibility having proved too frail for the harsh world:

> spirits, here, sublime,
> True sons of Genius, darlings of the Muse
> Have lov'd to wander. Such the luckless youth,
> That hymn'd the shade of Ælla and that sung
> The victor Norman: He, whose master-hand
> Call'd from his harp immortal tones; 'till Fate,
> Summon'd by dire Despair, his tuneful breath
> Stifled remorseless

(lines 14–21; pp. 243–44)

Among the Bristol poets alluded to here is Chatterton, who was thought to have killed himself having left Bristol and found himself without a supportive literary circle in London. Robinson is not mentioned by name, but when coming upon her poem just after this one, the reader of the *Anthology* views her as another Bristol genius who suffered when she left the city's "salubrious streams" for the false glamour and the mean streets of London—not least because she had bemoaned Chatterton's fate in *Walsingham*. Thus, the volume reclaims her by contextualizing her as a Bristol poet as well as a victim of capitalist commodification. It welcomes her to a radical Bristol circle and renews the newspaper partnership that she, Coleridge, and Southey had forged. It does, however broach her past immorality as an issue when it includes the poem that Coleridge had addressed to Robinson in the *Morning Post* in December 1797. "To an Unfortunate Woman" appears after "The Haunted Beach," once more contextualizing Robinson as a fallen woman redeeming herself by writing. Despite, or perhaps because of this framing, the *Anti-Jacobin Review* declared the *Anthology*'s style to be an effort "to debauch the passions of the lower and middle orders."[55]

Southey's poetic attempts to radicalize the lower classes had previously been parodied by the *Anti-Jacobin*.[56] In his company, Robinson's sensuous poetic style seemed socially and politically motivated. Her "Haunted Beach," it seemed, was read by Tory reviewers in the context of Southey's prior allusive response to the "Ancyent Marinere." Although it was not included in the *Anthology*, "The Sailor who Had Served in the Slave Trade" had appeared from Cottle's Bristol firm in February 1799 as part of an expanded edition of Southey's *Poems*. It anticipates "The Haunted Beach" in deriving the guilt that possesses the mariner from a recognizable cause in the familiar social world: Southey's sailor is haunted, mind and body, by having, under orders from his captain, flogged a slave woman to death; Robinson's fisherman is plagued by having murdered and killed a shipwrecked sailor for his treasure. At the root of both crimes is greed, as if both poets felt the need to provide a readily comprehensible motivation with relevance to topical issues, for the transgression that in Coleridge's ballad is terrifying because it is unexplained and apparently arbitrary. It is Southey who is most directly topical: his ballad is a graphic indictment of the slave trade that works by dwelling on the destroyed body of the black woman and by linking it to the destroyed mind of the white man: both are seen to have been exploited by the trade that reduces them to tools; and this exploitation is the more shocking because it offends against the code of chivalry that demands men should be kind to the "weaker sex."

> O I have done a cursed deed
> The wretched man replies,
> And night and day and every where
> 'Tis still before my eyes.

> I sail'd on board a Guinea-man
> And to the slave-coast went;
> Would that the sea had swallowed me
> When I was innocent!

And we took in our cargo there,
Three hundred negroe slaves,
And we sail'd homeward merrily
Over the ocean waves.

But some were sulky of the slaves
And would not touch their meat,
So therefore we were forced by threats
And blows to make them eat.

One woman sulkier than the rest
Would still refuse her food,—
O Jesus God! I hear her cries—
I see her in her blood!

The Captain made me tie her up
And flog while he stood by,
And then he curs'd me if I staid
My hand to hear her cry.

She groan'd, she shriek'd—I could not spare
For the Captain he stood by—
Dear God! that I might rest one night
From that poor woman's cry!

She twisted from the blows—her blood
Her mangled flesh I see—
And still the Captain would not spare—
Oh he was worse than me!
[…]

She groan'd and groan'd, but her groans grew
Fainter at morning tide,
Fainter and fainter still they came
Till at the noon she died.

They flung her overboard;—poor wretch
She rested from her pain,—
But when—O Christ! O blessed God!
Shall I have rest again!

(lines 53–100; SPW, V, 290–92)

If Robinson read Southey's poem (and of this we cannot be sure),
she may have found in it a means of bringing the violence and guilt

explored in Coleridge's "Ancyent Marinere" to more recognizably British shores and bodies: while Southey's allusively relocates the encounter between wedding guest and mariner to a groaning sailor met in a Bristol "hovel," Robinson, perhaps alluding to Southey's allusively Coleridgean ballad, finds the murderous fisherman in a "shed" on the beach. Allusion signals not just admiration but also indebtedness: it makes and marks Jacobin poems spring from each other.

In October 1800, Coleridge again acted to publicly include "The Haunted Beach" among the poems that defined his circle: he wrote to the *Morning Post* from the Lake District, sending verses by Wordsworth that he had lightly revised—declaring that they were tributes to Robinson. One of them, "The Solitude of Binnorie," appeared in the paper after a declaration that

> It would be unpardonable in the author of the following lines, if he omitted to acknowledge that the metre…is borrowed from "The Haunted Beach of Mrs. ROBINSON"; a most exquisite Poem, first given to the public, if I recollect aright, in your paper, and since re-published in the second volume of Mr. SOUTHEY'S Annual Anthology. This acknowledgement will not appear superfluous to those who have felt the bewitching effect of that absolutely original stanza in the original Poem.[57]

Here Coleridge was simultaneously puffing the *Anthology* and Robinson; he was also making Wordsworth her debtor—generously giving her in public the status of originator while obscuring her poem's allusive relationship to his own "Ancyent Marinere." If this gesture reiterates his need to extend friendships into coteries of poetic correspondence, it also demonstrates his desire to give his coterie a London base—as well as provincial ones in Bristol and the Lakes—without succumbing to the commercialism of the metropolis. It shows, too, his understanding that poets needed to act collectively to promote their work, using newspaper correspondence and anthologies rather than single-author volumes to claim the attention of a reading public. Coleridge left the authorship of "The Solitude" unidentified: Robinson may have assumed it was by him; the circle was, ideally, to be close enough for it not to matter which author originated what.

In December, Robinson continued the public correspondence by herself publishing a collection—*Lyrical Tales*—named in admiration of *Lyrical Ballads*.[58] This volume contained many poems that echoed Southey's, Coleridge's, and Wordsworth's[59] and several that took her own, sentimental, perspective on the commodification of people by contemporary culture. It also, to a degree not previously noticed by critics, responded to the emphasis in the *Anthology* on dramatic monologues spoken by native people, some exploited by British colonialism, some independent still and proud. "The Haunted Beach" reappeared, now given an antislavery and anti-empire context by its positioning close to "The Negro Girl" and "The Lascar"—a change that may have resulted from the recontextualizations produced by the *Anthology*.

"The Negro Girl" had had a prior existence, having been published as "The Storm" in the *Morning Post* in February 1796. Robinson rewrote it substantially for *Lyrical Tales*, changing the speaker from a white girl, Nancy, to the black woman Zelma.[60] The alterations reflect her tendency to transform her poetic voice by entering dialogue with those of the new poets she admired. Thus, the poem protests against slavery by focusing on the tortured body of the captured African and the heartless cruelty of the slave-ship crew, as Southey had done in "The Sailor who Had Served in the Slave Trade." Robinson writes of slavers who "with blood their hands embrue, / And mock the wretch's pray'r, / Shall guiltless Slaves the Scourge of tyrants feel, / And, e'en before their God! unheard, unpitied kneel" (lines 45–47; *Lyrical Tales*, p. 109). She also voices the colonized native's distress in a woman's words, as Wordsworth had done in "The Complaint of the Forsaken Indian Woman," while taking her maritime setting from the "Ancyent Marinere."

> "Be still!" she cried, "loud tempest cease!
> O! spare the gallant souls;
> The thunder rolls—the winds increase—
> The Sea, like mountains, rolls!
> While, from the deck, the storm-worn victims leap,
> And o'er their struggling limbs the furious billows sweep…"
>
> (lines 19–24; *Lyrical Tales*, p. 108)

Robinson traces the desperate scene she describes to economic causes. She indicts wealthy Britons for oppressing Africans in pursuit of further wealth:

> "O! barb'rous Pow'r! relentless Fate!
> Does Heav'n's high will decree
> That some should sleep on beds of state—
> Some, in the roaring Sea?

Some nurs'd in splendour deal Oppression's blow,
While worth and DRACO pine—in Slavery and woe!

Yon Vessel oft has plough'd the main
With human traffic fraught;
Its cargo—our dark Sons of pain—
For worldly treasure bought!
What had they done? O Nature tell me why—
Is taunting scorn the lot of thy dark progeny?"

(lines 25–36)

If the poem responds to Southey, Wordsworth, and Coleridge, contributing to their circle as an equal, it also sounds a new note of which the male poets were not capable. Robinson's attack on mercantile capitalism and imperialism utilizes her own history as a cast-off mistress abandoned by her lover, for her black speaker laments that the trade has torn her loved one from her. Her white owner, wanting to exploit her sexually, sends Draco, her beloved fellow slave, away. Exploitation here takes the form not just of confinement in a slave ship, or labor in the fields, but deprivation of one's beloved and prostitution to one's owner:

"Torn from my mother's aching breast,
My Tyrant sought my love—
But in the grave shall ZELMA rest,
Ere she will faithless prove;
No, DRACO!—Thy companion I will be
To that celestial realm where Negros shall be free!

The Tyrant WHITE MAN taught my mind—
The letter'd page to trace;—
He taught me in the Soul to find
No tint, as in the face:
He bade my Reason, blossom like the tree—
But fond affection gave, the ripen'd fruits to thee.

With jealous rage he mark'd my love;
He sent thee far away;"

(lines 66–79)

Here, Robinson brings a feminine and feminist perspective into play, linking the commodification of women's bodies in capitalism and in the slave trade as Wollstonecraft had briefly done in prose, but doing so with the emotional power accruing from first-person dramatic monologue. As such, "The Negro Girl" is a lyrical ballad of romantic confession, alluding to and influenced by the allusive verse of Southey, Wordsworth, and Coleridge, which in its emphatic immediacy advances upon the models for female antislavery verse—more distant, more generalizing—that Robinson inherited from the Bristol poets Hannah More and Ann Yearsley. This advance—Robinson's mature, original contribution to radical, Romantic poetry, was enabled by her participation in a common discourse in which one poem called out another in response—a virtuous circle of creativity in which allusion was both a compositional method and a hallmark of fellowship.

If "The Negro Girl" brands *Lyrical Tales* as a collection concerned like Southey to voice the suffering and anger of black slaves in the colonies,[61] then "The Lascar" shows that colonial exploitation began and ended at home. Here, Robinson brings to the forefront a theme that is in the background of Wordsworth's "Female Vagrant" and "Ruth" (also published in 1800)—the physical displacement and mental alienation suffered by those transported to and fro by imperial trade and colonial war. When she wrote, the plight of lascars—Indian sailors who manned the trading ships that plied between Britain and the east—was in the news. Thousands found themselves stranded in London and other ports such as Bristol, unable to find a passage back to India and desperately poor. It is the view of such a lascar, "home-less near a thousand homes"[62] that Robinson ventriloquizes

> "What is, to me, the City gay?
> And what the board profusely spread?
> I have no home, no rich array,
> No spicy feast, no downy bed!
> I, with the dogs am doom'd to eat,
> To perish in the peopled street,
> To drink the tear of deep despair;
> The scoff and scorn of fools to bear!
> I sleep upon a bed of stone,
> I pace the meadows, wild—alone!
> And if I curse my fate severe
> Some Christian Savage mocks my tear!"
> [...]
> "Was it for this, that on the main
> I met the tempest fierce and strong,
> And steering o'er the liquid plain,
> Still onward, press'd the waves among?

> Was it for this, the LASCAR brave
> Toil'd, like a wretched Indian Slave;
> Preserved your treasures by his toil,
> And sigh'd to greet this fertile soil?
> Was it for this, to beg, to die,
> Where plenty smiles, and where the Sky
> Sheds cooling airs; while fev'rish pain
> Maddens the famish'd LASCAR's brain?"
>
> (lines 25–36, 49–60; *Lyrical Tales*, pp. 31–32)

"Was it for this": here Robinson's language is, by an uncanny convergence, Wordsworthian. She uses the question that he selected in the winter of 1798–1799 to launch his own poem of homeless wandering and return—*The Prelude*.[63] It's possible that Coleridge had communicated Wordsworth's manuscript lines to her and the phrase was an allusion to them, but more likely that "The Lascar" was borrowing from Southey's poem "History," published in the *Morning Post*, January 16, 1799, which also featured in the *Anthology* (who, if either, of Southey and Wordsworth gave the phrase to each other is unclear). In Southey's poem, "Was it for this" is a question dramatizing Britons' falling off from the example offered by the past:

> Oh shame! shame!
> Was it for this I waken'd thy young mind?
> Was it for this I made thy swelling heart
> Throb at the deeds of Greece, and thy boy's eye
> So kindle when that glorious Spartan died?
>
> (lines 15–19; *Annual Anthology*, 2 [1800], pp. 88–89)

By publishing in the *Annual Anthology* Robinson's allusive poetry and his own poetry to which it alluded, Southey emphasized their common poetic language and purpose. Powerful by repetition, "Was it for this" became a motif of early Romanticism's political engagement with history, a rhetorical hallmark of the shared language that Southey, Robinson, and Wordsworth mutually developed. Rebuking the present by invoking the past from which the present has declined, "Was it for this" was itself a borrowing. Deriving from Ariosto and Virgil, it alluded to classical poets' strong denunciations of contemporary derelictions of the tasks imposed by history, thus bracing the poets of the 1790s to their task of moral teaching in their own age.[64]

By having "Was it for this" spoken by a lascar, Robinson allusively gives moral authority to a colonized, exploited subject—it is a destitute Indian sailor who utters Virgil's and Ariosto's famous rebuke. This challenges readers' assumptions about British moral superiority, prejudices that are further undermined when it is shown that mental growth is denied the lascar because he is an unwelcomed Other in Britain. Like a pariah, he internalizes his sense of racial difference as a feeling of inferiority.

> "Where'er I turn my sleepless eyes,
> No cheek so dark as mine, I see;
> For Europe's Suns, with softer dyes
> Mark Europe's favour'd progeny!
> Low is my stature, black my hair,
> The emblem of my Soul's despair!
> My voice no dulcet cadence flings,
> To touch soft pity's throbbing strings;
> [...]
> But what could worse to him betide
> Than begging, at the proud man's door?
> For clos'd and lofty was the gate,
> And there in all the pride of State,
> A surly Porter turn'd the key,
> A man of sullen soul was he—
> His brow was fair; but in his eye
> Sat pamper'd scorn, and tyranny;
> And, near him, a fierce mastiff stood,
> Eager to bathe his fangs in blood.

(lines 73–80, 123–32)

Turned away, the lascar wanders in the dark alone and is then wounded by a traveler, frightened of his blackness, who presumes he wants to rob him of his money. Lamenting bitterly, he is somewhat restored by the sight of a pastoral scene or rural domesticity—a scene verbally close to Coleridge's "Fears in Solitude" and Wordsworth's "Tintern Abbey":

> And now a Cottage low he sees,
> The chimney smoke, ascending grey,
> Floats lightly on the morning breeze
> And o'er the mountain glides away.
> And now the Lark, on flutt'ring wings,
> Its early Song, delighted sings;
> And now, across the upland mead,
> The Swains their flocks to shelter lead;
> The shelt'ring woods, wave to and fro;

> The yellow plains, far distant, glow;
> And all things wake to life and joy,
> All! but the famish'd Indian Boy!

(lines 289–300)

Virtuous rustics act differently from wealthy merchants and travelers: they come to the black man's aid when they see him fall. But the villagers are too late: he dies before they reach him. The poem ends bleakly, suggesting that the common humanity that overcomes the commodifying gaze of imperialism and capitalism is an unrealized possibility in contemporary England.

Lyrical Tales was Robinson's most innovative and radical achievement, a volume enabled by allusion to Southey, Wordsworth, and Coleridge that benefited from and also developed *Lyrical Ballads'* voicing of the experience of oppressed people alienated in England's green and pleasant lands (home and abroad). It was published in December 1800, just two months after she and Coleridge had continued their verse exchange; in October, Robinson sent him her "Ode, Inscribed to the Infant Son of S. T. Coleridge" (published in *The Morning Post*, October 17, 1800). This poem quoted from and alluded to Coleridge's nature poems; it revealed her extraordinary ability to make others' style her own—she wrote of Lake District fells in Coleridgean manner, without ever having been there. Coleridge then replied with "A Stranger Minstrel," welcoming Robinson as a corresponding member of a circle that centered on Wordsworth at Grasmere and alluding to her invocation of "Skiddaw's brow sublime."

> "I would, old Skiddaw, she were here!
> A lady of sweet song is she,
> Her soft blue eye was made for thee!
> O ancient Skiddaw, by this tear,
> I would, I would that she were here!"
> Then ancient Skiddaw, stern and proud,
> In sullen majesty replying,
> Thus spake from out his helm of cloud
> (His voice was like an echo dying!):-
> "She dwells belike in scenes more fair,
> And scorns a mount so bleak and bare."

(lines 9–33; CPW, I, ii, 651)

As he alludes to Robinson's allusions to his own poetry, Coleridge regenders and repoliticizes the natural sublime. Its masculine and

monarchical voice ("sullen majesty") relaxes into the words of
Robinson's poetry even as it pays tribute to the freedom of her song,
which

> Now to the "haunted beach" can fly,
> Beside the threshold scourged with waves,
> Now where the maniac wildly raves,
> "Pale moon, thou spectre of the sky!"
> No wind that hurries o'er my height
> Can travel with so swift a flight.
> I too, methinks, might merit
> The presence of her spirit!
> To me too might belong
> The honour of her song and witching melody,
> Which most resembles me,
> Soft, various, and sublime,
> Exempt from wrongs of Time!

(lines 55–67)

The words reflect upon their own allusiveness: their effect is to make
song suspend difference—Coleridge as Skiddaw as Robinson as
Coleridge—a grace dissolving place. A circle of quotation becomes
a spiral; melody returns echo; the poem is an epitome of Coleridge's
1790s' mobilization by, and achievement of, a shared and mutually
developed poetic language that sprang from and renewed domestic
intimacy both in manuscript, for the benefit of a coterie, and in print,
for the public to see.

"A Stranger Minstrel" alluded to Robinson's private life as well as
her poetry: it hinted at the "mortality" that, by winter 1800, faced the
gravely ill poet. On December 26, Robinson died, leaving Coleridge
to tell Thomas Poole—one of the stalwarts of the Bristol years—of
her nobility of being. He did not know it then, but her death was
a watershed: the extended Bristol coterie that he, she, and Southey
had forged, and that had brought a new kind of poetry into focus,
would never be reconstituted. Southey was away in Portugal, and his
projected third volume of the *Annual Anthology* would never appear.
Lloyd would come to the Lakes, but lapse into madness. Lamb would
stay in London, skeptical of Wordsworth's influence; Cottle be left
behind in Bristol. For all of them, the communal allusiveness of the
poetry of the Bristol years would sound again only in muted form, as
the Jacobinical critique of commercialism in the city and the empire
gave way to the exploration of the growth, or dejection, of the now-
northern poets' minds.

CHAPTER 2

BROTHERS IN LORE: FRATERNITY AND PRIORITY IN *THALABA*, "CHRISTABEL," AND "KUBLA KHAN"

The *Annual Anthology* was a product of the Bristol poetry workshop in which Southey and Coleridge took central places. Several of Coleridge's own contributions to it, however, had originated not in the city, and not in Southey's presence, but in Nether Stowey in Wordsworth's. That they reached the public for the first time in the *Anthology* reveals the renewed importance of Southey as Coleridge's friend and as the editor and organizer who brought the coterie's poems to print. Southey continued to be a creative force as well, and in this chapter I examine a rather neglected period in which his and Coleridge's mutual compositional influence had major results. I have three purposes in doing so: first, to intervene in debates about the genesis and nature of Romantic Orientalism; second, to reassess the importance of the Coleridge/Southey partnership in the careers of each and thus in Romanticism; third, to explore the uses of allusion in this partnership. If allusion served among the Bristol circle to acknowledge mutual influence and celebrate literary friendship, while obliquely satirizing enemies, it also acted, for Coleridge and Southey at the center of that circle, as a way by which each paid tribute to the published work of the other, and as a hallmark of the closeness of their creative partnership. In 1800 and 1801, however, it gradually changed to become a means of fashioning a new, lasting style, by each man's self-definition against the other. It is this change that I intend to examine in detail.

In mid-July 1799, Coleridge returned from Germany to Nether Stowey, the center, just two years earlier, of his most intense experience of the stimulating effect of his circle of poet friends. In mid-July 1797, excited by the arrival of the Wordsworths, who came to live nearby, and the visit of Charles Lamb, he had been inspired to write "This Lime-Tree Bower My Prison"—a breakthrough poem in which, buoyed by the presence of friends, he had first perfected the conversational style that appeared to be a spontaneous overflow of feeling. Throughout that poem of July 1797, Coleridge invoked the friends whose departure on a hill walk had prompted its writing: "My friends, whom I may never meet again"; "my Sister & my Friends! to whom / No sound is dissonant, which tells of Life!" (CL, I, 332–36). The poem was an acknowledgement and a gift: Coleridge left it unprinted but sent it in letters to two absent friends—Lloyd and Southey—its function being to show older members of the coterie the exhilarating effects of the just-arrived poets and thus ensure that the newcomers would be welcomed. In the letter to Southey, the poem seems an overflow into verse of Coleridge's chatty and excited prose: both aim to include Southey vicariously in a new experience of friendship and verse sharing. The prose tells Southey that Wordsworth offers him a "suit of rooms" if he wants to visit Alfoxden; the poem name checks their mutual collaborator Lamb (CL, I, 336). The letter effectively "publishes" the poem as a group-derived text within the larger group, and as a sample of the advances that community has allowed Coleridge to make over the poetry of his youth. Between the lines, Coleridge also uses the letter to show Southey the direction in which he wishes to lead the coterie. He praises the parts of Southey's poem "Mary, Maid of the Inn" that are "properly colloquial"; he disavows the manufactured, ignorant, and inflated style of his own "Songs of the Pixies" and "Monody on the Death of Chatterton," old poems that Southey wanted to publish in a volume he was compiling to raise money for Chatterton's impoverished family—a coterie project designed to honor the boy poet whom the Bristol poets revered. A conversational poetry arising from immediate, shared experience would be the new Coleridgean mode of the group: a few months later, Coleridge's parodies of Lamb's, Lloyd's, and Southey's deviations from this mode would cause it to split. Angry, the parodied friends dropped Coleridge; piqued, he instead developed his collaboration with Wordsworth.

Returning in summer 1799, Coleridge found Stowey a painful contrast to the heady days of July 1797. Southey, Lamb, and Lloyd were still estranged and the Wordsworths had not, and would not, come back. There was no circle of friends and poets; Coleridge was restless and unproductive. Southey, meanwhile, had begun to find Lloyd unreliable, and was himself unsettled. His wife—sister, of course, of Coleridge's spouse—then persuaded him to go with her to Somerset in search of seaside air to benefit her health. Once in the vicinity, the sisters engineered a reconciliation between the poets. By August 20, Southey was staying in Stowey. He had with him a new poem he was drafting, an Oriental romance concerning sorcerers and the Arabian youth who destroys their empire of evil spells. The youth is named Thalaba—meaning "seeker after truth," a term usually used of religious zealots (the plural form of the noun is Taliban). He also brought his commonplace book in which he had copied extracts from Eastern travel narratives and histories. Coleridge, meanwhile, had his own Oriental draft to show Southey—some verses later published as "Kubla Khan." Western Somerset became a meeting point of Eastern fantasies.

The reconciliation led to a renewal of creative energy for both poets: they worked together at the same table on their own poems and also on joint ones. They began a collaborative Oriental epic on the life of the prophet Mohammed. This poem grew out of the same material that Southey was using for *Thalaba*—George Sale's translation of the Koran (1734) as well as D'Herbelot's *Bibliotheque Orientale* (1697). The idea was that Coleridge would write the first book, Southey the second, and so on. But of this dramatic scenario, all that Coleridge completed was the opening invocation:

> Utter the Song, O my Soul! The flight and return of Mohammed,
> Prophet and Priest, who scatter'd abroad both Evil and Blessing,
> Huge wasteful Empires founded and hallow'd slow Persecution,
> Soul-withering, but crush'd the blasphemous Rites of the Pagan
> And idolatrous Christians.—For veiling the Gospel of Jesus,
> They, the best corrupting, had made it worse than the vilest.
> Wherefore Heaven decreed th' enthusiast Warrior of Mecca,
> Choosing Good from Iniquity rather than Evil from Goodness.
>
> Loud the Tumult in Mecca surrounding the Fane of the Idol;—
> Naked and Prostrate the Priesthood were laid—the People with mad shouts
> Thundering now, and now with saddest Ululation
> Flew, as over the channel of rock-stone the ruinous River
> Shatters its waters abreast, and in mazy uproar bewilder'd,
> Rushes dividuous all—all rushing impetuous onward.

(CPW, I, i, 568–71)

The poem seemed more typically Southeyan than Coleridgean: the empire-building power of religion, the self-righteous relish for religious violence, the destruction of idolatry by an austere monotheist in the grip of his own vision had featured in Southey's first epic *Joan of Arc* (1796) and in the joint work *The Fall of Robespierre*. But "Mohammed" also bore a certain similarity to the first part of "Kubla Khan"—in which an eastern potentate also founds a civilization by force of arms. I'll return to this similarity later in the chapter.

Southey was more successful: he wrote a hundred and more lines of the second book—and what he wrote was very promising—exciting, suspenseful, dramatic, fast moving, engaging the readers' sympathies for the hunted refugee Mohammed.

> Cloakd in the garment of green, who lies on the bed of Mohammed,
> Restless and full of fear, yet semblant of one that is sleeping?
> Every sound of the feet at his door he hears, & the breathing
> Low of inaudible words: he knows their meaning of murder,
> Knows what manner of men await his out-going, & listens
> All their tread, & their whispering, till even the play of his pulses
> Disturbs him, so deep his attention. the men of the Koreish
> Fix on the green-robed youth their eyes; impatiently watchful
> Wait they the steps of his rising, the coming of him whom they
>   hated.
> He rises & makes himself pure, & turning towards the Caaba,
> Loud he repeats his prayer: they hear, & in eagerness trembling,
> Grasp the hilts of their swords—their swords that are sworn to the
>   slaughter.
> But when the youth went forth, they saw, &, behold! it was Ali!
> Steady the hero's face: it was pale, for his life was a blessing;
> It was calm, for in death he lookd on to the crown of the Martyr.
> Dark as they were of soul & goaded by rage disappointed
> They shed not the blood of the youth; but remember'd their
>   Chieftain his father,
> Abu Taleb the good, & respected the virtue of friendship.
> Baffled, & full of wrath, through Mecca they scatter the tidings:
> "He has fled, has discover'd our plans, has eluded our vengeance.
> Saw ye the steps of his flight? where lurks he, the lying blasphemer?"
> Now to the chase, to the chase! seize now the bow & the quiver;
> Now with the sword & the spear,—ye stubborn of Mecca! pursue
>   him,—
> Seek him now to the North & the South, to the sunset & sunrise,
> Follow, follow the Chosen one's flight! They rush from the city
> Over the plain they pursue him, pursue him with cries & with
>   curses—
> Sounds that rung o'er the plain, & rung in the echoing mountain;

And Mecca received in her streets the din of their clamorous uproar.
But the voice of the Moslem, the silent prayer of the faithful
Rose to the throne of God; & tears of the heart overflowing
Interceded for him whom they lovd & believed his Apostle.

(SPW, V, 475–76)

Despite the promise of Southey's beginning, "Mohammed" ground to a halt and, by January 1800 was in effect abandoned. Its failure is instructive, however: the project showed the two poets more clearly their respective strengths and interests; it clarified what kinds of Orientalist poets Southey and Coleridge were. Southey was inhibited by his skepticism about whether Mohammed himself believed his own claims. An epic on a male Joan of Arc, who believed his own inspiration even if others did not, Southey was prepared to write. One on an imposter, who pretended to an inspiration he did not feel, he was not. And so the failure with "Mohammed" established the direction of the Islamic poem Southey had already begun—*Thalaba*. Over the next 18 months, he worked on a story of an austere prophet who believed himself chosen by God and who destroyed the sensual civilizations that had perverted monotheism into idolatry. *Thalaba*'s theme, like that of "Mohammed," is the power of religious faith— enthusiasm—to create revolutionary movements and the ability of these to topple empires. It is an historical East—a place where civilizations rose, came into conflict, and fell—that interests Southey, with religion as the motive power. His subject is not the nature of belief as such, but belief's social and political power as an ideology. It follows that the psychology of his characters, and the landscapes they inhabit, are of less importance to him than historical events— pursuits, battles, conquests. It is these that *Thalaba* dramatizes— the hero's escape across the desert strongly resembling Mohammed's. The poem is shaped by Southey's central poetic drive to deal, in narrative form, with the effects of religious conviction on the historical stage. Southey is essentially a narrative poet.

Narrative epics were not Coleridge's forte; the "Mohammed" experience would confirm him as a different kind of poet—especially a different kind of Oriental poet. He did not get far before abandoning the joint poem. In 1823 he recalled that, if he had completed it, he would have focused on a theological debate between different kinds of believers. The psychology of belief fascinated Coleridge, not its social and ideological effects—and his failure to progress in the "Mohammed" project reflects the fact that it was to be a narrative poem of battles, conquests, defeats, and victories before it was a debate about the relation of mind, world, and God as conceived by people of different faiths. This failure, moreover, is related to that of "Kubla Khan"—another poem that begins, but does not progress far, with a narrative about an Eastern man of power and empire builder. "Kubla Khan" turns aside from the mode in which it commences— a historical narrative about the building of a pleasure dome, and its prophesied destruction by war—and looks instead at the mental conditions required to make dreams seem real—to build that dome in air. It was as if, then, "Mohammed" reaffirmed Coleridge's direction by repeating a failure: he could begin, but not sustain, narrative poems. He would not be able to complete an Oriental epic; for him the Oriental poem was, instead, a genre in which exotic beliefs could be dramatized—a zone of dream, spells, magic, and enchantment, where strange relationships of mind and world could be played out. From failure came a new, internalized Orientalism of the imagination.

Nevertheless, each poet did borrow something from the other through the intense period of collaboration of which "Mohammed" was one outcome. Their time together in August–September 1799 was not just a period when their different directions became clarified but was also a period of influence—of conversation and of reading merging together, so that who originated what scarcely mattered, and each borrowed from the other images, stories, and ideas that seemed, for a while, to belong to both—the coterie language of the earlier 1790s renewed and intensified after the breakdown had been repaired.

The results of this borrowing of images, stories, and ideas are evident in both "Kubla Khan" and *Thalaba*. Although both existed as unfinished drafts when the poets came together, both were changed by the meeting: as a result, each alludes to the other. We cannot be certain exactly what happened in which order, so I'm going to conjecture two scenarios of influence—alternate versions of how the poems were shaped and reshaped in late summer 1799.

Scenario One: "Kubla Khan" was, Coleridge wrote in 1816, composed in 1797 but left unfinished. There is however, no evidence of what state it had reached before May 1799, when one of Coleridge's companions on his hiking tour of the Harz mountains noted in his journal that Coleridge had quoted, "from a Poem of his own" the lines "And here were Forests, ancient as the Hills, / Enclosing Sunny Spots of greenery."[1] Southey had certainly not seen this poem before the reconciliation in Somerset. But it seems that it was shared that August in Nether Stowey because its opening lines, "In Xanadu did

Kubla Khan a stately pleasure dome decree," are alluded to in lines that were eventually published in Book I of *Thalaba*:

> Where high in air a stately palace rose.
> > Amid a grove embowered
> > Stood the prodigious pile;
>
> [...]
> Here studding azure tablatures
> > And rayed with feeble light,
> Star-like the ruby and the diamond shone:
> > Here on the golden towers
> > The yellow moon-beam lay,
> Here with white splendour floods the silver wall.

(lines 103–19; SPW, III, 9–10)

This passage is Southey's description of the illusory garden of Irem that appears before Thalaba in the desert. The obvious inference to draw is that in August 1799 Southey heard Coleridge recite "Kubla Khan" and, in response, introduced this passage to his poem: the "stately palace," in particular, seems too close to Coleridge's "stately" pleasure dome not to be related to it. If so, we can see Southey's narrative poem about the clash of religious ideologies being reshaped by Coleridge's descriptive set-piece of an Eastern pleasure garden. Southey suspends his narrative drive so as to introduce an episode in which he lingers on an exotic landscape—a place of enchantment like Xanadu. Coleridge has nudged Southey toward a less austere, more languorous Orientalism in which the East is a zone of unreality, an exotic locale for sensual, magical paradises. Behind both stand Spenser's bower of bliss, Milton's evocation of Eden and especially Sir William Jones's 1767 poem "The Seven Fountains, an Eastern Allegory," in which "stately," "palace," and "dome" appear together in a description of an eastern king's landscape garden:

> The nymphs returning with the stately car,
> O'er the smooth plain with hasty steps they came,
> And hail'd their youthful king with loud acclaim;
> With flow'rs of ev'ry tint the paths they strow'd,
> And cast their chaplets on the hallow'd road.
>
> At last they reach'd the bosom of a wood,
> Where, on a hill a radiant palace stood;
> A sumptuous dome, by hands immortal made,

> Which, on its walls and on its gates, display'd
> The gems that in the rocks of Tibet glow.
>
> (lines 82–91)[2]

Later in *Thalaba*, in parts of the poem written after the 1799 reconciliation with Coleridge, more such enchanted palaces and gardens
appear: they are illusory Edens designed by evil sorcerers to tempt
Thalaba away from the path of rectitude, his road of dedication to an
invisible, abstract God. But they all bear the marks of "Kubla Khan"—
registering how strongly Southey was impressed by his friend's verse.
Coleridge, it appears, provided a Jones-derived Orientalism of dream-
like descriptions and scenes that suggest hallucinatory mental states
and these tempted Southey away from the direct plot of his action-
packed narrative poem. Ultimately the dreamy paradises prove false,
as Kubla's pleasure dome also does, because their peace and beauty
is built on violence. Whereas Kubla's paradise garden is threatened
by ancestral voices prophesying war, Thalaba's turns out to be a sorcerer's illusion.

If the pleasure garden reveals the poets' partnership—their sharing of ideas, images, and forms—what supersedes them demonstrates
their incipient difference. While for Coleridge the true pleasure dome
is that built in the imagination of the poet, for Southey pleasure
comes instead from the justification of the righteous. Thalaba's dedication to his austere God is rewarded when, guided by his faith, he
avenges the killing of his father, at the cost of his own life. Right has
prevailed, through violence, and the knowledge that it is has prevailed
is its own reward. Thus, in Southey's poetic scheme, the Coleridgean
paradise garden provides scenery and decoration and is not essential to the moral action of the poem. Nevertheless, the Coleridgean
effect is shown in the difference of *Thalaba* from the abandoned
"Mohammed," for "Mohammed" would have been faithful to a real
person and real historical events—its purpose being verisimilitude to
the actual, as if Southey could take the reader beyond the texts from
which he gleaned his knowledge, to offer a transparent view of history.
Thalaba, taking up where "Mohammed" left off but mostly written
after the meeting with Coleridge, is more a mixture of genres—an
epic that pretends to realism like "Mohammed" though the events
narrated are fictional, but also a romance that foregrounds its own
fictionality, telling tall stories of magic spells and exotic realms, as if
the Orient was a fantastical world summoned up by the geographical fantasies and travelers' tales of Western texts. It thus fits the bill
of Orientalism as Edward Said defined it[3]—a Western construction

taken from old books, knowing and caring little for present-day conditions on the ground—that was then projected onto the East, as if the construction could be mapped onto reality. Yet, at the same time, it undercuts this process of mapping a textual fantasy-world onto reality, by foregrounding its own textuality in its notes, which openly reveal it to be a conglomerate of travelers' tales and stories, and, therefore, unreliable as a guide to the real.[4]

The second scenario turns the chronology and the course of influence around and places Southey as a crucial source of the poem that became "Kubla Khan." It goes thus: What if the lines in *Thalaba* preceded those of "Kubla Khan"—if Southey's "stately palace" was the chief source of Coleridge's "stately pleasure dome"? If, in effect, much of "Kubla Khan" was a response to *Thalaba*? To argue thus, we have to set aside the 1797 date that Coleridge, nearly 20 years later, gave for his poem—or at least believe that, when he heard Southey's lines in 1799, he modified what he had already drafted. It's a possible scenario: we know Southey had drafted Book I of *Thalaba* already when he arrived at Nether Stowey, because he tells us so in letters and in a dated copy of the manuscript.

What does it matter if Coleridge misdated his poem—or omitted to mention his 1799 revisions—when he came to publish it in 1816? It matters because if he modified or developed his lines on a paradise garden in the wake of reading Book I of *Thalaba*, or the Orientalist excerpts transcribed in Southey's commonplace book, then his relationship with Southey is as significant on one of his greatest poems as that with Wordsworth was on "Dejection: An Ode"—and this is an influence we—and he—have failed to account for. It matters too because it helps explain where Coleridge's Orientalism came from and of what kind it was. It's a question of both adoption and rejection, about Coleridge learning the lesson of the failure of "Mohammed" and jettisoning Southey's narrative machinery so as to create, from Southey's paradise gardens, a new kind of Orientalist poem—an internalized poem about the way in which the imagination dreams up exotic fantasies in response to its reading of travelers' tales. In effect, "Kubla Khan" becomes a self-reflexive and self-conscious meditation on the East as a purely textual realm—a dreamworld that westerners make up in response to their reading of unreliable travel accounts. It is not Edward Said's projection of fantasies derived from old books onto the real Orient, but a reflexive commentary on the making, from our reading, of fantasy worlds that stay fantastical: domes in air. The process of making-up this dreamworld as one reads is what interests Coleridge, not any real Orient that might be reached beyond the text. His Orientalism, sharpened as he borrowed from but also understood his difference from Southey, does not just internalize the quest romance (Harold Bloom's definition of the romantic lyric[5]) but also reflects upon that internalization—with Thalaba's pursuit of his goal through the Arabian desert transformed into a quest within for the source of imagination's creative power.

The textuality and internality of Coleridge's Orientalism is not simply a matter of a likeness between a few lines of Southey's verse and a few of Coleridge's: Southey's commonplace book, which he brought with him to Somerset, contained passages transcribed from European stories about the paradise gardens of Aloadin, Irem, and of Kublai Khan to which Coleridge's poem is verbally close. Indeed, after a long note from Samuel Purchas on a paradise garden, *Thalaba* cites Odoricus's tale of

> a certaine countrey called Melistorte, which is a very pleasant and fertile place. And in this countrey there was a certeine aged man called Senex de monte; who round about two mountaines had built a wall to inclose the sayd mountaines. Within this wall there were the fairest and most chrystall fountaines in the whole world: and about the sayd fountaines there were most beautiful virgins in great number, and goodly horses also, and in a word every thing that could be devised for bodily solace and delight, and therefore the inhabitants of the countrey call the same place by the name of Paradise.

> (SPW, III, 259)

Southey's notes acted as sources for Coleridge, as the commonplace book was no doubt open on the table as the friends started work on "Mohammed" in Nether Stowey. They then decided to travel together to Coleridge's birthplace, Ottery St. Mary in Devon, walking south past Porlock and the overgrown walled gardens near Culbone and discussing Oriental travel books on the way. From Ottery they proceeded to Exeter, where Southey made more excerpts from travel books in the cathedral library.[6] In September, they parted and Coleridge took the same route back to Stowey—with Oriental travels still on his mind. It may have been on this trip that, ill with dysentery, he rested at a farmhouse a quarter of a mile above Culbone church, dosed himself with opium, and reworked his poem on a paradise garden in the light of the reading matter and conversation that the weeks with Southey had brought him. Certainly, no sooner did he arrive home than he wrote to Southey about *Thalaba* and about Niebuhr's travels in Arabia (CL, II, 533). It's at least possible then, that although a draft of some of "Kubla Khan" existed, it took firmer shape in late summer 1799. As Elizabeth Schneider showed, some very powerful textual evidence suggests much of the text dates from this time.[7] For instance, as Schneider reveals, the phrase "midway on" appears elsewhere in Coleridge's oeuvre only in writing that dates from autumn 1799–spring 1800 (it appears in "Love" and, as "midway on the ocean,") in *The Piccolomini* (CPW, III, i, 487; Act III, scene iii, 64). The phrase alludes to Walter Savage Landor's *Gebir* (1798)—a poem to which Southey introduced Coleridge after their reconciliation at Stowey: "midway on the wave" is Landor's locution. The word "momently" also appears for the first time elsewhere in Coleridge's work in late 1799 in his translation of *Die Piccolomini*: "the whole scene moves and bustles momently" (CPW, III, I, 255; Act I, scene iv, 92). Wordsworth picked this word up, as if he were alluding to a recently encountered "Kubla Khan," in a letter he wrote to Coleridge on Christmas Eve 1799 about his visit to the Yorkshire waterfalls and caverns: "The stream shot from between the rows of icicles in irregular fits of strength and with a body of water that momently varied" (WL [EY], p. 279). Then there is the phrase "deep delight": aside from "Kubla Khan," Coleridge uses it for the first time in "Lines Written in a Concert Room," composed while the poets were together in Exeter: "Such songs in such a mood to hear thee sing, / It were a deep delight" (CPW, I, i, 598). But it also occurs in a passage originally intended for Book II of *Thalaba*, which was written in autumn 1799 (Southey later moved it to Book IX): "That with such deep and undefined delight" (IX, 536; SPW, III, 515). If this reveals the allusive relationship between the two poems, highlighting the poets' renewed mutual influence, it also suggests that much of "Kubla Khan" was developed in autumn 1799. Schneider also notes that William Taylor, in a letter to Southey that Coleridge may have read in Stowey, states "I am glad...you are intending to build with the talisman of song a magic palace on the site of the Domdaniel of Cazotte." Taylor's letter also included some verse, later published in the *Monthly Magazine*, which mentions a girl and an Abyssinian bishop.[8] And Schneider (pp. 207–8) points out that the second volume of Southey's *Annual Anthology* (1800), in preparation during autumn 1799, contains Joseph Cottle's "Markoff: a Siberian Eclogue," featuring the line "I, who in caves of ice have oft reclined." Was Cottle alluding to what he had just seen in Coleridge, or did Southey introduce Coleridge to Cottle's poem?

A third scenario is also possible, in which the influence is mutual and each poet develops his poem in the light of the other's draft and the excited conversations that followed as they renewed their friendship: not so much make-up sex as make-up text. Indeed, the famous 1816 preface in which "Kubla Khan" was said to have been composed in a farmhouse near Culbone is a semi-fictionalized account that, if it relates to his return without Southey from Exeter in 1799, tellingly locates Coleridge's inability to continue the poem to the end of that period of intense creative partnership. In favor of this conjecture is that fact that it's highly unlikely that Coleridge found a copy of Purchas's *Pilgrimage* in such a farmhouse—it was a rare and learned book—or that he possessed a copy and carried it with him (there's no record of his owning the extremely large and heavy tome). But he may have been reading extracts from it in Southey's hand. It was not until he visited Grasmere, the following year, that he encountered a copy—Wordsworth's—in a country cottage—Dove Cottage. His 1816 preface compresses and conflates different moments of his past creative life into a potent myth about the creative mind and the Orientalist poet. Within that myth are allusions that hint, in disguised form, at the text's debts to others, a practice that, notoriously, Coleridge followed when borrowing from Schlegel and Schelling in his *Biographia Literaria* (drafted over the same period as the 1816 preface).

Whichever scenario we adopt—and it will probably never be possible to decide which is correct—what is clear is that their collaboration allowed each of the poets to experiment with different versions of Orientalism, so that Coleridge became, for a while, a more Southeyan writer—and vice versa. The result of this was that each was able to develop a new direction, in which their existing strength was clarified after having been modified by what they learnt from the other as they traded ideas, stories, and images for a month of intense friendship.

The larger significance for accounts of English poetry is twofold—that the collaboration with Southey was more important than critics have often allowed for, reminding us that Coleridge's Romanticism was nearly always a collaborative discourse—whether with Wordsworth, Southey, Sara Hutchinson, or J. H. Green. But also that Orientalism in English verse was refined in the process, with *Thalaba* and "Kubla Khan," the two most influential Oriental poems of the era, each pushed by the collaboration in the direction of an Orientalism marked by exoticism and fantasy derived from travelers' tales, and explicitly or implicitly a self-reflexive meditation on the effects of reading these texts—a literary Orientalism, rather than a narrative aiming transparently to portray verifiable historical events. In *Thalaba* a narrative of action was still strongly present but overlaid with dreamy passages; in "Kubla Khan" the narrative of action is truncated, and the dreamy passages become allegories of the poet's creativity. The former, of course, is more Saidian than the latter since it is at least partly mapped onto a supposed real Orient; neither, however, offers to tell a truth about a real historical place in the way the abandoned epic "Mohammed" would have done.

After Coleridge's return home, Southey stayed in Exeter and the south. There, he found his mental health failing him and eventually fled to Bristol, where he put himself under the treatment of Dr. Thomas Beddoes. A trip to a warmer climate and a change of scene was recommended, and so in spring 1800 he set sail for Portugal. He took with him the *Thalaba* manuscript so as to continue drafting it. The collaboration with Coleridge was still an essential support: as soon as he arrived in Lisbon on May 1, he wrote requesting Coleridge to send him the manuscript of *Christabel*—still a work in progress.

It appears that Coleridge did send him the manuscript, although he was still working on the poem in autumn 1800, for in December Southey wrote verse of his own in response to it—nothing less than a prequel to *Christabel*—of several hundred lines. He intended these lines to be the last book of *Thalaba*; clearly he was so powerfully energized by Coleridge's poem that he chose to make the climax of his Oriental romance a backstory that renewed the collaboration of autumn 1799 from lonely exile. But Southey's prequel was also motivated by puzzlement and critique, as if he needed to dramatize in more straightforward narrative terms the moral ambiguity of *Christabel*—where action gets suspended and who is innocent and who guilty cannot be decided. Thus *Thalaba*, an Oriental tale, gets sidetracked into the chivalric world of Coleridge's poem as Southey tries to resolve, to create a narrative of public actions and reactions to explain—what, in *Christabel*, is an internalized, psychological trauma—the cause of the fall from innocence into guilt, and the redemption from this guilt.

The prequel contains a sub-Spenserian knightly tournament, described in archaic diction, in which the hero Thalaba fights Sir Leoline. Leoline, it is explained, was once the champion of the virtuous damsel and her mother who ruled the land; however, he has been enchanted by the evil sorcerer—the hell hag—who has usurped the throne. He now fights on the hell hag's side against the damsel and her mother. Clearly, this is a displaced version of the plot of Coleridge's tale in which Leoline is enchanted by the witchlike Geraldine to turn against his own daughter and her virtuous mother. Southey may well have read the line that Coleridge omitted from the poem when he published it in 1816, comparing Geraldine's body to the "sea wolf's hide" (CPW, II, i, 659)—that is, identifying her as a foul hag, a werewolf who has changed shape into a beautiful woman. Southey's "hell hag" is certainly foul in body and deed:

> An {old} & hideous ~~blind old~~ Hag
> Hath brought this evil on us; she hath made
> Her giant son our tyrant & by spells
>   {So} ~~Hath~~ won the many to her cause
> That from their loyalty and ancient faith
> Recreant, bewitched to ruin, they themselves
> Give their own children for her sacrifice.
>   ~~Strong is her giant son,~~
> ~~Yet is his trust in {illeg. word} & wizard guile,~~
>   ~~A fraudful enemy~~
> And daily at their Tyrant idols feet
>   With hymns of adoration & of joy
>   They shed the life of man.

(SPW, III, 313)

Southey's story of witches, knights, and enchantment is a Spenserian response to Coleridge's Gothic romance. It explains Leoline's retreat to his lonely castle in the woods by creating a story about his shameful past. Evidently, Southey was trying to work through the mysterious relationship of innocence and guilt in Coleridge's poem, for he turns Thalaba into a figure who performs the same role as Bard Bracy would have performed in *Christabel*, restoring the proper relationship of damsel-daughter and knight by helping to free Leoline from the evil spell that has him fighting against the virtuous. Thalaba's archery lures Leoline onto the holy ground under the oak tree, a spot sacred to the damsel's mother, and there the damsel's innocent words have power to lift the spell:

> On rushes Leoline.
>   And now beneath the Holy Oak
>   He lifts the sword to strike!
>   The Damsel caught his arm,
>   She looked him in the face—she called his name—
> The well-known tones awakened him—
> The spell that had abused his noble soul
> Lost all its power, he dropt the impious sword.

(SPW, III, 315)

It is significant that in Southey's conventional chivalric version, it is the knight and not the innocent damsel who is enchanted and guilty;

the damsel's virtue is not compromised as it is in Coleridge's poem: it restores Leoline. In Coleridge's poem, the restorative power of innocence is in much more trouble, for Christabel is tainted by her complicity in her seduction by Geraldine, and must herself be redeemed before her father can be freed from the spell that binds him. Southey effectively rewrites Coleridge's version of the chivalric tale with a more orthodox morality and more conventional understanding of gender and sexuality.

Having awoken to his true self, Leoline immediately joins Thalaba in fighting on the damsel's side against the usurping hell hag and her son. Southey gives him no interiority; he is simply a fighting champion: evil is to be destroyed by good on the battlefield; the two do not coexist within a character unless that character is bewitched. Leoline at least redeems himself but has to content himself with the supporting role, for it is Thalaba who is the appointed remedy and who destroys the hell hag. The damsel and her mother are restored to rule their rightful realm, but the poem then displays no further interest in them: Thalaba leaves them behind as he journeys underground to the source of all evil spells, which he will destroy. The *Christabel* characters form merely an episode in his larger mission: they are introduced to Southey's poem to narrate, in terms of external, dramatic action, questions about shame, complicity, sin, and guilt that Southey will not explore by giving his hero a morally ambivalent internal dimension. There is no psychological complexity in Thalaba—nor in the damsel, her mother, and Leoline: it is never explained *why* the knight is so susceptible to evil spells. But his shameful actions act as a prequel giving a narrative precedent for his susceptibility to Geraldine's spell in Coleridge's poem. And the prequel, as an allusive intervention in Coleridge's poem, suggests that muscular deeds can redeem guilt. Southey needed to resolve *Christabel*'s moral and narrative suspense—its summoning of guilt as an arresting power—by creating redemptive action. Here then, on the fantasy Oriental stage allowed by *Thalaba*, he imagines might restoring right, and his own input reshaping Coleridge's indulgence of paralyzing moral ambiguity and narrative stasis as it had the year before when the "Mohammed" project, the *Thalaba* draft, and the poets' walking and talking had changed Coleridge's direction in "Kubla Khan." This was now not a coterie trading of images, ideas, and stories but an attempt to recreate such a coterie style from a distance—an attempt that, the distance being so great, inevitably failed and that revealed more about the poets' growing differences than what they had in common. Southey was trying, but not succeeding, except by force, to guide his friend—the prequel was both an allusive tribute and a corrective to a manuscript poem on which, Southey knew, Coleridge was still working. He aimed to give Coleridge impetus in a new direction even as he was himself altering the direction of his own Oriental poem by suddenly introducing Coleridge's characters into it.

Southey knew he had been sidetracked by his fascination for Coleridge's new poem, and by his desire to resolve what Coleridge's fragment left unresolved. He dropped Leoline, the tournament, and the damsel because they introduced new elements and characters just as his poem approached resolution, thus displacing its hero and his quest to the margins. In a letter to a friend, he declared "You will I know not be displeased at the total omission of the Queen & Leoline—a bungling piece of botch work at which my own conscience and taste revolted very soon" (SL 567). So he pruned the new characters out of the published poem.

Nevertheless, if the draft was ultimately omitted and Southey's prequel to *Christabel* never published, the decision to write it in the first place is telling. It reminds us—as does the earlier relationship with "Kubla Khan"—that *Thalaba* is a poem whose genesis was intimately bound up with the relationship with Coleridge, as a poem shaped by Southey's desire to generate, from Coleridge's fragments, historical romances that combined fantasy and action and that would act out in external events (and in the process create a causal explanation of), the moral ambivalence and psychological complicity that Coleridge kept discovering in the old genres of ballad and romance. Both "Kubla Khan" and *Christabel*, then, were seminal for Southey's poem—just as it, in its early books and sources—had been influential on Coleridge. And *Thalaba*, blending the historical and the fantastical, was seen by critic Francis Jeffrey as *the* defining example of the "new system" that Southey, Coleridge, and Wordsworth had together introduced into English poetry. Its hallmarks included "an affectation of great simplicity and familiarity of language." It combined "perpetual exaggeration of thought" with "splenetic and idle discontent with the existing institutions of society."⁹ What we now call Romanticism—what Jeffrey called Lake poetry, that is to say—emerged in its quintessential form from the allusive collaboration—both an intimate exchange and a mutual differentiation—of Coleridge and Southey as they reformed, as a duo, the Bristol coterie in the hills of Somerset and Devon in 1799.

CHAPTER 3

SIGNIFYING NOTHING: COLERIDGE'S
VISIONS OF 1816—ANTI-ALLUSION
AND THE POETIC FRAGMENT

What does it mean when a text seems to confess, but exactly what it confesses to is not apparent? Many of Coleridge's later poems present themselves as confessional pieces, in the manner pioneered by Coleridge and Wordsworth in 1797, but stop short of actually revealing the circumstances that generate the emotional states they explore. Cryptic suggestions, pregnant phrases, and arch hints substitute for plain exposition; the writer seems coy; readers feel tantalized or even cheated. The text has shifted under their gaze: what seemed as if it would be autobiographical turns out to be allusive—it hints rather than reveals, refers rather than details—but what it hints at and refers to is not within readers' knowledge. There is no prior discourse available that, with some effort, a reader could locate and so resolve the present one: the poem raises the expectations of allusion but fails to fulfill them. The later Coleridge, it seems, operates by teasing—preparing to confess but confessing nothing, seeming to allude but alluding to nothing. His poems seem fragments severed from some larger context that the reader has no means of reading. Was this a proto postmodernist playfulness, designed to demonstrate how generic expectations construct readers' notion of reality by raising, but refusing to meet, those expectations—reminding us how texts condition, rather than reflect, the world?[1] Or was it an inevitable consequence of the quest for all-encompassing organic unity?[2] Perhaps. It was also more than that: Coleridge's anti-confessional and anti-allusive fragments had particular causes—political, social, and biographical—and were designed to make a specific political intervention in the political sphere. In what follows, I explore anti-confession and anti-allusion in two texts of 1816 and 1817 that modern scholarship enables us to understand as being related to each other and to some texts of 1803, a privilege not available to readers at the time.

The 1816 text—"The Pains of Sleep"—was published by Coleridge in a small volume of fragments accompanied by "Kubla Khan" and "Christabel." Coleridge tells us there that "Kubla Khan" is a "vision" in a "dream," and that what appears on the printed page is the remnant of "two to three hundred lines" composed, but not written down, in a reverie brought on after taking an "anodyne" (a manuscript preface identifies the anodyne as opium) (*Christabel*, p. 52). Of "Christabel," Coleridge likewise tells us, "I had the whole present to my mind, with the wholeness, no less than with the liveliness of a vision; I trust that I shall be able to embody in verse the three parts yet to come" (*Christabel*, p. 52). Of the three poems in the volume, it is only "The Pains" that is left without any explanation of what the whole of which it is a part might look like—whether it too existed in the poet's mind, or on paper. Coleridge merely states: "I have annexed a fragment of a very different character, describing with equal fidelity the dream of pain and disease" (*Christabel*, p. 54). In a letter of 1814, however, Coleridge had supplied, if not a picture of the whole of which "The Pains" was part, at least an indication of its hidden cause and subject matter: the poem was "an exact and most faithful portraiture of the state of my mind under influences of incipient bodily derangement from the use of Opium" (CL, III, 495). Opium, it would then be reasonable to conclude, was, as the material cause of the mental states of which the 1816 poems were fragmentary pictures, the love whose name Coleridge did not dare to speak in public but to which he alluded by his passing remark about having composed "Kubla Khan" after taking an anodyne. "Vision," it follows, was Coleridge's public euphemism (and private allusion) for a complex of bodily and spiritual causes and effects dependent on opium eating. The *Christabel* volume was an allusive collection of fragments because to spell out the whole story—that the "psychological curiosit[ies]" that it contained illustrated the mind of an addict—was too shameful (*Christabel*, p. 51).

Drug addiction was not the only context that did not explicitly appear in the 1816 volume: there were others surrounding "Kubla" and "Christabel" to do with rivalries with Southey and Wordsworth and to do with the Lake poets' public reputation for Jacobin radicalism. These contexts became pressing when the "The Pains of Sleep" was composed, on a walking tour of Scotland, in 1803. In the letters and notebooks that Coleridge wrote on that tour, the poem emerges from commentaries on his disturbed sleep, his bodily ailments, his drug and alcohol use (opium, ether, and camphor; whisky, rum, and porter), and, lastly, his encounters with the Scots Highlanders he meets on the way. It is these contexts that I want to explore because I think they hold the key to an issue with which Romantic Studies has been occupied ever since Marjorie Levinson's controversial 1986 discussion of Wordsworth's "Tintern Abbey": the relationship of confessional poetry to political issues and historical events that it does not explicitly discuss. "The Pains of Sleep," I suggest, had such a relationship, evident in the letters and notebooks in which it took shape in 1803 (although this has hitherto been unperceived by critics). Was Coleridge, as Levinson suggested about Wordsworth,[3] culpably omitting from the version of it that he published in 1816 and, therefore from its portrait of the self, issues and events that were essential to its genesis and meaning—that were, in effect, part of the whole of which it was a "fragment"? And if so, why? In the opinion of Hazlitt, Coleridge's fiercest critic in 1816, the Jacobin radical of the 1790s now had recourse to various rhetorical obfuscations, evasions and self-abasements in order to pretend that his reactionary present was consistent with a political past that had never really been revolutionary.[4] Was the publication of "The Pains of Sleep" as a fragment that fails to fulfill the confessional expectations that it raises one of these evasions? Was its anti-allusiveness—its cryptic reference to prior discourses that the reader had no means of accessing—a result of craven self-censorship? Bad faith? Or is the case more complicated—especially since the poem is about nightmares whose content and meaning is not fully declared to the dreamer poet? Might the formation of that content by the matters recorded in the poem's context remain unknown to the poet—be, in other words, the poem's political unconscious? Germane to these questions is the fact that, later in 1816 after the hostile critical reception of the *Christabel* volume, Coleridge did prepare some of the poem's context for publication—but shorn of all reference to the poem. He reported his 1803 encounters with Scots Highlanders in his *Lay Sermon*, an explicitly political work. 1816, then—a year in which revolution was widely expected, so poor, hungry, and discontented were the laboring classes—saw Coleridge putting into print for the first time his poetical and political writings of 13 years earlier, but keeping them separate from each other, even though they had once been intertwined.

"The Pains of Sleep" in 1803

"The Pains of Sleep" was the product of a poet who flourished in and longed to renew a coterie. Full of reference to humiliating bodily and mental suffering, it was meant not for print but to engage the sympathy of friends—fellow poets. Its descriptions of nightmare battles allude to the vocabulary that, in the Dejection texts of 1802, Coleridge had employed to depict himself to the circle of friends around Wordsworth—Dorothy and Mary Wordsworth and, above all, Sara Hutchinson—as a sick man dependent on their love for his recovery. In "Dejection. An Ode," the violent images are metaphors applied to the wind, heard outside the room in which the poet is writing:

> 'Tis of the rushing of an host in rout,
>> With groans, of trampled men, with smarting wounds—
> At once they groan with pain, and shudder with the cold!
> But hush! there is a pause of deepest silence!
>> And all that noise, as of a rushing crowd,
> With groans, and tremulous shudderings—all is over—
>
>> ("Dejection. An Ode," Part VII, lines 111–16,
>> CPW, I. ii, 702)

These imaginings are curable, the poem suggests, by recollecting Sara's love and writing to her about it. In "The Pains," however, similar imaginings of a "trampling throng" overwhelm the poet's dreaming consciousness—he retains no distance from them (line 18; *Christabel*, p. 62). As a result, the poem suggests that the language Coleridge formulated within the Wordsworth circle was now in crisis. Coleridge's self-portrait leans toward terror and horror for want of the coterie sympathy that had formerly kept him from slipping over the edge. The poem does not, as the Dejection texts had, expect reassurance; it emerges from a breakdown in the supportive circle, a crisis caused when tensions between Coleridge and Wordsworth led to a separation. Coleridge composed it as a verse-letter sent not to the Wordsworth coterie but to Southey, as an attempt to make common cause with a friend also suffering acute mental distress and thereby to persuade him to come and live in Keswick. The poem was a desperate bid to renew the partnership that predated friendship with the Wordsworths—the Bristol circle of poetry and pantisocracy centered on Coleridge, Southey, Robert Lovell, and their wives—the three Fricker sisters. As such, it was successful: "publication" by letter within the now-dispersed coterie reassembled the circle; Southey and the Fricker sisters did come to share a house with Coleridge and his wife. Having served its function, Coleridge laid it aside: it did not see print for a further 13 years.

The crisis that led to "The Pains" began on a wet tour of Scotland that Coleridge, Wordsworth, and Dorothy undertook in autumn 1803. In unrelenting rain, tensions with his travelling companions grew to such a pitch that, on August 30, after just a fortnight, Coleridge parted from them at William's suggestion, noting "My words & actions imaged on his mind, distorted & snaky as the Boatman's Oar reflected in the Lake" (CN, I, 1473). Feeling misunderstood by the Wordsworths, whose loving companionship made him all the more conscious of his own inability to be with the woman he loved, Sara Hutchinson, Coleridge feverishly embraced his enforced solitariness. Sleeping little, fuelled by a cocktail of drink and drugs, he walked 263 miles in eight days across the moors and through the glens, bleeding and blistered, pushing himself to and beyond the limit of endurance. After a particularly long day on September 2, he reached Fort William only to collapse at the inn in "hysterical weeping" (CN, I, 1487). The following night, anticipating "another Attack of Gout in my Stomach," he took opium—"a violent Stimulus, which kept me half-awake the whole Night" (CN, I, 1488). Semi-wakefulness, however, was better than the terrible nightmares that plagued him when fully asleep: these, he noted, were "Horrors…I truly dread to sleep / it is not shadow with me, but substantial Misery foot-thick, that makes me sit by my bedside of a morning, & *cry*" (CL, II, 982). Using opium to procure rest yet knowing that "opiates produce none but positively unpleasant effects" (CL, II, 979), Coleridge was, and knew himself to be, in a vicious circle in which his dreams turned the temporal occurrences of the day into a spatial drama "by which the smallest Impulses… *aggregate* themselves—& attain a kind of visual magnitude, with a correspondent Intensity of general Feeling" (CL, II, 974). Among the occurrences thus dramatized were undoubtedly his worry that he was diseased, his anxiety about opiates, and his fear of sleep itself, mixed with repressed resentment of the Wordsworths and guilty longing for Sara Hutchinson.

Sleep-deprived and hysterical (he recorded three attacks altogether during the tour), Coleridge found himself by day in a peculiarly heightened state of attentiveness. A solitary walker, he recorded in intense detail what he encountered on the way—the almost surreal capacity of the bleak landscape to engender in his mind strange reflections and weird analogies. On September 7, for example, he exclaimed to his notebook "O Christ, it maddens me that I am not a painter or that Painters are not I!—the *chapped Bark* of the lower part of the Trunk, the Bark like a Rhinoceros rolled in mud & exposed to the tropic Heat" and "Let me not, in the intense *vividness of the Remembrance, forget to note* down the bridging Rock, cut off alas! from the great fall by the beaked promontory, on which were 4 Cauldrons, & a small one to boot—one at the *head* of a second Fall, the depth of my Stick, reflected all the scene in a Mirror—Gracious God" (CN, I, 1495).

If the landscape was so maddeningly self-transformative in his mind that he had to call on God to steady it within himself, the people he encountered in it also produced disturbing mental images. Everywhere he went, he was shocked by the poverty, the primitive living conditions, the lack of cultivation—all signs of a defeated culture and depopulated country. On September 5, he was near Fort Augustus noting "The Women at work / in about a mile from this, on a savage piece of uncultivated ground...8 miserable Huts, a neighbourhood! The best of which would have disgraced a Beaver, or republic of Termites. & out of their low slanting Door *come with a clip five* tall men, wearing on their backs & limbs cloathes—masks of the present Century!—a little way on, another Cluster of Turf Huts with Peat Roofs, wretched as the former" (CN, I, 1490). Here, the Highlands become vertiginous, alien places: he describes a hut as a Canadian beaver lodge, then an African termite mound. He no longer feels within his native land, but transported to foreign, primitive places and times—and back again—hence his shock that the men who emerge from the hut wear modern clothes, which seem "masks," as if their true apparel should be that of "savages."

Again and again the Highlands played tricks on Coleridge's mind. Near Inverness he saw fieldworkers getting in an oat crop so poor "I thought *they were weeding*—low Oats, so meagre!—and the Harvesters so lazy & joyless!" (CN, I, 1496). Incredulous at a degree of demoralization beyond his experience as an Englishman, he was appalled at Scotland's difference from the Lake District: "Deludingly like Ulswater...(alas! too few Houses, too little motion)" (CN, I, 1469). Faced by this delusive landscape—its beauty concealing terrible poverty, primitiveness, and depopulation—the hysterical Coleridge found his Britishness, his pride in national identity, unraveling—a process accelerated by what he witnessed the locals say. Thus on August 26, he and the Wordsworths were rowed out to Rob Roy's cave by a "Jacobin Traitor of a Boatman" (CN, I, 1469). Coleridge did not record the boatman's treasonable speech, but on August 31, he met "three good Highlanders, two understood & talked Gaelic, the third, an intelligent man, spoke low Scottish only"... "I talked much with the Scotchman—the oppressions of the Landlord—& he used these beautiful words—'It kills one's affections for one's Country, the Hardships of Life, coming by change, & wi' injustice'" (CN, I, 1475). Evidently, as the adjective "beautiful" suggests, Coleridge sympathized with the Highlanders' plight and their response to it: they could not be patriots when forced off their patrimonial land by owners who found that they could gain more profit from sheep grazing than from villagers' rents. The clearances reduced the Highlanders to grinding poverty and to mass emigration, emptying the landscape, destroying clan loyalty, and killing patriotic virtue. The boatman, this later note implies, had good cause for his sentiments: the "intelligent" Scots speaker sounds, in his cadenced lament, like the shepherd of Wordsworth's "Last of the Flock"—another victim who protests the political system that impoverishes and deracinates the rural laborer. But the boatman was, nevertheless, not only a Jacobin—as Coleridge himself was still regarded by many—but a traitor. Coleridge's plain words reveal that to protest social injustice was, in the repressive climate of 1803, not just to be political but also to seem treacherous. War had been renewed with France in 1802, and in autumn 1803 a Napoleonic army of 200,000 men waited near the channel ports while a fleet of barges was constructed to launch an attack on Britain. In these tense circumstances, discontented, disloyal Highlanders were, to English patriots, a real threat to the nation: after all, such men had been the soldiers who, with French support, invaded England in 1745. Once a Jacobite, now a Jacobin: the auld alliance of Scotland and France might be renewed under the revolutionary cockade.

Coleridge had been identified as a revolutionary democrat in the early 1790s but had recanted his support for France and declared his loyalty to his native land in 1798, when Napoleon's first army of invasion had gathered on the channel coast. By 1803, the renewed prospect of invasion threatened to bring these dual loyalties to crisis point by forcing him to take one side and so betray the other—as if the coming violence were designed to punish him, whoever won. Thus, his encounters with Highlanders were troubling: while they strengthened his sympathy for men made jacobinical by injustice, they also left him guilty that such sympathy made him complicit with treachery to the nation to which he had publicly dedicated his love.

On September 10, Coleridge arrived at Perth footsore yet exhilarated, exhausted yet sleepless, edgy, and in extremis. He reported his arrival in a letter meant to comfort Southey, whose only child had just died and who, grief stricken and far from his friends, was desperate.

He told Southey he must come and live with him in Keswick: the two lonely, unhappy poets would strengthen each other by companionship; their broken circle would be renewed—as in 1799 when he had previously turned to Southey in the absence of the Wordsworths (CL, II, 982). He also told Southey how he too had suffered—from appalling health and "dreadful" spirits brought on by "the Horrors of every night"—and sent the lines that became "The Pains of Sleep"—as if to say, "I too am desperate." The next day he wrote to his wife that Southey's news had left him "weeping—vomiting—[in] wakefulness the whole night" as if he had overdosed on "some narcotic Drug" (CL, II, 985). Thus the poem was avowedly a product of the "hysterical" derangement of body and mind that Coleridge attributed to his morbid sensitivity and that he had hoped to heal, but had in fact worsened, by exercise and by sedatives. Anticipating Southey's disapproval of these methods, he declared, a little guiltily, that he had "abandoned all opiates except Ether be one... & when you see me drink a glass of Spirit & Water, except by prescription of a physician, you shall despise me" (CL, II, 982). Other letters and notes, however, suggest that this "abandonment" was recent, partial, and short-lived.

The letter says nothing about his encounters with "Jacobin traitor[s]," but relates in passing an extraordinary incident that suggests how politically tense Scotland was: "I have been a wild Journey," Coleridge declares, "—taken up for a spy & clapped into Fort Augustus" (CL, II, 982). One of several garrison towns built by the English after the Jacobite rising, Fort Augustus was a military stronghold. Evidently, to authorities made jumpy by the prospect of Highlanders joining a French invasion, the arrival there of a dusty pedestrian, who was curious about everything he saw and made notes in a book, was deeply suspicious. Respectable gentlemen rode on horseback: unkempt and on foot, Coleridge looked like a Jacobin and/or French agent (as indeed he had in 1797 when a government agent was sent to Somerset to report on his "spying" activities there). And of course, if the authorities had made enquiries, he had a history of published admiration of the French revolution and attacks on the British government, as well as friendships with men who had been tried for sedition. Indeed, in 1795 he had been in danger of arrest when he lectured in Bristol condemning the show trial and transportation to Australia of Scots radicals whom the authorities regarded as republican revolutionaries. Thus, to the fort authorities it would not have been a difficult decision to arrest a public defender of notorious traitors Joseph Gerrald and Maurice Margarot, who was interviewing local discontents and recording the defenses of every fort that he visited (see CN, I, 1490).

Coleridge had reason to know of the dangers of imprisonment for radical activities. In 1801, his Cambridge mentor Gilbert Wakefield had died from typhus caught when he was jailed for writing a seditious pamphlet. Apparently, Coleridge talked his way out of trouble: he was allowed to leave after a breakfast interview with the governor of the Fort, but not before one of the letters he had been writing had been seized—as he reported anxiously to Southey in the same paragraph as that describing his terrible dreams and enclosing "The Pains of Sleep." Given this textual and temporal proximity, it's likely that the nightmares described in the poem—that the poem's very existence as a means of representing his desperate state of being—were shaped not just by the fallout of his separation from the Wordsworths but also by his imprisonment and by the dangers of Jacobinism and loyalism that the imprisonment dramatized on both personal and national levels. Unspecific though the poem is, it describes dreams that play out dramas of injustice, revenge, conspiracy, and complicity, in which Coleridge is both the ashamed perpetrator of guilty violence and a sufferer from it at the hands of his enemies:

> the fiendish Crowd
> Of Shapes & Thoughts that tortured me!
> Desire with Loathing strangely mixt,
> On wild or hateful Objects fixt:
> Pangs of Revenge, the powerless Will,
> Still baffled, & consuming still
> Sense of intolerable Wrong,
> And men whom I despis'd made strong
> Vain-glorious Threats, unmanly Vaunting,
> Bad men my boasts & fury taunting
> Rage, sensual Passion, mad'ning Brawl,
> And Shame, and Terror over all!
> Deeds to be hid that were not hid,
> Which, all confus'd I might not know,
> Whether I suffer'd or I did
> For all was Horror, Guilt & Woe,
> My own or others, still the same,
> Life-stifling Fear, Soul-stifling Shame!
>
> (CL, II, 983)

Clearly, this is no more a poem *about* political encounters than it is a portrayal of any one dream. But nor is it a *avoidance* of political occurrences or social issues (the poet averting his gaze from what the landscape he travelled through should have shown him, as

Wordsworth is supposed to have done in the Wye valley). Rather, it is a commentary on the nature of dreams and the cause of nightmares. "Desire with loathing" is the contradictory mixture that, according to Freud, leads material to be so traumatic that the conscious mind represses it, only for it to return in disguised, symbolic narratives in dreams. On Coleridge's own theory, events that occur in temporal succession are redistributed spatially in dreams—hence the "everything happening at once" effect he describes in this passage. Yet, if the confused sequencing and abrupt transformations disguise the traumatic material from Coleridge himself, the poem's context suggests its true nature to readers of his letters and notebooks. The trauma stems from his ashamed love of opiates, certainly, but also from his divided political loyalties, brought to crisis point by the feverish encounters with landscape and people that, in his "hysterical" state of being, he endured on his Highland walk. Coleridge both desired and loathed to be a Jacobin revolutionary and to be a British loyalist: he sympathized with the Highlanders' plight and admired their political diagnosis of their disloyalty to the Crown, yet feared being involved in traitorous violence and being suspected of treachery to a country to which he had declared his patriot loyalty. He respected the would-be rebels and their cause, but left them behind on the road, only to find himself imprisoned, needing to reassure men of power whom he despised that he was on the government's side. Surely these compromising and terrifying events induced the guilty desire, frightened anger, and ashamed betrayal that the poem portrays as the emotions produced by his nightmares. As he notes, his own contradictions are the cause of the restless mental energy that generates his dream visions of violence and crime:

> Still to be stirring up anew
> The self-created Hell within;
> The Horror of their Crimes to view,
> To know & loathe, yet wish & do!

Here, Coleridge's analysis of guilty complicity with transgression is close to that of his explicitly political poem "France: an Ode," in which he depicted the French people's support of Napoleon's imperialist militarism as a masochistic desire for subservience to a tyrannical master who exploited them.

> The Sensual and the Dark rebel in vain,
> Slaves by their own compulsion! In mad game

They burst their manacles and wear the name
Of Freedom, graven on a heavier chain!

(lines 85–88; CPW, I, i, 467)

An inability to raise themselves above the dictates of their senses left
them enslaved, yet ready to assist in the enslavement of the hitherto
free Swiss (conquered by French armies in 1798), thereby betraying
revolutionary liberty even while acting in its name. In "The Pains of
Sleep" political events are not the ostensible subject matter, but complicity and transgression are once more shown to be at work. They
occur in Scotland, not France, and in Coleridge himself rather than
the French people—too close to home for him to acknowledge their
cause. Like the French, however, he too is gripped by the sensual in
that he is overwhelmed by the power of dream images—derived from
sight, hearing, and touch—over which the conscious mind has no
control. He is enslaved to his nightmares, which symbolically refract
daytime experiences in terms of power and powerlessness: Coleridge's
unconscious delivers to his sleeping self a sensory image-stream
derived from his traumatic political involvements. His poem recovers
what it can, and reshapes, in meter, the symbolic language of these
dreams: it is a displacement and condensation of dreamwork that is
already a displacement and condensation.[5] The poem is left confessing
and alluding to nothing specific, not because Coleridge consciously
severs it from the context it hints at but does not detail, but because
that context undergoes repression and returns, condensed and disguised, in dreamwork.

"THE PAINS OF SLEEP" IN THE
CHRISTABEL VOLUME 1816

In 1816, when Coleridge finally published "The Pains of Sleep," it
was for his political involvements that he was chiefly known. Living in
London and attempting to manage his opium addiction, he appeared
before the public as a political journalist writing anti-Jacobin articles
in the government-funded newspaper *The Courier*—to the dismay of
his onetime friends among the radicals. He had produced no book of
poems for 18 years and was anxious about his new volume—*Christabel, Kubla Khan, The Pains of Sleep*—being merely a belated printing of some old poems that were already familiar in literary circles
(he had long been reciting them as party pieces and circulating them
in manuscript). The volume, published at Byron's instigation, was a
poetic foray into a metropolitan print culture of which Coleridge was

both hopeful and suspicious. In 1816, a reading public more numerous than ever before was capable of bringing a writer huge sales, turning him into a celebrity—as in the cases of Scott and Byron—whose private life then became a matter of public interest. It was, Coleridge declared, an "age of personality" and he feared that his own personal failings would be made subjects of gossip (*Friend*, II, 286–87).

The reading public was not only hungry to know about writers' private lives, it was also influenced by reviewing journals to a degree unknown in the 1790s, and these journals were bitterly opposed to each other on political lines. The public sphere was disputatious and partisan—and not just in explicitly political publications, for literary culture itself was politicized—hence the damning reviews of the so-called Cockney poets for vulgarizing the traditional literary language of the educated elite; hence also the vilification of Wordsworth's and Southey's literary experiments in the *Edinburgh Review*.

It was to avoid such vilification that the *Christabel* volume surrounded Coleridge's old poems with new prefaces designed to set out a favorable mode of reception—a reception theory in embryo; in the same breath, they also tried to place the author above the fray of a print culture both contentious and in thrall to the fickle tastes of a mass reading public more interested in ephemeral magazines and romances than in traditional poetry. They imagined readers as a select audience entranced by a bard; they depicted Coleridge as a dreamer not consciously in control of his writing; they denied that the verse amounted to poetry—as if to excuse him in advance and preempt criticism that the contents were unfinished. Marketed as "visions" and "fragments," "Christabel," "Kubla Khan," and "The Pains of Sleep" were not quite "poems" and their writer was too dreamy to be held to account in the partisan public sphere: Coleridge, that is, avoided appearing in the volume either as a poet to be judged against other poets, or as the contentious political journalist who had once been a radical critic of government and who now wrote articles calling for radical critics to be arrested.

The effect of the 1816 publication of "The Pains of Sleep" was to make it doubly a depoliticized poem: if politics was implicitly present in the 1803 poem at the level of nightmare images that symbolize the uneasy Scottish encounters recorded in the context, that context is completely removed in 1816, so that even an unconscious refraction of political encounters is impossible to detect. The *Christabel* volume renders the poem safe, distancing the haunted self that Coleridge portrays in it from his guilt about his attraction to and abandonment of revolutionary politics. The poem's final question about "Wherefore fall on me" the terrible "punishments" of nightmares can emphatically not be answered "Because I have been complicit with these would-be rebels and still sympathise with them yet such sympathies involve treachery to my country endangered by French invasion." Nor can guilt at his gradual abandonment of those sympathies, and his breaking of alliances with radical friends, be adduced as a cause. Instead, the poem appears as a confessional fragment recovered from a visionary's mind, with the social and material influences upon that mind not, as expected, spelled out but only hinted at—as by the anodyne "anodyne" allusion to opium. Indeed, in a circular argument (albeit one left implicit), the volume suggests that fragmentation is proof of the writer's visionariness: if his mind was not possessed by images and scenarios beyond conscious control it would be possible to render it more comprehensively on paper. What those images and scenarios were, beyond the fragments published, was not explained. Readers are left hanging—the poem, full of sound and fury, signified nothing, or, at least, nothing traceable to a political past.

THE CONTEXT IN *A LAY SERMON*

Coleridge's attempts to preempt hostile criticism of the *Christabel* volume did not work. The publication was heavily attacked by reviewers: the authorial persona of its prefaces, far from lifting Coleridge above the partisan public sphere, was thought unmanly and weak. The *Edinburgh Review* judged the poems to be "raving and driv'ling" and "utterly without value."[6] Noting that a recommendation by Byron had helped get the volume published, it belittled this alliance as a marketing strategy—a public relations campaign in which one poet's praise of another was a favor to be called in so as to boost sales when a new volume was to appear. Unable to accept poets' sincerity, or see beyond commercial opportunism, the *Edinburgh Review* justified Coleridge's fear of reception in print. And it drew attention to a political context about which the volume had remained silent. Those who had echoed Byron's praise of Coleridge, it declared (67), were "the mean tools of a political faction" who lauded the volume because they approved of Coleridge's journalism (in April 1816 he was terming radical campaigners who occupied positions similar to his own in 1795 "incendiaries," "illiberal bigots," and "anti-patriotic patriots" [EOT, II, 433–34]). It proved impossible in a polarized public sphere for Coleridge to prevent his volume being judged by association with his reactionary newspaper articles. The published poet and the political pressman were not separable roles.

It was perhaps in acceptance that his poetry would inevitably be colored by his journalism that, toward the end of 1816, Coleridge reworked some of the models of the author/reader relationship that he had used in *Christabel* in a pamphlet of social and political argument, *A Lay Sermon*. This publication once more tried to preempt criticism and rise above the fray, beginning with a tortuous prolegomenon designed to justify the mode of address that Coleridge would employ. Coleridge both beseeched the higher and middle classes to look favorably upon his language, and declared that this language was consistent with his past career: from the start, he stated, he had tried to address political matters through the principles embodied in the language of the Bible. But this strategy was counterproductive: it protested too much, revealing Coleridge's fear that readers would judge his style obscure and his politics inconsistent. He turned, instead, to another mode of discourse—an "allegoric vision"—that models an ideal scene of oral instruction and reception. Paradoxically, the vision turns out not to be seen but heard and in this respect it remodels the prefaces of the *Christabel* volume—which depict the relationship between author and reader as an oral inspiration of an audience by a chanting bard.

The "allegoric vision" was a self-borrowing, a text Coleridge had published before.[7] For the author, it acted as a strengthening allusion, bolstering him against the anxiety of appearing in print because it derived from a previous publication wherein he had successfully appeared before the public as a man of political principle. In its new incarnation, it begins with a gothic tale about journeying through the Apennines with a pilgrim:

> We had not long been fellow-travellers, ere a sudden tempest of wind and rain forced us to seek protection in the vaulted doorway of a lone chapelry: and we sate face to face each on the stone bench alongside the low, weather-stained wall, and as close as possible to the massy door. After a pause of silence: "Even thus," said he, "like two strangers that have fled to the same shelter from the same storm, not seldom do despair and hope meet for the first time in the porch of death!" "All extremes meet," I answered; "but yours was a strange and visionary thought." "The better then doth it beseem both the place and me," he replied. "From a visionary, wilt thou hear a vision? Mark that vivid flash through this torrent of rain. Fire and water. Even here thy adage holds true, and its truth is the moral of my vision." I entreated him to proceed. Sloping his face toward the arch and yet averting his eye from it, he seemed to seek and prepare his words: till listening to the wind that echoed within the hollow edifice, and to the rain without, which

> stole on his thoughts with its two-fold sound,
> The clash hard by and the murmur all round,

he gradually sank away, alike from me and from his own purpose, and amid the gloom of the storm and in the duskiness of that place he sate an emblem on a rich man's sepulchre, or like a mourner on the sodded grave of an only one, an aged mourner, who is watching the waned moon and sorroweth not. Starting at length from his brief trance of abstraction, with courtesy and an atoning smile he renewed his discourse, and commenced his parable.

(LS, p. 133)

This scene of instruction resembles the preface to "Kubla Khan" in that it highlights vision and trance, and makes a self-authorizing citation of Coleridge's own poetry (the "Ode to the Rain"). If the setting is gothic—the chapel porch, the storm, the comparison to the moonlit atmosphere of "Christabel"—then so is the "visionary": like an emblem on a tomb and a mourner on a grave, he is a marker of death. In this, he resembles the ancient mariner—a man who has a spectral authority, an uncannily familiar Other who has seen what ordinary men cannot. His wisdom, therefore, is not assailable by normal social debate. By hearing it, Coleridge gains an otherworldly sanction—a knowledge from the borders of life and death that he can repeat to others—as if he were the mariner's wedding guest turned willing proxy. Thus, by a fiction about oral inspiration that associates him with a wandering seer, he bolsters his authority as a print author preaching about society. A means of establishing his credentials for readers, the scene is an allegory that, as in the *Christabel* volume of a few months earlier, narrates inspiration and transmission as being oral, personal, and outside print culture, betokening Coleridge's suspicion of that culture and need for aid in entering it. If not as entrancing as verse, his political writing would at least be a ritualized and potentially holy speech act—a sermon—and if he himself was a lay preacher only, he could claim to have received inspiration from his pilgrim visionary.

The visionary imparts to Coleridge, and then Coleridge imparts to his readers, a "parable"—this effectively begins a lay sermon with an instructive story: Coleridge gives priority in his publication to a religious discourse that, because it is in narrative mode, is less easily challenged than are the moral lessons and social arguments of didactic preaching. Thus, he licenses himself to address the oppositional public sphere, in which everyone's sincerity is suspected and discourse attacked on party grounds, from a vantage point above it. And the parable, it turns out, is about the necessity of avoiding extremism—a point made argumentatively in the sermon proper, even if there Coleridge has to defer to, rather than successfully renew, the entrancing one-to-one oral communication of the visionary in the Gothic chapel. Thus, the *Lay Sermon* delivers a political application of vision but only by virtue of a rhetorical device that derives authority from beyond the sphere of politics and print, and that defers to discourses that, in their orality, cannot easily be commodified within those spheres.

If "vision" is a rhetorical strategy borrowed from the *Christabel* volume, citing his own poetry is another (he had done so in the preface to "Kubla Khan"). The effect of this citation of oneself as an authority is to assert continuity—an unbroken chain between the past and present textual self and between this prose and past poetry. Thus the expectation is created that, in the text proper, Coleridge's past will be drawn on fully; allusion aids a strategy designed to give readers confidence in the author as one delivering a coherent political authority derived from his past. Thus, the introductory tale gives Coleridge, by association, a visionary authority that, even if borrowed and flawed, offers him more purchase than did the dreamy, forgetful persona of the "Kubla" preface or the divided nightmare sufferer of the 1816 "Pains of Sleep." It enables him to launch a social critique that is not reducible to the agenda of any one party. He benefits from the rhetorical strategy for coping with print culture that he pioneered uneasily in the *Christabel* volume; that volume itself, in retrospect, acquires a political resonance that would not otherwise have been apparent, as an anticapitalist, anti-print culture publication.

In argumentative prose rather than tale, parable, or verse, the main body of the *Lay Sermon* identifies and resists the commodifying tendencies of capitalism and criticizes the aristocracy for adopting notions of value that allowed them to enrich themselves at the expense of their tenants' mental and physical health ("Persons are not *Things*" [LS, p. 206]). And it introduces what had, in 1803, been the context of "The Pains of Sleep"—the reports of encounters with Scots Highlanders derived from Coleridge's letters and notes. These reports appear with no indication that they had once surrounded the poem he had published only a few months previously: poetical and political author are kept separate from each other as if association with the guilty, terrified, and desperate self recorded in the poem would undermine the carefully constructed sermonizer who seeks a consistent position above implication in party conflicts. Nevertheless, having created that position, rhetorically at least, Coleridge can discuss the Highlanders more frankly than he did in 1803. He gives more details of their plight. The clansmen, he shows, are being forced from their rented homesteads to make way for sheep grazing that will accrue more profit to the lairds. This capitalist turn by the land-owners is destroying the last vestiges of the loyalty that the chivalric code and the feudal system had perpetuated to the benefit of social harmony and national security. Coleridge then reports more of their speech: their rebellious and violent intentions are now more directly declared—albeit from a perspective whose sympathy is qualified by distance. He quotes one of the disaffected clansmen:

> "If the—should come among us, as (it is said) they will, let him whistle to his sheep and see if *they* will fight for him!" The frequency with which I heard, during my solitary walk from the end of Loch-Lomond to Inverness, confident expectations of the kind expressed in his con-cluding words—nay, far too often eager hopes mingled with vindictive resolves—I spoke with complaint and regret to an elderly man, whom by his dress and way of speaking, I took to be a schoolmaster. Long shall I recollect his reply: "O, Sir, it kills a man's love for his country, the hardships of life coming by change and with injustice!"

> (LS, p. 211)

Coleridge is both more vehement and more cautious in this pas-sage than in his 1803 notebook. He substitutes allusive dashes for the word "French" so as not to raise the specter, in the revolutionary year of 1816, of treasonable sympathy for Britain's enemy. Likewise, "Eager hopes mingled with vindictive resolves" is a detached, abstracted way of hinting that the Highlanders welcomed French inva-sion and expressed revolutionary intentions of taking revenge on the lairds and masters (though, tellingly, its phrasing echoes the paired adjective/noun combinations of "The Pains of Sleep") "Spoke with complaint and regret" is a similarly distanced means of suggesting that Coleridge, far from espousing their sentiments, was disgusted by them—and therefore loyal to his king and country, as he expected others of better education to be (the schoolmaster). That the school-master explicates, rather than condemns, their rebellious declarations allows Coleridge to place in another's mouth an implied sympathy for them and a criticism of the governing classes. Rhetorically, the passage delivers a strong critique but leaves Coleridge's own position in the scene veiled: his persona in the *Lay Sermon* of being a disinter-ested observer is thus maintained at the expense of any exploration of his own political dilemmas, past and present. There is no allusion to the texts—notebooks, poem—which showed that the encounter left him with political nightmares from which—in the opinion of critics who believed he had betrayed his former beliefs—he had still not escaped. This omission was ultimately limiting: Coleridge was unable to write with a sincerity seen to stem from a principled involvement in the issues of the day—from a spelled-out account of his experience of political and social changes—because he was not willing to come to terms in public with his personal history of Jacobinic sympathies and divided loyalties, nor with the full extent of his change to anti-Jacobin journalist. His carefully constructed position of visionary insight depended on reviving his political past only in fragments, rewritten so that they seemed scarcely even to allude to the onetime contexts from which they had been detached.

Disingenuous he may have been; confessional he certainly was not, but Coleridge's partial printing of his 1803 Scottish texts did at least, by keeping his former Jacobinism hidden and putting his loyalty on show, let him articulate a trenchant attack on the changing social mores of the governing classes. His cited schoolmaster—like one of the local authorities who speak in *Lyrical Ballads*—demonstrates that the contemporary equivalent of the feudal world of "Christabel" is in collapse: no warriors or bards will save the day, any more than Bard Bracy did. For all of Scott's idealizations of the highland past, chivalry, Coleridge implies, will not be retrieved in face of the naked commercialism of modern Scotland's Sir Leolines. The *Lay Sermon* is not the *Lay of the Last Minstrel*: Coleridge is not content, as Scott was, to cover contemporary capitalism in the appealing plaid of the old cultural values it had helped destroy. The world of "Christabel" remains in opposition to a modern world that, Coleridge shows, only replaces chivalry with a more self-interested ideology that is epitomized by the heartless "laws" of political economy that justify the greed of the commercialized ruling classes.

TEXTUAL SEVERANCE

His critique limited by his fear of criticism and the need to defer to the reading public that this fear induced, Coleridge's political vision had limited scope in 1816. He could dramatize, by reworking his 1803 texts, the effects of the exploitation of the poor by the rich, but he could not take a stance on a solution, lest, by advocating reform, he revive his reputation as a 1790s radical and undermine his newfound conservatism. Hazlitt recognized this limitation, and its causes, when reviewing the vision of society expressed in *The Statesman's Manual* as a "voluntary self-delusion" and "hallucination" by which Coleridge hid from himself, and from the reading public, the details of the very different practical political measures he had advocated when a democrat and now, as an anti-Jacobin.[8] Hazlitt probably did not know that both the Highlanders in the *Sermon* and "The Pains of Sleep" derived from the same letters and notes (although he visited Coleridge just after the Scottish tour in October 1803 and shared many an evening party with him in the 18 teens). Now that we do know this, however, we can read the poem and the sermon as complementary texts, whose 1803 intertwining Coleridge could not afford to acknowledge in 1816. Published separately from each other, the two textual fragments suggest that Coleridge's traumatic, drug-conditioned Scottish encounters in 1803, and his anxiety about the reception of his writing in the partisan public sphere in 1816, made him unable to explore explicitly the way his relationship to the political contributed to a self in which guilt, fear, and shame were deeply rooted: the poem presents such a self but cannot spell out the political context, refracted as it is through dreamwork; the prose includes the political but eschews exploration of a haunted self in favor of the persona of a detached though sympathetic witness of the Highlanders' sufferings. In the end, both the published poem and the prose are flawed by this: Coleridge, as both Hazlitt and De Quincey saw, was unable, in print, to live up to the confessional promise his texts began by making. He could at best allude obscurely to, but not explicitly examine a whole historical self in which the guilt, shame, and division caused by his political career and his opium eating was deeply inscribed. Their bare-all autobiographies—*Liber Amoris* and *Confessions of an English Opium Eater*—were (among other things) Rousseauvian answers to Coleridge's strategy of publishing himself—his textual past—as a visionary alluded to in fragments only.

-

Chapter 4

Positioning *The Missionary*: Poetic Circles and the Development of Colonial Romance

In this chapter, I investigate the pioneering of a new Romantic genre that, in the hands of Byron and Scott, would become one of the most popular of the era. The colonial romance—the verse narrative that told a story of love and hate between colonizer and colonized in a country undergoing imperial conquest—was a cousin of the Oriental tales that I examined in the second chapter, but was much more clearly related to contemporary power struggles across the globe. Scott's *Vision of Don Roderick* (1811), for example, used the eighth-century conflict for control of Spain to allegorize the Peninsular War between Napoleonic France and the allied forces of the Spanish resistance and of Britain. Byron's *The Giaour* (1813) set a love story between a Christian and a Muslim in the Greek islands, long the possession of Venice and coveted by the Turks and currently the object of both French and Russian/Ottoman ambition. "The Island" (1823), meanwhile, portrayed the recently discovered Tahiti, setting the love of an island girl and a mutineer from the *Bounty* against the colonial order imposed by the British navy.

Byron's colonial romances were best sellers; they were anticipated, however, by a less popular tale from which he learned and to which he paid tribute—William Lisle Bowles's *The Missionary* (1813). Bowles's romance was set not in the East, but in the West: it depicted cross-cultural love in South America during the Spanish conquest—a topical subject in 1813 because of the liberation struggles, supplied and financed from Britain, being fought there. *The Missionary* was itself a response to Southey's 1805 epic on the conquest of America, *Madoc* (Bowles publically praised this poem and sought Southey's approval for his new work, which supplied the love plot that *Madoc* had signally failed to include). And in its turn *Madoc*, a poem drafted over a ten-year period, bore the hallmarks of Southey's and Coleridge's response to 1790s' songs and tales about indigenous people—songs by poets of sensibility including William Hayley, Helen Maria Williams, and Bowles himself. Bowles was particularly influential: the colonial romance was in part an outgrowth of the "Indian" poems that Southey and Coleridge had developed in answer to him, the poet they lionized when, from 1794 to 1796, they first established the "Bristol" language to which Lamb, Lloyd, Robinson, and Wordsworth also contributed. It was an outgrowth produced not just by imitation, however, but by creative modification: in a kind of literary corbeling, the Bristol poets developed new kinds of colonial poetry by building out from the platform Bowles provided; Bowles, the mentor learning from his acolytes, was then enabled to add a new layer further extending theirs. Byron, for his part, added a more exotically and erotically ornamented layer over both. The process was marked by verbal echo and thematic borrowing as well as by self-conscious and demonstrative allusion, including tributary adoption of each other's hallmark metrical and stylistic effects; by these means the shared terms and favored forms of the 1790s Coleridge/Southey/Wordsworth coterie were developed into a genre designed to respond to the great historical events being played out in the early 1800s.

BOWLES AND THE INDIAN SONG

Writing to a friend in November 1794, Southey asked "Have you read Bowles's sonnets? They are most beautiful. I know no poems that ever went so much to my heart" (SL 114). It was their melancholy revisiting of favorite places that endeared these sonnets to the young poet, and led him to imitate in his own work Bowles's delicate reflections on the passing of time. When he met Coleridge in June 1794, he found his enthusiasm shared—so much so that in autumn 1796 Coleridge put together an anthology of sonnets by himself, Southey, Lamb, Lloyd, and Bowles and had it privately printed (price 6d). Intended to be bound together with Bowles's own poems, the anthology was a tribute in which Coleridge aligned his friends as Bowles's acolytes and summoned him as their companion in print—they not only imitated Bowles's style but also made allusions to him as their father-figure. Pleased at having, by becoming editor and publisher, fulfilled his wish of sharing the page with his hero, Coleridge gave copies to friends, spreading his enthusiasm and widening the circle of influence to which the volume testified. This was social authorship in action—Coleridge creating a group publication in which individual identities were pooled.

Bowles's was a formative influence, powerful enough for both poets to remember their debt 20 years later. In 1815, Southey told Bowles, "I am indebted to you for many hours of deep enjoyment, and for great improvement in our common art,—for your poems came into my hands when I was nineteen and *fed* upon them" (SL 2558). In 1817, Coleridge declared that Bowles was (with Cowper) "the first who combined natural thoughts with natural diction; the first who reconciled the heart with the head" (CBL, I, 25). And though it was Bowles's sonnets that impressed him most,[1] the lyric poems were also seminal, for both their "natural" diction and rhythm, and their imagery and themes. Bowles favored songs and tales featuring native peoples—Indians and Africans; his evocation of the Pacific islander Lee Boo, a poem whose "marked beauties" Coleridge noticed in a letter,[2] influenced "To a Young Lady with a Poem on the French Revolution" (1794), a piece wherein Coleridge declares "My soul amid the pensive twilight gloom / Mourned with the breeze O Lee Boo! o'er thy tomb" (CL, I, 104). Here Coleridge, alluding to Bowles's poem, takes Bowles's trademark stance of melancholy brooding over suffering, and adopts wholesale his trick of making noble "savages" symbolize the destruction of innocence when it comes into contact with "civilized" society. Similarly, in his "Greek Ode" on the slave trade, composed for a prize competition at Cambridge, Coleridge adapted lines from Bowles's "The African," a poem in which the slave is comforted in his bondage by his fellows' vision of an idyllic afterlife in the spirit world.[3]

> Fleeter than the hurricane,
> Till thou view those scenes again,
> Where thy father's hut was rear'd,
> Where thy mother's voice was heard;
> Where thy infant-brothers play'd
> Beneath the fragrant citron's shade;
> Where through green savannahs wide
> Cooling rivers silent glide,
> Or the shrill sigarras sing
> Ceaseless to their murmuring;
> Where the dance, the festive song,

> Of many a friend divided long,
> Doom'd through stranger lands to roam,
> Shall bid thy spirit welcome home![4]

Rather than induce guilt in his readers by detailing slavery's cruelty—as Southey was later to do—Bowles offers them a vision of posthumous pastoral bliss that renders the slave more enviable than pitiable. Africans' spirit world, in Bowles's harmonious couplets, is an exotic idyll in which busy commercial Britons can imagine themselves at rest, free of care.

Africans and "Indians" proved somewhat interchangeable in Bowles's songs: his recipe was innocent, noble savagery and an approximation, in print, of native people's oral poetry—a song. In one such lyric, Bowles adopted the voice of a primitive South American forest dweller. Bodily at one with nature, Bowles's Indian is guided by tribal tradition. He is governed by an oral memory of the speech of his fathers but is otherwise a free inhabitant of the idyllic forest:

> Home returning from our toils,
> Thou shalt bear the tiger's spoils;
> And we will sing our loudest strain
> O'er the forest-tyrant slain!
> […]
>   By the river's craggy banks,
> O'er hung with stately cypress-ranks,
> Where the bush-bee hums his song,
> Thy trim canoe shall glance along.
>
>   To-night at least, in this retreat,
> Stranger! rest thy wand'ring feet;
> To-morrow, with unerring bow,
> To the deep thickets fearless we will go.

> (lines 15–32)[5]

Pastoral fantasies of this kind showed Indians as Rousseauvian nature-children. They made them autochthonous beings in whom word and deed, and mind and body are one. They turned them into symbols of the natural wholeness that European civilization seemed to have lost—symbols attractive enough for Coleridge to borrow them for his lyrical ballad "The Foster Mother's Tale," which features a youth "Who sung a doleful song about green fields, / How sweet it were on lake or wild savannah, / To hunt for food, and be a naked man, / And wander up and down at liberty." A prisoner in the old world, the youth escaped by boat, along one of South America's great rivers, and "liv'd and died among the savage men" (lines 61–64; 81, CPW, I, i, 229–33).

Southey's enthusiasm for Indian songs surpassed that of his mentor Bowles, taking the form not of generic idylls but of a more culturally specific cycle of National Songs published in *The Morning Post* between August and October 1799. The first and most important to appear was the "Song of the Araucans During a Thunder Storm"; others in the sequence included "The Huron's Address to the Dead" and "The Old Chikkasah to his Grandson": together they constituted a public assertion of patriotism and assertion of Southey's expertise on Native American culture (SPW, V, 372–74, 385–86, 387–89, 395–97). Where Bowles's Indians were generic, Southey's would be ethnographic.

They were ethnographic because Southey wanted to respond to contemporary politics—both in Europe and America, where Indians were increasingly under colonial pressure. The Araucans interested him because they seemed to have realized on the historical stage, in terms of patriotic resistance to conquest, the rustic independence and savage self-reliance that Bowles had idealized in unspecific terms. They had first impinged on European culture in an epic poem, *La Araucana*, written by one of the conquistadores, Don Alonso de Ercilla in 1589; they appeared in English in 1785 when William Hayley part-translated Ercilla's poem. In Hayley's hands, the Araucans became warrior heroes for a Romantic age since they not only fought nobly but also loved deeply, suffered pathetically, and wept passionately. Figures of sensibility, they combined the independent vigor of the "ancient Germans" in Tacitus with the natural tenderness of Rousseauvian noble savages. Hayley's translation represented them as epic heroes and lovelorn protagonists, in some respects worthier of praise than the Spanish.[6] As Hayley recorded, the cruel Spanish governor Valdivia was killed in battle by Lautaro, an Araucan whom the Spanish had brought up as a page boy and who had reverted to his native loyalty.

The reputation given to the Araucans by Ercilla had fueled British fantasies of gaining wealth and power by liberating the riches of South America from the grip of the Spanish. In 1740, a naval expedition commanded by George Anson sailed for the Pacific coast intending to give "due encouragement and assistance" to "those gallant Chilean Indians who have long set the whole Spanish power at defiance, have often ravaged their country, and remain to this hour independent."[7] This expedition failed to raise the Indians, but succeeded in capturing the Spanish treasure galleon.

Attacks on South America were fueled by and in turn refueled a venerable and self-serving British myth, that the Spanish and Portuguese were uniquely rapacious imperialists, in contrast to the mild, commercial British. This "black legend" stereotyped the Spanish and Portuguese as superstitious and cruel and used their treatment of Indians as evidence of the inherent brutality of their empire. So tyrannical was their rule, it was assumed, that the Indians, would, if assisted, rebel, welcoming colonization by the rational, Protestant, commercial British rather than by the descendants of Cortes and Pizarro. The Araucans were living proof: they continued to reject Spanish ambitions upon their territory.

Hayley's translation reflected Britons' historical interest in the Araucans. But it was not until the end of the century that South American Indians became topical, and for a reason close to home, as Britons suddenly found themselves threatened by invasion. In April 1798, Napoleon's French and Spanish fleet began amassing in the Channel ports, ready for the conquest of Britain. Faced by so imminent and serious a threat, political radicals were left with a dilemma. They had long opposed the war with France and its Iberian ally that the ministry had pursued since 1793, and had persisted in upholding the ideals of the French Revolution (even if they had criticized some of the actions carried out in its name). For this they were now pilloried in the press and were pressurized into publicly declaring their allegiance to Britain and enmity to the invading French. On April 20, the radical leader Sheridan affirmed his loyalty to the country, if not to the governing ministry, in a parliamentary speech that was rapturously received as the epitome of nonpartisan, disinterested patriotism. Coleridge followed suit in his poems "Fears in Solitude" and "France: An Ode" a few months later (dating the composition of the former April 20, in allusion to Sheridan's already-famous declaration).[8] And in the following winter, Sheridan also turned to verse, mounting at Drury Lane a drama about imperial conquest and native resistance that was widely seen as an allegory of the contemporary European situation. *Pizarro* dramatized the Incas' fight against the conquistadors, portraying the Spanish as rapacious villains.[9] It was as an anti-French play that *Pizarro* succeeded: it featured patriotic rhetoric recycled from Sheridan's own parliamentary speeches, which united the audience as patriot Britons by turning their anxiety into fortitude and formulating the moral superiority of native defenders to foreign invaders. Sheridan's play was a runaway hit; but in Southey's eyes its success was not deserved: "It is impossible to sink below 'Pizarro'" he wrote in 1799 (SL 443, October 10). His

"Song of the Araucans" was an attempt, like *Pizarro*, to demonstrate his loyalty to his country but on a different model from Sheridan's play: whereas Sheridan had simply transferred his own parliamentary oratory into the mouths of his characters, who were Indian in name only, Southey was determined to create a poem that was ethnographically accurate as well as a patriotic allegory of native Britons trying to resist French imperial aggression. He attempted to get as formally and tonally close to real Indian songs as he could, and followed the historical evidence that the Araucans sang of their heroes in an allegorical verse that was reminiscent of the Celtic Bards and Danish Scalds, being unrhymed and written in anapestic trimeter and tetrameter:[10]

> We gaze on your warfare in hope,
> We send up our shouts to encourage your arms—
> Lift the lance of your vengeance, O Fathers! with force!
>   For the wrongs of your country strike home!
>
> Remember the land was your own
> When the sons of destruction came over the seas;
> That the old fell asleep in the fullness of days,
>   And their children wept over their graves.
>
> Till the Strangers came into the land
> With tongues of deceit and with weapons of fire,
> Then the strength of the people in youth was cut off,
>   And the father wept over his son.
>
> It thickens! the tumult of fight!
> Louder and louder the blast of the battle is heard!...
> Remember the wrongs that your country endures!
>   Remember the fields of your fame!
>
>   (lines 21–36; SPW, V, 372–74)

No simple-minded "savages," Southey's Araucan speakers urge their nation to victory in the name of the "forefathers" whose spirits they detect in the wind. Inspired by their patriarchal bond with nature, they seek restoration of what is their own, displaying a complex awareness of what about their society is worth defending. These Indians are heroic resistors of imperialist violence, a people whose bodily bravery is not some inexplicable innate ferocity but the expression of their self-conscious sense of their political right—Jacobin heroes, as we saw in chapter 1.

The context in which the poem appeared made its contemporary relevance crystal clear. *The Morning Post* was the house journal of the radical opposition. On the day of the poem's publication, August 10, the paper carried news of the flight of Bonaparte from Acre, and relayed rumors that he had "been mortally wounded." It also informed readers that a huge Secret Expedition was embarking for the invasion of the continent: news of patriotic war against would-be invaders dominated its pages. Nevertheless, there was room for advertisements, one of which told readers of a forthcoming spin-off from Sheridan's popular play. Astley's Royal Amphitheatre was producing "an entirely New Operatical Ballet of Action, interspersed with Song, Recitative, Dance and, Chorus...called ROLLA AND CORA; Or, THE VIRGIN OF THE SUN" (August 8). The allegorical import of Southey's verse, and its emulation of Sheridan's, could not have been more apparent. Yet, despite the political context provided by the newspaper publication, Southey's Araucans are not simply allegorical of noble Britons resisting French/Spanish conquest. Projections they are, but ambivalent ones, marked by at least two further contexts. One of these was Southey's continuing opposition to Britain's government, which was expressed in his private writings of the period: in May 1799 he paid a jail visit to Gilbert Wakefield and Benjamin Flower, who had been imprisoned for publishing political critiques, and declared "These are evil times and I believe I may write the epitaph of English Liberty!" (SL 408). Wakefield's arrest was particularly shocking because he was not an agitator who harangued the common people to rise in rebellion, but a gentleman-scholar who published pamphlets full of classical and biblical allusions. That the government thought fit to have him tried for his writings showed that it would no longer permit extra-parliamentary debate even in the print media of the educated classes. The personal freedom of those who defended liberty in the press could not be guaranteed: Southey knew that if Wakefield could be imprisoned, he himself easily could be too. Any opposition to government would have to be either private or oblique.

Southey's "National Songs" are both oblique opposition and expressions of despair about the degeneration of print culture. Southey does not set his songs in Britain but chooses, as other radicals did at this time, a remote but clearly allegorical location. He also, however, locates liberty and patriotism beyond the published—and indeed written—word. These national virtues do not stem from a free press and parliament debating the actions of monarch or ministers but from a rural, uncivilized people's bond with the land, a bond vouchsafed by their communal and oral poetry. In other words, Southey asked the readers of the *Morning Post* to take a more radical step than Sheridan asked the playgoers at Drury Lane. He asked them to align themselves with an unlettered, "primitive" people who relied upon an animist religion of nature, as the opening of the "Song of the Araucans" reveals:

> When it thunders, these People believe that the Souls of their Ancestors are engaged in battle with the Souls of the Spaniards.
>
> The storm-cloud grows deeper above,
> Araucans, the tempest is ripe in the sky;
> Our forefathers come from their islands of bliss,
> They come to the war of the winds.
> The souls of the strangers are there
> In their garments of darkness they ride thro' the Heav'n;
> The cloud that so lurid rolls over the hill,
> Is red with their weapons of fire.

(lines 1–8)

Nowhere does Southey allow readers to dismiss this interpretation of nature as superstition. On the contrary, it is the Araucans' centeredness in their worldview that gives them the communal confidence to resist the invaders. It is in the belief of an organic rural community, and not the debate of educated urbanites, that a reliable sense of national liberty is found: here Southey, like the Lyrical Balladeers, expresses a social radicalism that reflects his distrust of the middle classes who had so easily gone along with the alarmist anti-Jacobinism that lay behind Wakefield's and Flower's imprisonment. Like Wordsworth and Colcridge, Southey endorsed the rural and oral in conscious opposition to the destruction, by anti-Jacobin invective and government repression, of an oppositional print culture in which he had a powerful voice. Writing for newspapers still enticed him because it offered him the chance of influencing public opinion; it also frustrated him because that opinion seemed so easily manipulated by lies—hence the strange gesture of publishing newspaper poems that located freedom and loyalty beyond print and beyond literacy. Freedom and loyalty inhered in the Araucan community, and the rustic, Wordsworthian Britons to whom it alluded, because it was beyond the influence of the very medium in which Southey was publishing his poem: unlike the readers of newspapers, the Araucans were not a reading public whose firm convictions had degenerated into fickle opinions because it had consumed, day after day, new scare stories planted in the press by a cynical government determined to destroy all opposition. The readers of the newspaper, however, were given a gestural participation in this community that existed beyond print culture, since, as they sat at their breakfast tables reading the poem, they found themselves joining in a mass recitation. The Araucans speak or sing the poem together as one and so the silent and individual act of private reading pretends to the status of communal and choral speech.

The second context in which the poem resonated was the debate among poets about oral poetry. Southey's National Songs resembled *Lyrical Ballads* in their response to the situation of the late 1790s; they remind us that critical concentration on *Lyrical Ballads* has blinded us to the importance of the "Indian" poem to a poetic coterie that took its lead from Bowles, Hayley, Helen Maria Williams, and other Whig poets of sensibility—a circle that comprised Southey and Robinson as well as Wordsworth and Coleridge. Yet, Southey's songs were also departures from the exotic pastorals of Bowles's Indian and African verse; Bowles's idylls were reforged as the threat of invasion put radicals' political loyalties under intense pressure. And Southey also differed from the common language that he shared with Wordsworth and Coleridge in one respect: his Indian poems were more culturally specific, historically informed and communally expressed—speaking not for a romanticized individual but for a group who came into solidarity by uttering their words together. They were, in fact, indicative of Southey's historicist alternative to Wordsworth's introspection—he attempted both to make the British reader share (his approximation of) the psychological space of indigenous people (as in Wordsworth's "Complaint of the Forsaken Indian Woman") and also to trace that psychological space to its temporal and spatial origin—its historical moment. This double effort made him, implicitly, the kind of critic of Wordsworthian Romanticism that Marjorie Levinson and Jerome J. McGann later became—his songs do not aim to transcend the speaker's implication in historical events but to reveal it. This willing acceptance of multiple relationships to political events present and past was demonstrated by the poems' newspaper publication but also by their formal affiliation to Indian models and by the addition of footnotes giving extra information about Native American customs.

Southey's songs are an alternative lyrical ballad cycle that rejects the individualism of Wordsworth's appropriation of rustic voices and, in the process, counters the direction in which that individualism was taking the Bristol coterie—as Coleridge became closer to Wordsworth and his sister. Southey speaks not singly but for/as a named organic community in an approximation of their style and form. The effect is political as well as social: not only are so-called primitive oral rustics shown to be deeply moral but also their collective consciousness is shown to perpetuate a history of resistance to oppression. Thus, while Southey had intervened in British politics by locating liberty beyond the city and beyond the written word, he had also created Indian figures who were neither noble savages—Bowlesian children of nature—nor ignoble ones—ferocious beasts. If he had projected British dilemmas and desires onto Native Americans, he had also strived for authenticity. Of course, that authenticity was limited by the fact that he knew Araucans only from books written by other white men and also used them allegorically to comment on British events. Nevertheless, although an appropriation of Indians' culture, Southey's poems were an advance upon the stereotypical and ignorant depictions that preceded him. He had given his Indian speakers a consciousness that was not only heroic but also believably human. Such Indians, fictional though they were, gave Britons a political education rather than an exotic show of inferior Others. Southey had achieved the first complex representation of Native Americans—or tribal people generally—in English verse.

ROMANTIC SOUTH AMERICA

After 1799, the Bristol poets, for whom Bowles was so important, dispersed: he was no longer a mentor who helped bind them together as a group. Over the next few years, the image of the South American Indians they had idealized in Bowles's wake also underwent significant changes as a result of world politics. Britain became first the enemy and then the ally of the Indians' colonial masters—Spain and Portugal. From 1803, it was at war against the Napoleonic empire: Spain and Portugal and their American colonies, as France's allies, became its enemies. In 1807/1808, the sides switched: Napoleon invaded his southern neighbors and Britain allied itself to the Spanish and Portuguese, who rebelled against French rule. At the same time, independence movements in South America began, with London the European center in which the would-be liberators met, sought allies, and publicized their cause. It was from Britain that the leaders sailed on their voyages of liberation, followed by British soldiers, equipped with British supplies, and financed by British loans.

The British interest in South America was not a matter of selfless idealism but of the desire for advantage. Before 1807, wresting the colonies from Spanish control would be a blow struck against Napoleon; it would also, many hoped, vastly enrich British trade.[11] A heady blend of political ambition and commercial fantasy is apparent in the advertising copy published by authors such as William Burke, who wrote in 1807, in the course of declaring *South American Independence: or, the Emancipation of South America,* [to be]*the Glory and Interest of England.*[12] Burke was an advocate for British assistance to be given to the South American revolutionaries who were gathered in London to lobby for support. He revived, for this new cause, the old British hope that the Araucans could be used to destroy Spanish power. In effect, he praised Native American resistance, not through any genuine sympathy with their cause but for reasons of *real politik*: the Araucans might make the liberators' work easier for them and thus make more likely the achievement of an independent South America from which British manufacturers could profit. The merchants and manufacturers were able to win greater support from government when Napoleon invaded Iberia in 1807. Faced with French Revolutionary domination of the South American colonies' mother countries, and the closing of Europe's markets to British goods, Britons began to approve of revolution in South America. Ministers overcame their skepticism about commercial prospects and their antipathy to revolutionary movements, and raised an expeditionary force, commanded by Sir Arthur Wellesley, to assist in South America's liberation.

Before it could set sail, matters altered again when, in May 1808, the Spaniards rose in revolt against Napoleon, after he forced their king, Ferdinand, to abdicate in favor of his brother Joseph Bonaparte. Britain now allied itself to the Spanish; Wellesley's force was diverted from South America to Spain itself. The government favored attacking Napoleon directly in Iberia, and would not countenance aiding the liberation of its new Spanish ally's South American colonies.

In many of those colonies, the occupation of Spain led the Creoles to take control of affairs while proclaiming their loyalty to Spain's exiled king—thus gaining experience of self-government. In Britain, liberal journalists and eager manufacturers continued to campaign for assistance to be given them, despite the new and, for them, unfortunate alliance of Britain with Spain. They did so in concert with the would-be liberators who used London as their base. Among these men were Simon Bolivar, Francisco de Miranda, and Jose de San Martin—who had fought against Napoleon in the peninsula but had resigned from Spanish service. As an experienced officer, San Martin was welcomed by the revolutionaries, of whom Miranda, a charismatic veteran of the French Revolution, was the figurehead.[13] It was Miranda's expedition to liberate Venezuela that Wellesley's force had been raised to assist, and it was his vision that the young J. S. Mill promoted in the press.[14] In 1809, for example, Miranda and Mill together reviewed a book whose publication demonstrated the excitement about South American independence.[15] The English translation of Juan Ignacio Molina's *History of Chile* appeared because Britons now wanted to be informed about the lands that might soon be freed for their goods and investments. And Miranda and Mill singled out Chile as the country that offered the most enticing prospect of trade: its wool would supply the manufactories of Britain, its produce would feed half Europe.

The review concentrated so heavily on advocating British support for liberation that it said little about Molina's book itself. Yet, the *History* was itself a significant contribution; edited by Southey from Molina's comprehensive histories in Italian, it offered Britons a more detailed historical understanding of Chile and of the Araucans than ever before.[16] In translation, Molina reflected Southey's own biases. He attributed to the Araucans the social and martial virtues that Britons wished to believe they themselves displayed. At the root of their character was environment: following Montesquieu and Robertson, Molina argued that the harsh climate of Chile led its inhabitants toward cooperation and effort. The Araucans derived their hardihood, their determination to overcome obstacles, from the battle against their environment. From this struggle they developed, just as John Locke had argued Britons developed, laws that fostered property, progress, and patriotism. Foremost was the "right of private property" and of "hereditary succession." This "fundamental principle gave rise to the first arts" (II, 20), stimulating industry and giving each man a reason to want to defend the land against invaders (II, 56). In summary, they resembled no people more than the romantic rural Britons idealized by Wordsworth:

> They never form towns but live in scattered villages or hamlets, on the banks of rivers.... Their local attachments are strong, each family preferring to live upon the land inherited from its ancestors, which they cultivate sufficiently for their subsistence. The genius of this haughty people, in which the savage still predominates, will not permit them to live in walled cities, which they consider as a mark of servitude. (II, 59)

Molina also admired Lautaro, the Araucan who had been brought up by the Spanish as a page boy. He was "the Chilean Hannibal" (II, 168) who had led the Araucans to victory after victory, restoring "the liberty of his native country." He had begun his career at the tender age of 16, when, at a crucial stage in battle, he turned on his Spanish masters. "The Araucans, ashamed at being surpassed by a boy, turned with such fury on their enemies, that at the first shock they put them to rout, cutting in pieces the Spaniards and their allies" (II, 148). Noble as well as brave, Lautaro then solicited for the captured Valdivia's life, though to no avail. To complete his heroic credentials, Lautaro was "endowed with singular beauty and affability" (II, 152) and was cool and resourceful under fire.

Innocent, honorable, masterful, and intelligent, Lautaro was the embodiment of the noble and chivalric martial culture that made the Araucans different from all other South American Indians. So determined were they to defend their liberty, Molina noted, that only 17 years after first encountering horses, they had formed an effective cavalry of their own. Accustomed to hardship, trained in war from earliest youth, the Araucans were new Spartans. They were, in fact, idealized twice—first by their sixteenth-century Spanish enemies who admired their courage, second by Romantic writers who were steeped in the cult of the rural primitive. To Molina, as edited by Southey, they resembled not only the Celts and Vikings but also the Scottish clans described by Ossian.

It was in the wake of Molina's romanticization of the Araucans that Bowles wrote his long poem on the conquest of Chile, *The Missionary* (1813; revised 1815). He intended it to engage "interests on this side of the Atlantic,"[17] as the preface explained:

> A Spanish commander, with his army in South America, was destroyed by the Indians, in consequence of the treachery of his page, who was a native, and that only a priest was saved, is all that has been taken from history. The rest of this poem, the personages, father, daughter, wife *et cet.* (with the exception of the names of Indian warriors) is imaginary…The place in which the scene is laid, was selected because South America has of late years received additional interest, and because the ground was at once new, poetical, and picturesque.
>
> (*Missionary*)

America was new ground for Bowles—he had omitted discussing its conquest in his first long poem *The Spirit of Discovery* (1804) in deference to "such poets as Mr. Southey and Mr. Rogers."[18] He might have added Coleridge to his list, for if Southey was gaining prominence as the author of *Madoc* (1805), his epic on the Welsh conquest of America, the author of "Kubla Khan" and "The Ancient Mariner" was receiving plaudits, in the salons and dining rooms of London, for his inspiring recitations of his exotic verse. This praise gave the erst-while disciples confidence in their own authority, and changed their relationship with their hero. In 1806, Southey reviewed Bowles's *Spirit* in disappointed tones.[19] He disapproved of the episodic and disconnected nature of the work as a whole, criticized some of its phrasing and noted errors of fact (while praising the parts that were in Bowles's former manner). The onetime admirer was now disillu-sioned and querulous—all too keen to correct his mentor's faults in public.

Responding to this criticism, Bowles sought out a circle of youn-ger poets to support both the composition and the publication of *The Missionary*. He asked Samuel Rogers (author of the *Voyage of Columbus*) for help; he entreated Southey's and Coleridge's advice, particularly as he revised the poem toward a second edition. Southey wrote, declaring "I love your missionary: tho the priest who in reality shared Valdivia's fate most probably heartily deserved it. The clergy who accompanied the first conquerors were as bad as the conquer-ors themselves."[20] Coleridge, meanwhile, enjoyed being Bowles's Wiltshire neighbor and advised his hero in person on the revisions— an assumption of power that, he later wrote, was not without tension: "I injured myself irreparably with him by devoting a fortnight to the correction of his Poem—he took the corrections and never forgave the Corrector" (CL, IV, 694, 570). Apparently, Bowles found the experience of a disciple becoming an equal partner—and assuming the superiority implicit in offering corrections—an uncomfortable one. The exercise was not repeated.

Despite such risks, Bowles continued to look for help. He asked John Murray to persuade Byron to add lines that would emphasize his poem's relevance to the Spanish struggle against Napoleon.[21] Byron did not provide the lines, but the request reveals Bowles's strategy plainly. *The Missionary* was to be helped to public notice by its associa-tion with the most fashionable poets of the younger generation and as an allegory of empire in which the immorality of Spanish conquest of America would reflect upon contemporary Napoleonic imperialism.

It was not only in Europe that imperialism was being fought out. Between 1811 and 1816, the period in which *The Missionary* was being composed and received in Britain, the fate of the Spanish empire in America hung in the balance—and nowhere more so than in Chile. In September 1810, Creoles in Santiago announced that they would govern until Spain's deposed king was restored. Although they pro-claimed loyalty to Ferdinand, they effectively became an independent government, opening the country to free trade, to the satisfaction of

British merchants. Self-government did not bring peace, however, for the Creoles soon divided over whether they should pursue complete independence and republican status, or whether they should maintain their affiliation to the monarch. The dictatorial rule of José Miguel Carrera Verdugo (president, 1812–1813), was opposed by the republican faction led by Bernardo O'Higgins, who had been educated in Britain and, in 1798, radicalized there by Miranda, fresh from revolutionary Paris.

The republicans, or "patriots," as they became known, used the Araucans' resistance to the Spanish conquest as an inspiring example for their own independence movement. They sought to unite Creoles against royalist "peninsulares" by taking on the Araucans' mantle—as if they were a politically and racially distinct native group resisting foreigners (although in practice continuous intermixture between Creoles and Spaniards had occurred). The patriots, they claimed, were simply continuing the essentially Chilean resistance to Spanish domination: they were all Araucans now. This propaganda campaign was a vital tool in the production of a nationalist ideology: O'Higgins and Bolivar both encouraged it, despite the paradoxical fact that there were no actual Araucans in their movement, which remained in the hands of an educated Creole elite that prided itself on its freedom from Indian blood. Meanwhile, forces loyal to the Spanish crown continued to fight the liberators. In October 1814, a Spanish army from Peru defeated the Chilean army, forcing O'Higgins to flee across the Andes to Argentina. It was there that he joined forces with San Martin, who had arrived from London and set about training an army capable of crossing the Andes and retaking Chile, and then wresting Peru from royalist control. Part of his strategy involved gaining Indians' assistance—or at least ensuring they did not oppose him.[22] Having won Araucan approval, San Martin and O'Higgins moved over the Andean passes in early 1817 to again clear Spanish troops from Chile and Peru. They did not, however, take the Araucans with them: San Martin cultivated the Indians largely so as to spread disinformation about his attack plan via them to the Spanish.

In this revolutionary context, it was no wonder that Bowles both lauded Chilean resistance to the Spanish and concluded with a vision of postwar harmony. His idealized depiction of the Araucans' struggle against the original conquest allowed him to paint a hopeful scenario for present-day independence without having to adhere to the confused events reported by the newspapers. It helped him to suggest the possibility of a postcolonial South America ruled by cooperation between peaceful Europeans and grateful natives—exactly the possibility that Britain's businessmen hoped would come about. Thus it served what might be called a neocolonialist free-trade agenda, in which, investors hoped, Britain would have sufficient influence in independent South America to make good profits, without having to take colonial control. However, the means of acquiring this influence, in Bowles's romanticized vision of politics, would be neither financial nor military, but religious and romantic. Bowles, himself a vicar, imagined a Christian priest preparing the way for a postindependence, internationalized Chile as he blessed the marriage of a Spanish girl with an Indian boy.

The hero of the poem is Lautaro, derived from Molina, but softened by his susceptibility to love. As a boy, Bowles's Lautaro is abducted from his Andean valley by the Spanish. Brought up to be the page of the Spanish commander Valdivia, he loves, and eventually marries, a Spanish girl, Indiana. His sister Olola, who remains in her native valley after his abduction, falls in love with the Spanish minstrel Zarinel, who leaves her to return to the Spanish armies. She follows, but dies despairing; he finds her body washed up on the beach. In the battle that immediately follows, Lautaro reverts to his Indian loyalty and fights against his Spanish masters. Only Anselmo, the Spanish missionary, is unharmed, and lives to join the hands of Lautaro and his Spanish bride in marriage.

The overall moral of these sentimental events is clear: Europeans can succeed in assimilating Indians only through love rather than war. Lautaro's and Indiana's love triumphs over their cultural difference, and Anselmo's paternal love for Native Americans is rewarded as his life is spared. It is also endorsed as he blesses the Spanish and Indian love match. Thus it is Anselmo, with his Christian ethics of love and forgiveness, who is the real hero, even though Lautaro's cross-cultural education is the main focus of attention. Bowles said as much in his preface: "The chief event of the poem turns upon the conduct of Lautaro; but as the Missionary acts so distinguished a part, and as the whole of the moral depends upon him, it was thought better to retain the title which was originally given to the poem" (*Missionary*, p. viii). The poem, then, was attractive not as an accurate rendition of history but as a romanticization of events made in the interest of promoting a society based on paternalist Christian love.

That the love of a guerilla boy and colonist girl triumphs may seem like wish-fulfillment fantasy. Yet, it was also a response to the epic poem on the colonization of America to which Bowles had deferred in the preface to *The Spirit of Discovery*. Southey's *Madoc* had also rewritten history so as to imagine European colonization of America not as the brutal enslavement of one people to another but as the arrival in the New World of liberals fleeing the tyranny of the old. Madoc, the hero, sails across the Atlantic with a band of Welsh refugees from Saxon power; after landing in America they befriend, and liberate, an Indian tribe, the Hoamen, that has been subjugated by the local imperialists—the Aztecas. Defeating the Aztecas and forcing them into exile, Madoc, his troops and his Indian allies are left masters of the field, ready to found a new Welsh/Indian hybrid civilization. Yet, at just this point, Southey fails to take the necessary step—necessary in terms of both the historical narrative he has constructed and the emotional expectations he has aroused. Madoc does not marry the Indian queen; there is no depiction of love triumphing over war and uniting the colonists and the indigenes. The result is, as Lynda Pratt has written, "a foundation epic in which nothing is founded and in which male friendship takes the place of the breeding of future citizens."[23]

The romantic failure puzzled Southey's friends. Southey defended himself by declaring that Madoc was too old to make a romance believable. To this, Anna Seward replied that in the reader's mind he was "some years under thirty...Is it at that age, at life's high noon, that men lose the propensity to love and marriage? I thought it the season at which men feel and inspire ardent passion."[24] Reviewers made this skeptical reaction public: Francis Jeffrey belittled Madoc's inability to display "amorous propensities either towards the ruddy damsels of Wales, or the olive princesses of America."[25] Nor did the other characters fall in love or experience passion: the poem was sexless.

Bowles learned from the faults of *Madoc*. Southeyan in other respects, *The Missionary* shows the very fate of Chile to depend on passion, on the overcoming of the enmity of colonizer and native by love. Their capacity to love gives Bowles's characters a psychological complexity and dramatic appeal that Southey's do not possess, because it exposes them to cross-cultural conflicts of loyalty. In this respect, *The Missionary* is a critical reworking of Southey's poem that, while borrowing Southey's idea of allegorizing contemporary colonialist possibilities by rewriting the first colonization of America, supplies the absence at the center of *Madoc*.

The Missionary differs from Southey only after having borrowed Southey's theme, echoing his words, and alluding to his hallmark metrical effects. Bowles worked by creative modification rather than rejection of the "Indian" verse that Southey had developed in the 1790s and early 1800s (partly from Bowles's own models). In what is effectively an allusive spiral, Bowles's picture of the natives of the

Andes is derived from the travel accounts Southey cited in *Madoc*, from Molina, which Southey edited, and from Southey's own Indian songs—as when, in canto VIII, Bowles's "Song of the Indian Maids," rather than present the pastoral idyll of his own Indian songs of the 1790s, echoes Southey's in tone, diction, and even meter:

> Oh, shout for Lautaro, the young and the brave!
> The arm of whose strength was uplifted to save,
> When the steeds of the strangers came rushing amain,
> And the ghosts of our fathers looked down on the slain!
>
> 'Twas eve, and the noise of the battle was o'er,
> Five thousand brave warriors were cold in their gore;
> When, in front, young Lautaro invincible stood,
> And the horses and iron-men rolled in their blood!
>
> As the snows of the mountain are swept by the blast,
> The earthquake of death o'er the white men has passed;
> Shout, Chili, in triumph! the battle is won,
> And we dance round the heads that are black in the sun!
>
> (VIII, 13–24; *Missionary*, pp. 156–57)

Bowles has in mind Southey's Chilean poem—the "Song of the Araucans." Like that piece, his is a choral chant, a communal voicing of patriotic fervor and proud independence. Like Southey, Bowles has his speakers communally invoking their ancestors and identifying the landscape as a source of native power. And if these echoes are clues to his source in Southey's more ethnographic Indian song, then the prosodic imitation is close enough to be an act of tribute—a self-conscious allusion to the anapestic meter of "The Song of the Araucans" that was Southey's hallmark as a poet of indigenous forms (it featured in his English folk ballad "Poor Mary" and his "Botany Bay Eclogue" "John, Samuel and Richard"). Bowles's prosodic allusion strengthens his bloodthirsty evocation of native people's resistance to conquest by calling to mind Southey's prior evocation of Chileans' strong-minded, united, fierce otherness: the unusual meter makes the Indians sound alien to English ears. They are not like us, and not to be patronized by the usual exotic idealism. "Maids" they may be, but they do not conform to the gender role expected of English maidens: these are no meek, innocent, submissive damsels, but nor are they savages. The cultural construction of femininity is, for a moment, brought into focus.

For a moment only: Bowles's Southeyan disturbance of convention is, as the poem moves to its close, subsumed under a familiar paternalism, through the missionary after whom the poem is named. Anselmo is a Romantic version of the sixteenth-century Dominican friar Bartolomé de Las Casas who, in many books and speeches, defended the Indians as innocents needing protection rather than savages deserving extirpation. Las Casas's courageous condemnations of Spanish cruelty in South America echoed through the works of historians and propagandists right into the Romantic period. They established him as the prototype of the benevolent paternalist whose compassion redeemed the colonial project. Anselmo follows this pattern: opposed to Spain's secular conquistadores, he also resists the church authorities. Crucially, he has been unjustly imprisoned and tortured by the Inquisition in Spain—an enslavement to tyrannical power that, in the poem's logic, aligns him with the Indians. He has fostered a Spanish daughter left orphaned by the Inquisition's activities, whom he has symbolically named Indiana. It is she whom Lautaro marries, forming a Spanish/Indian family united under the benevolent Christian father.

It is when Lautaro has to fight on the Spanish side that his divided loyalties can no longer be borne. He chooses to turn against his masters because he recognizes "a faint resemblance of his father's face" in an Indian warrior (VII, 228; *Missionary*, p. 148). He intervenes to save him. Taking the Indian side is a matter of returning to his true family. Thus, Lautaro is a model hero because his absorption of Christian virtues redeems him from warrior fierceness while his Indian respect for fathers prevents him betraying his race. Since respect for fathers is also a European value, this "Indian" characteristic does not alarm readers, especially since Lautaro's respect for his own father is subsumed under his love for the Christian Father.

The Missionary is concerned with daughters as well as sons. Lautaro's story is mirrored by the story of his sister Olola. Her character is also established in relation to her father. She "soothed his cares" and "kissed the tear he shed" (I, 174, 181; *Missionary*, p. 18). Dutiful, compassionate, innocent, Olola is an idealized daughter tending an aged father. She is allowed little active will and no successfully realized relationships outside the family save with other women. When she falls in love with Zarinel the Spanish minstrel, she is shown as a victim to "hopeless love a prey" (I, 182). And although she walks from mountains to shore in search of her beloved, she despairs and dies, like Ophelia, in the water. Her companion on the walk turns out to be Indiana, the foster daughter of Anselmo, who has been

separated from Lautaro (though Olola does not know of their relationship). Thus, Bowles brings together two lovelorn women, defining them as lost daughters and disappointed lovers who lament their
loss and helplessness.

INDIAN
It is an Indian maid, who chanced to hear
Thy tale of sorrow, as she wandered near:
I loved a white man once; but he is flown,
And now I wander heartless and alone.
I traced the dark and winding way beneath:
But well I know to lead thee hence were death.
Oh say! what fortunes cast thee o'er the wave,
On these sad shores perhaps to find a grave?

SPANISH WOMAN
Three years have passed since a fond husband left
Me and this infant, of his love bereft;
Him I have followed; need I tell thee more,
Cast helpless, friendless, hopeless, on this shore.

(V, 58–69; *Missionary*, p. 108)

To increase the pathos, it is her brother Lautaro who overhears her
sing a death song by the seashore. Realizing too late her identity and
intention, he is unable to intervene before she drowns herself.

Olola's death song alludes to Wordsworth's "Mad Mother," who
had also been deserted and contemplates drowning herself.

I heard the song of gladness:
    It seemed but yesterday,
But it turned my thoughts to madness,
    So soon it died away:
I sound my sea-shell; but in vain I try
To bring back that enchanting harmony!
    Hark! heard ye not the surges say,
Oh! heartless maid, what canst thou do?
    O'er the moon-gleaming ocean, I'll wander away,
And paddle to Spain in my light canoe!

(VI, 75–84; *Missionary*, p. 123)

Bowles also alludes here to Southey's "Botany Bay Eclogue" (itself
a poem based on Bowles's earlier evocations of Indian noble savagery).[26] The "light canoe" invokes Southey's "The savage thrusts his

light canoe to shore / And hurries homeward with his fishy store"
(lines 3–4) as well as the "trim canoe" of Bowles's own "American
Indian's Song" (line 28). *The Missionary,* however, revises as well
as pays tribute to its sources in the Romantic Indians of the 1790s'
poets. By extending their short lyrics into a narrative of cross-cultural
contact, Bowles explicitly considers—and apologizes for—the consequences of colonialism. Here, he positions the Indian as a victim who
deserves from the reader the compassion and protection denied by
the Spanish. This merely entails a general regret; it demands no action
and positions the reader as a benevolent paternalist, a would-be chiv-
alrous knight who would save Indian damsels if he could. It is over the
Indian maid's dead body that paternalism triumphs: Olola has to die,
and has to sing of her death, to let readers feel good by feeling sad.
Southey advised Bowles as much: "I could have wished your Indian
maid had been spared,—because I am arrived at that age when men
like to be spared from as many painful feelings as possible;—in our
youth we love to shed tears over fictitious sorrows,—as we grow older
we have none to spare for them, and find too much cause for melancholy thoughts ever to have them willingly excited. But you could not
have disposed of her otherwise, and when happiness has been rendered impossible, death becomes the desirable termination."[27]

Death was the desirable termination because it excited compassion
and compassion, as Southey acknowledged, aligned the reader with
the "compassionate" colonialism that the poem sought to vindicate.
Olola exists in the poem to provide pathos, to offer sentimental epi-
sodes designed to arouse readers' pity. Byron learnt from this. But
Byron did not, like Bowles, limit his heroines to roles of passivity,
in which innocence is maintained by a refusal to envisage daughters
becoming independent of their fathers. Bowles has Olola die rather
than transfer her loyalty from her father to Zarinel or find independence. In this way, he preserves her affiliation to patriarchy in the
guise of demonstrating the danger of alliance with the colonists. She
apparently stays Indian by affiliation, but is made to conform to a
European paternalism that insists that women remain their fathers'
daughters. Thus Bowles only *seems* to endorse her Indianness and
warn against the love of warlike Spaniards, while in fact shaping her
in the form of European fathers' desire. Olola fulfils one romantic
idea of women as Indians, as innocent and passive spirits of nature
who are dependent on men and who are naturally subordinate within
the family, in which their function is to nurture, care, and heal.

With the Spanish defeated, Lautaro is reunited with Indiana and
they return with Anselmo to Lautaro's native valley, where Anselmo

decides to remain until he dies. The conclusion is Wordsworthian in its perception of a country graveyard as a community shared by the dead and the living:

> Here lay my bones, that the same tree may wave
> O'er the poor Christian's and the Indian's grave.
> Oh, may it (when the sons of future days
> Shall hear our tale and on the hillock gaze),
> Oh, may it teach, that charity should bind,
> Where'er they roam, the brothers of mankind!

(VIII, 302–7; Missionary, p. 177)

Here, the chiming couplets help make Anselmo's anticipation of his own death a moving—because harmonious—emotional apprehension of the brotherhood of man. And this brotherhood is sanctified by a nature that is blithely indifferent to racial difference and that extends its protective care to Indian and incomer alike ("the same tree"). In these circumstances death is, as in Wordsworth's poems, a continuing participation in the organic world, which preserves the dead for the community of the living. Poetry's role is to spread the news of this continuing community and so perpetuate it ("shall hear our tale"). But the ethic on which this community depends is not romantic passion but charity, and in this respect the passage exemplifies what David Fairer has called "that reconciling, harmonising dynamic that marks Bowles's lifelong commitment to the principle of active charity."[28]

The lesson of Bowles's tale was that Europeans should not enslave and exploit, but assist the native people's independence struggle, and then civilize and intermarry with them. Here, South American Indians were heroic liberators and noble warriors but also willing candidates for cross-cultural love. Anselmo's concluding vision is of a time "when wildest tribes shall hear / Thy voice, O Christ! and drop the slaughtering spear" (VIII, 308–9; *Missionary*, p. 177), echoing the endorsement of missionary colonialism in *Madoc* where the conquering hero, his own "spear and sword, / ... hauberk and the helmet laid aside" (VIII, 16–17; SPW, II, 160), converts the spear-wielding Hoaman Indians to Christianity. *Madoc*, however, lacks a convincing account of how conversion might be achieved; Bowles revises what Southey had begun by adding the motif of intermarriage and the figure of the paternal priest, so as to produce a version of colonialism that displaces the conquest of nations into the conquest of hearts. He uses the Romantic Indians of South America to assuage colonial guilt: on their supposed willingness to love Christian fathers and to marry Christian husbands the fantasy of a postcolonial society of liberty, fraternity, and, if not equality, then paternalism, is set out.

Bowles's poem was retrospective; its setting was the Chile of the sixteenth century. Yet the author may have hoped that its vision of harmony between native Indians and an enlightened Catholic priesthood turning against its Spanish heritage could be reenacted in the colonies of his own times. Yet, if *The Missionary* heralded the actual liberation of Chile, it also resonated in another colonial context, feeding a debate about Britain's proper role with regard to the people it had recently incorporated into its empire. The debate focused on India, with so-called Anglicists opposing the "Indianist" government of the East India Company pre-1800, which had administered by adapting British codes and practices to those of the Indians. The company had, for instance, kept Christian missionaries out of its territories for fear of arousing opposition among the Hindu and Muslim population. Back in Britain, however, Anglican evangelicals had become determined that the Church of England should participate in the missionary movement that the dissenting churches had been pioneering since the 1790s. In 1813, William Wilberforce pushed a bill through parliament, forcing the East India Company to assist missionaries in its colonies.[29] Southey added his voice to the campaign in the *Quarterly Review*, arguing that it would be better for British power to spread Anglicanism rather than promote Baptist Christianity with its demotic appeal. He also claimed that proselytization would be more successful among "primitive" tribes than in India, in which ancient religious civilizations were still deeply entrenched.

Bowles's poem was written while the campaign that led to Wilberforce's bill and to an Anglican missionary drive was at its height. And if there is an irony in the fact that Bowles, a Church of England priest, should have made a Catholic father his hero, Anselmo is in fact a very Anglican missionary: learning from *Madoc*, which had been criticized for making its hero (in the interests of period verisimilitude) too Catholic, Bowles expresses no specifically Papist doctrine. His Spanish priest, for example, rejects the authority of the Inquisition, the institution whose continuing power in late eighteenth-century Iberia horrified British visitors. No mere propaganda piece, *The Missionary* nevertheless played a part in winning hearts and minds to Anglican missionary endeavor or, to be precise, to a softened version of it that imagined Christianization occurring through a gradual, generational accommodation of beliefs and loyalties instead of by immediate mass conversion. Intermarriage and filial piety, rather than indoctrination and discipline, were to be the means, and they allowed colonial conversion to seem a benign and sentimental harmonization of cultures, achievable through love. Thus, *The Missionary* was a new kind of poem, a Christian colonial romance, product of a reconstituted Romantic coterie in which Bowles took the advice of his younger admirers Coleridge and Southey, as did Mary Russell Mitford, whose *Christina, the Maid of the South Seas* (1811) incorporated their suggestions for revision. Like Southey's *Tale of Paraguay* (begun 1814, published 1825) Mitford's pious poem also made an interracial love match heal colonial violence in a Christian marriage. There was, in effect, a group of pro-missionary poems emerging under Southey's and Coleridge's influence that cast a paternalist glow over the hard slog of conversion, making the Christianization of native peoples seem a peaceful, benevolent, and eminently *possible* process. The antislavery and anti-imperialist attitudes of the 1790s were revised in these poems for a new era: they simultaneously assuaged the guilt Britons felt when they discovered the naked exploitation of Indians and Africans by their countrymen and reconciled them to further colonial expansion. In this context, it was not the poem's actual setting that mattered so much as its portrait of Indians. In showing the Araucans as finally willing to accept paternalist and ostensibly peaceful Christian incomers, Bowles gave Britons hope that among the "primitive" peoples they had lately encountered—Maoris, Aborigines, Polynesians, and Melanesians—they might become revered bringers of religion and civilization, rather than reviled seizers of slaves and loot. Civilizers rather than commodifying capitalists.

Less than five years after *The Missionary*'s publication, Chile had indeed been liberated: O'Higgins and San Martín, having led their army over the Andes, defeated the Spaniards on the Chilean side at the Battle of Chacabuco on February 12, 1817. Independence was formally declared the following year after San Martín beat the remaining Spanish army at the Battle of Maipú. O'Higgins then became the new country's first leader, while San Martín took his soldiers north to liberate Peru, the last bastion of Spanish power in the Americas. Byron saluted their achievement of independence in *The Age of Bronze* (1823): for him Chile was an inspiring example of the liberation he wanted to achieve in Greece. Byron also singled out *The Missionary* for praise,[30] and Bowles's harmonious vision of intercultural love assuaging colonial conflict is reflected in his own poem about the Pacific—*The Island* (1823). In this poem about events after the Bligh mutiny, Byron set on a Pacific atoll a fantasy similar to Bowles's—a fantasy that cross-cultural love could create a harmonious postcolonial community living out the Western ideal of liberty. He also included a hymn to freedom fighters in Europe and America—exactly what Bowles had hoped he would provide for *The Missionary*.[31] The hymn thus links not only the two regions but also the two poets, as Byron alludes to Bowles's verse (*Missionary*, II, 33–48, p. 33) in his own:

> Columbia rears
> Twin giants, born by Freedom to her spheres,
> Where Chimborazo, over air, earth, wave,
> Glares with his Titan eye, and sees no slave.

(The Island, II, 75–78; ByPW, VII, 37)

Despite the salute to Bowles's vision of South American liberty, Byron's choice of so remote and exotic a home for postcolonial harmony as a South Sea atoll suggests that he knew the harmony was too idealistic a fantasy to be located any place people actually knew in detail (since if they did know, they would be more deeply aware of the political complexies and racial divisions that dogged newly liberated postcolonial societies). It also suggests that for Byron, as for Bowles, Indians were attractive because it was possible to assume they were Rousseauvian noble savages ready to accept sincerely offered love from Europeans who were themselves rejecting civilization's and colonialism's evils. For Bowles, the European in question was a renegade priest who rejected the institution of the Spanish church; for Byron, it was a rural laboring-class Scot—his hero Torquil—who escapes the institution of the Royal Navy through mutiny. Bowles's father found his paternal love rewarded by the Araucans; Byron's hero found his romantic love repaid by a Tahitian maid. And, as in Bowles's tale, the ending is happy: for the first time in Byron's exotic tales, the loving couple remains united, an embodiment of the hope for a postcolonial society of liberty. *The Island* thus constitutes a turn from Byron's earlier depictions of lovers failing to bridge the divided loyalties produced by colonial struggle, suggesting that the poetry that Bowles pioneered in respect of Chile was mappable onto other regions where imperial Britain was encountering indigenous people.

The indigenous people had ideas of their own not envisaged in the idealized view that Bowles offered his fellow Romantic poets. Nor were Indians' opinions canvassed by Chile's Creole liberators, for although O'Higgins declared the Araucans to be equal in the independent nation, they remained, in fact, at the bottom of a society in which the elite Creole families took over the roles formerly exerted by the Spanish crown, without a redistribution of power or a revolutionary reform of race relations. Despite the fact that the liberators had claimed to be continuing an essentially Araucan love of liberty and rejection of Spanish dominance, actual Araucans had not been part of the independence struggle and were no more willing to cede power over their own region to the new governors in Santiago than they had been to the Spanish. For them, O'Higgins was neither their heir nor their liberator, but another would-be colonist. And so they remained hostile, joining forces with the royalist officer Vicente Benavides and keeping the southern part of the country at war. In face of this violence, Chile's leader proposed a British colonization scheme that casts an ironic light upon Bowles's, Southey's, and Byron's fantasies, however powerful they were in winning Britons' support for missionary empire and cross-cultural liberty. O'Higgins proposed to the British consul that the United Kingdom's poorest and most oppressed people—a people themselves subject to colonial domination for hundreds of years—should form a new colony between Araucania and the rest of Chile. The inhabitants of this buffer zone would be emigrant Irish. O'Higgins was himself the descendant of an Irishman who had emigrated first to Spain and then to its American colonies. But his scheme smacked of desperation rather than a commitment to better the lives of the Irish. The consul, sanguine about O'Higgins's need for a human shield to separate Chile's governing creoles from the Indians who rejected their government, replied "The barrier of the Irish against this savage horde, and the sort of commitment of Great Britain to give a protection to the settlers, would undoubtedly be a very desirable object for the Chile government; but the poor Irish peasant... will soon find that he must hold the ploughshare in one hand and the sword in the other to defend his industry and his life."[32] This, it goes without saying, was one of the few occasions that a British official opposed the emigration of the Irish poor from their homeland. But then it was he, as the official on the spot, who would have to deal with the resultant problems in Chile. Those who remained in Britain were much more eager to envisage, in Southey's words, "shipping the refractory savages off to the colonies" (SL 1315). As Wordsworth put the idea in *The Excursion*, the Britons whom capitalist agriculture had rendered a landless "excess" would sail for the New World, to mingle with the indigenous population and thereby civilize it:

> ...the wide waters, open to the power,
> The will, the instincts, and appointed needs
> Of Britain, do invite her to cast off

Her swarms, and in succession send them forth;
Bound to establish new communities
On every shore whose aspect favours hope
Or bold adventure; promising to skill
And perseverance their deserved reward.
"Yes" he continued, kindling as he spake,
"Change wide, and deep, and silently performed,
This Land shall witness; and as days roll on,
Earth's universal frame shall feel the effect;
Even till the smallest habitable rock,
Beaten by lonely billows, hear the songs
Of humanised society; and bloom
With civil arts, that shall breathe forth their fragrance,
A grateful tribute to all-ruling Heaven."

(*Excursion*, Book IX, 375–91)

Wordsworth's fantasy acts as a fitting conclusion to this chapter, for it encapsulates the process that I have documented. By the mid-1810s, the 1790s' Romantic circle drawn together, in the image of Bowles, Cowper, and Hayley, to oppose the exploitation of native people, was advocating, as an alternative, colonization as a civilizing mission. While this was a prospective reformation of the empire of slavery and commodification that they opposed—a political shift from earlier arguments that empire was inherently sinful—it still depended on the poeticization of Indians, who were thus more rhetorically powerful than ever as counters in political debates and as objects of fantasy. Poetic Indians fueled anti-Spanish and French propaganda; they fomented hopes of commercial profit; they helped define radical patriotism; they stimulated a new definition of empire as a Christianizing and civilizing mission; they allowed postcolonial society to be envisaged. Appropriated in order to renew old genres, they shaped the subject matter of Romantic verse and featured as the subjects of allusive practices by which a 1790s' poetic coterie was reconstituted in the 1800s—its onetime father figure now calling on his former disciples, renewing his own and their verse in the process. An allusive circle spiraled, as it imagined Indians in response to the pressures and anxieties attendant on colonialism, into new poetic genres: Sheridan projected his own parliamentary speeches onto Indians as he strove to make historical drama into an allegory of current affairs; Southey reinvigorated Bowles's Indian songs by approximating Araucans' communal and tribal speech; Bowles assimilated Southeyan Indians into a benign postcolonial romance of universal brotherly love. But almost nobody let them speak or write for themselves; their own opinions, desires, and needs remained obscure, hidden behind their usefulness in arguments about social and political changes in Britain and Europe. In the event, Wordsworth's emigration fantasy did not become reality in South America: it was the Canadian Indians who experienced a flood of impoverished Irish, Scottish, and Welsh emigrants. The Araucans had the advantage of their remoteness and maintained their *de facto* independence until the end of the nineteenth century, when their lands were taken from them by land-hungry Chilean speculators in a bloody campaign made possible by the repeating rifle. The systematic violence of this campaign—indeed its very existence as a campaign—is still denied by many Chilean historians, so sensitive is the idea that the white nation, having first romanticized the Indians and having claimed independence in their image and their name, raped, robbed, and murdered them less than a hundred years later.[33]

PART II

THE "RURAL TRIBE": LABORING-CLASS
POETS AND THE TRADITION

CHAPTER 5

THE PRODUCTION OF A POET: ROBERT BLOOMFIELD, HIS PATRONS, AND HIS PUBLISHERS

In the Romantic era, poets from the laboring class enjoyed popularity, and faced difficulty, on a scale undreamt of by their predecessors. With the expansion of the literary market, it was possible to sell books by the tens of thousands: if this prospect offered riches it meant allowing oneself to be marketed by commercial-minded publishers as a naïf "peasant poet"—a phenomenon or prodigy. It also created a new tension, leaving the poet pulled in one direction by the demands of the market (as interpreted by his bookseller) and in another by loyalty to his patrons (typically gentlemen who expected a supervisory role over what the poet published). Added to these pressures was an older problem: becoming published tended to isolate the laborer poet: giving up laboring for writing meant losing contact with his fellow laborers—his friends and workmates—without giving him a new social milieu in which he fitted. The poet, as he now was by trade, might still write about life as a laborer, but he lacked a circle of fellow writers and readers of his own class and was left on the margins of middle- and upper-class literary culture. Anxiety and alienation often resulted.

In these circumstances, allusion took on particular significance. For laboring class poets, it became a tour de force means of *willing* a supportive literary coterie into being where one did not otherwise exist. Summoning other poets—past and present—in one's poetry offered, like posting letters to oneself—a vicarious correspondence—an

imagined circle of fellow writers and readers to compensate for an actual position of isolation. If this promised confirmation of one's poetic vocation, it also bespoke anxiety, both about the lack of real contact with contemporary poets one admired and about reception: would a literary public from the higher classes accept allusion's implicit claim that the laboring-class poet properly shared a poetic language with established poets from the educated classes? Would allusion be seen as the self-vaunting presumption of an arriviste poetaster? In what follows, I explore the poetry of Robert Bloomfield, arguing that the peculiar intensity of its kinds of allusiveness is revelatory of both the particular social pressures that shaped laboring-class poetry and the sophisticated literary practices he evolved to cope with these pressures. In Bloomfield, allusion bespeaks acumen and artifice as well as anxiety and alienation. It is a subtle practice that references both past poets and present friends; at its best, it is a formative part of two genuine innovations in English poetry—one an Augustanism revised as was only possible for a poet able to survey, in retrospect, the entirety of Augustan verse—a poet with the radically different perspective of a laborer; the other a hudibrastic, colloquial, tourist verse that represents landscape through the conversation of intimate companions. The former reworks Pope, Dyer, Darwin—the neoclassical tradition; the latter melds Butler and Wordsworth—unlikely fellow authors of excursion poems. Both have been critically neglected; I aim to recover them here as vibrant contributions to Romantic poetry, while also revealing why allusion became a battleground with Bloomfield's patron and how, by the 1820s, it led him to a conservative remodeling of *Lyrical Ballads* akin to Wordsworth's own.

When Bloomfield took a tour of the Wye valley and the Welsh borders in 1807, he was already established as the best-selling "pastoral poet" of the age. Indeed, in the eyes of contemporaries, it was Bloomfield, rather than the two West Country and Lakeland poets we now call "Romantics," who had revived both landscape verse (the dominant poetic genre in the 1700s) and rural tales (the title of his second, 1802, collection) for the new century. But he had not done so by harvesting the already-poetic landscape of the Wye valley, which hundreds of tourists had already traversed and which Uvedale Price and William Gilpin had made the epitome of picturesque beauty. For Bloomfield had not written about the West Country: it was the flatter area of Suffolk that inspired his poetry. Suffolk because it was there, in a small village, that Bloomfield had spent his boyhood and there, in that same small village, that his family still lived. Bloomfield himself, however, did not: *The Farmer's Boy* (1800) (the long poem that made his name) detailed his Suffolk youth from a distance and highlighted his indebtedness to the gentlemanly georgics of Thomson, Cowper, and Dyer but was, nevertheless, a modification of their work—a poem for the new urbanizing Britain because it recalled the country from the position of a villager who had, like so many thousands in the early nineteenth century, emigrated to London. And it did so not from the gentleman's point of view but from a world of sweated labor: Bloomfield's boyhood was an emotion recollected not in tranquility but in the workshop; he composed verse in his head while laboring for hours a day as a shoemaker in an East End garret.

If Bloomfield's poetry gives the lie to Wordsworth's fear (expressed in the preface to *Lyrical Ballads*) that mechanical labor and Cockney culture corrupts, by its very repetitiveness, the taste of the laborer, it nevertheless displays many of the same characteristics as Wordsworth's own verse—a matter of similar responses to times in which a commercial and manufacturing culture left many people deracinated and yearning for a half-remembered place of origin—a childhood land in which the power of capital had not yet disturbed the culture or the consciousness. These similar responses included the organization of verse according to the work rhythms of shepherds and laborers, the penning of rural tales based on popular ballads and songs, and the addressing of poems to favorite landscapes. Not surprisingly, Bloomfield was an early supporter of Wordsworth's "feeling and Nature":[1] he had read "Tintern Abbey" by 1802.

Despite the similarities, Bloomfield occupied a different position from Wordsworth. Whereas the latter was a Cambridge University gentleman, Bloomfield was a journeyman shoemaker who had been, as a child, a rural laborer. And whereas Wordsworth came into his poetic self by traveling into the already-poetic West Country, Bloomfield arrived at his by dwelling on his former home, the largely unpoetic East England (which had not been previously identified by travelers, tourists, and poets as hallowed ground). Bloomfield, that is to say, had to *make* his locality an authentic site from which Englishness could be derived without the aid of a local tradition in art and letters on which Wordsworth, near Tintern on the much-toured Wye, could draw.

In making Suffolk a place in which a laborer's participation in a traditional rural Englishness could be celebrated, Bloomfield satisfied the pastoral desires of urbanites with sufficient disposable income to buy lavish publications—an expanding market in the early nineteenth century. He also attracted the patronage of the local Whig landowners whose ideology committed them to the idea that they held obligations toward the "lower orders" who worked on their estates. And it was these men, seizing on Bloomfield's poeticization of an area, much of which they owned, who propelled him into renown. Bloomfield was, in fact, a joint production—a poet placed before the public by a combination of gentlemanly patronage (as was typical of many poor poets in the eighteenth century) and astute marketing by a commercial bookseller (a new phenomenon created by and for what was rapidly becoming a highly capitalized book market). He would suffer from the tensions inherent in this new position—as Clare and other laboring-class writers later would too. Bloomfield, indeed, was one of the first to bear the pressure of the fast-changing conditions of literary production that gave booksellers new opportunities for profit and with them new power and independence. Like Scott's, his popularity with an expanded reading public brought his publishers wealth and renown; it made them intensely interested in perpetuating his success. Confident that sales figures proved they understood the market, they did not feel the need of a gentleman amateur to tell them and the public of the poems' merits. They no longer saw it as their role to produce volumes for a small circle of educated subscribers procured for them by a patron's name: they no longer required an intermediary who recommended the poetry by his social status and reputation as a man of taste.

The problem for Bloomfield was that he did not speak alone—at least not when *The Farmer's Boy* was published: the others involved in producing him as a "peasant poet" all had a stake in his text. Only in his head was it his alone, for he had composed it not on paper, but under his breath while in the workshop making shoes. Once written down, the poem received the assistance of Bloomfield's elder brother George (also a poet). George was a father figure and supporter: it was he who brought the manuscript to the attention of booksellers and of Suffolk gentleman and poet Capel Lofft. Lofft then used his connections to secure a publisher.

A Foxite radical, a Whig of advanced liberal views, Lofft regarded it as part of his duty to represent the interests of the laboring classes but assumed, as did many such Whigs, that he knew what those interests were better than the laboring classes themselves. He wanted to show that the common people, if properly encouraged, could produce as sophisticated forms of poetic expression as their social superiors. The issue was the nature of this encouragement: Lofft wanted both to edit Bloomfield's verse to fit his own notions of taste and to gain the credit for having shepherded the prodigy into print. He added to *The Farmer's Boy* a preface complaining that his championing of a poor woman unjustly sentenced to hang for theft had led to his removal from the magistracy. Clearly, Bloomfield's publications provided him with the platform he craved to show his worth as, in the phrase favored by the Foxites, a "friend of the people"—a friend, moreover, who had suffered for his friendship. Lofft was, in effect, a new kind of patron—not a great aristocrat supporting a poet as part of his duty to the talented poor of his locality but an amateur with his own political and literary career to promote. He published his sentimental poems in literary magazines and also appeared there as the promoter of new verse by writers who lacked the social position to get into print by themselves—women and laboring-class poets. Byron mocked him for this as "a kind of gratis Accoucheur to those who wish to be delivered of rhyme, but do not know how to bring it forth." This gendered gibe made Lofft a man midwife, an effeminate aide of a feminized literary culture.[2] It satirized Lofft's association with what Byron viewed as an unmanly literature of excessive sensibility that was flowery in diction, winsome in emotion, and vapid in thought. This feminized literature was epitomized by Lofft's frequent contributions to the magazine *The Ladies Monthly Museum* and by his 1804 anthology of sonnets, *Laura*.

Laura was a renewal of (or, to Byron, a throwback to) the feminine literary circles of the 1780s and early 1790s. Lofft included a allusive tribute to Mary Robinson written in her trademark language.[3] He also addressed sonnets to Anna Seward (declaring himself "charm'd" by her "Poesy"), to Charlotte Smith (the "sweet, tender, melancholy Melodist" "softly warbling" her "pathetic Lay"), and to Coleridge (who "bathd" his "Locks in pure poetic Dews").[4] These tributes revealed his aspiration to become a member of literary circles of which he had not been a formative part, and which, in the cases of Coleridge, Robinson, and Smith no longer functioned. His allusiveness was a form of name-dropping: the tic of a gate-crashing latecomer to the poetry of sensibility.

It was toward the consumers of the poetry of sensibility that Lofft pushed Bloomfield's *Farmer's Boy*—without seeking Bloomfield's consent. Bloomfield found himself not so much at the center of a supportive circle as a producer of raw material that others refined into a marketable commodity. Lofft not only obtained a publisher for the poem, but also revised the manuscript so as to suit the taste of what he knew as the main readership for verse—the middle-class women who bought the magazines in which he published, and who themselves wrote sentimental verse as an amateur "accomplishment." The patron/editor replaced with polite circumlocutions many of the

Lofft proposed "gentrified" ("The Farmer's Boy")

earthier vernacular words that featured in Bloomfield's modification of the polite, distanced Georgic poetry on which he drew. The farmer's boy was dressed up to appear before the ladies, so as not to offend or appear uncouth. For example, as Peter Cochran notes,[5] Lofft altered the lines "Each sturdy Mower emulous and strong / Whose writhing loins meridian heat defies" to "Each sturdy Mower emulous and strong / Whose writhing form meridian heat defies" (*Farmer's Boy*, "Summer," 141–42). The writhing loins of sturdy working men were not to be gazed at by polite females. Lofft also saved ladies their blushes by removing dialect forms that were too redolent of Suffolk laborers' speech and deleting details of rural distress: the published poem might describe the lives of farmhands, but it would observe from a distance as had the gentlemanly Georgic poets of the eighteenth century who were then admired.

In emending Bloomfield's words so that they became more distant and decorous, Lofft undid some of the renovation of past poets that was central to them. Bloomfield did not simply name check or sample: he modified the models he alluded to by taking them in a colloquial, earthy, graphic direction. For instance, the mower who defies the heat of the day—his loins writhing with his energetic labor—is a virile but also suffering figure because, regardless of the sun, he is forced to work by the need to make hay. He is an informed corrective of the figure he is intended to recall—the mower in Thomson's "Summer" who has time and leisure to rest when the day is hot:

> 'Tis raging Noon; and, vertical, the Sun
> Darts on the head direct his forceful rays.
> O'er heaven and earth, far as the ranging eye
> Can sweep, a dazling deluge reigns; and all
> From pole to pole is undistinguish'd blaze....
>   ...the mower sinking heaps
> O'er him the humid hay, with flowers perfum'd;
> And scarce a chirping grass-hopper is heard
> Thro' the dumb mead.[6]

In giving the Georgic a reality check—allusively juxtaposing his close-up descriptions to the distant scenes of his poetic models—Bloomfield endangered the entire genre, undoing its idealizing perspective by making its focus the laboring bodies of fieldworkers. The poet-narrator was now aligned, as Bloomfield reworked Georgic poets' words, with hands-on work rather than with distant prospects. Rural life was less pastoral, less pleasingly picturesque, and less aesthetically available for sentimental generalization when the sweat that produced the waving harvests and verdant meadows so beloved of nature poets was at the center of the account. In this respect, Bloomfield was embarking on a revolution similar to, though quieter than, Wordsworth's: he was correctively modifying the language, and with it the social attitudes, of eighteenth-century verse, if not replacing it wholesale as *Lyrical Ballads* aimed to do.

Bloomfield's allusive verse made Georgic poets rub noses not only in sweat, but also shit. Lofft bowdlerized a phrase that alluded to Cowper's famous set-piece sentimental narrative of "Crazy Kate," the rural lass driven mad by unrequited love. Cowper describes her as one who

> roams
> The dreary waste; there spends the livelong day,
> And there, unless when charity forbids,
> The livelong night. A tattered apron hides,
> Worn as a cloak, and hardly hides, a gown
> More tattered still; and both but ill conceal
> A bosom heaved with never-ceasing sighs.
> She begs an idle pin of all she meets,
> And hoards them in her sleeve; but needful food,
> Though pressed with hunger oft, or comelier clothes,
> Though pinched with cold, asks never.—Kate is crazed.
>
> (*Task*, I, 13–23)

Bloomfield picks up both the scenario—the lovelorn maid—and the diction. His "lovely Poll" also goes mad.

> The heath, the Common, or the fields to roam:
> Terror and Joy alternate ruled her hours:
> Now blythe she sung and gather'd useless flow'rs,
> Now pluck'd a tender twig from every bough,
> To whip the hov'ring Demons from her brow.
>
> (*Farmer's Boy*, "Autumn," 120–24)

Alluding to Ophelia gathering flowers as well as to Kate roaming the commons, Bloomfield is nonetheless less idealizing than either Cowper or Shakespeare. He turns pastoral fantasy about rustic innocence and betrayed beauty into a picture of the sordid effects of depression. Self-harming, self-disgusted, the girl sleeps in the pig sty and leaves herself unwashed; she also refuses the proffered help of good Samaritans: she is not available for pity.

> oh how much more forlorn
> Her night, that knows of no returning dawn.
> Slow from the threshold, once her infant seat,
> O'er the cold earth she crawls to her retreat;
> Quitting the Cot's warm walls in filth to lie,
> Where the swine grunting yields up half his sty.
> The damp night air her shivering limbs assails;
> In dreams she moans, and fancied wrongs bewails.
> When morning wakes, none earlier rous'd than she,
> When pendant drops fall glit'ring from the tree,
> But nought her rayless melancholy chears,
> Or sooths her breast or stops her streaming tears.
> Her matted locks unornamented flow;
> Clasping her knees and waving to and fro;
> Her head bow'd down, her faded cheek to hide;
> A piteous mourner by the pathway side.

(*Farmer's Boy*, "Autumn," 133–48)

As if sensing that Bloomfield's explicit portrait undid the decorous distance on which Cowper's sentimentalism depended, Lofft sanitized the pig sty: whereas Bloomfield had written of the girl lying "in filth" "Where the swine grunting yields up half his sty," Lofft published "Quitting the cot's warm walls unhous'd to lie, / Or share the swine's impure and narrow sty" ("Autumn," 136–38). Thus, Bloomfield appeared in print as poet whose allusions paid tribute to, and placed him in the line of, Latinate landscape poets—but without the modification of that line produced by his unique laboring-class idiolect and perspective.

The first Bloomfield saw of the published poem was when he was shown a copy on visiting the Duke of Grafton. He had had no opportunity to participate in the editing process or to see it through the press: he was in ignorance of Lofft's preface, which contained embarrassing remarks about his bucolic appearance when he first came to London. Despite this high-handedness, as a young unknown laborer who had composed a poem but had little experience of publishers and booksellers, he was genuinely grateful to Lofft. Later, when more experienced and confident, he became so vexed by the process of bowdlerization to which Lofft had subjected the poem that he reconstructed the manuscript as he had originally composed it, so that there should be a record of the poem shorn of Lofft's alterations.

Bloomfield's next work was a reaction against the production job by which the bowdlerizing Lofft and the commercializing publishers had successfully marketed *The Farmer's Boy*. The publication had made him a cult figure—a phenomenon—but in the artificial form of "peasant poet," at best worth reading as an unaffected imitator of Georgic and, at worst, as a naïf genius, interesting chiefly because he managed, despite a scanty education, to write at all. The skill and artifice of his allusive art, its modification of the poetry it invoked—and the implicit criticism of the idealizing tendency of that poetry—had been obscured. He turned to a very different kind of verse, yet a still more allusive one, in an effort to escape his public image and to show himself to be as sophisticated a craftsman and as authoritative a moralist, in areas of literature and life far removed from his experience as a farmhand, as were the classically educated poets of the previous century. Allusion was now assertive, a means of claiming the right to stand alongside the practitioners of the loftiest verse form, the most remote from the farmyard—the ode. Bloomfield titled the new poem "To Immagination" and may have been prompted by Wordsworth's hymn to imagination in "Tintern Abbey," which he had recently encountered in the 1800 *Lyrical Ballads.* In contrast to "Tintern Abbey" however, imagination in Bloomfield's poem, though stimulated by the view of nature, is personified but not self-consciously related to the poet. Instead, "immagination" takes a topographic flight, a departure indeed for Bloomfield, formerly bard of a single Suffolk village, and a token of his desire to escape the "peasant poet" tag (since laborers' views were held to be confined to the local range within which their experience was confined). It is as if Bloomfield deliberately sets out to elaborate upon Dr. Johnson's maxim that the poet should "let Observation with extensive view / Survey mankind from China to Peru"[7]—since in rhyming couplets and eighteenth-century diction he takes a shifting but apparently omniscient view of nature and humanity in South America and Africa. Bloomfield's is a less egotistical response to nature than Wordsworth's, but nevertheless derives from it a comparable emotional and moral pressure. Bloomfield disengages the poetic imagination from the personality of the poet and from his own limited viewpoint, allowing him vicariously a greater scope of comment. The voice allows the narrator to seem to rise above his own personal interest and moralize: this is not the egotistical sublime but a new version of the eighteenth-century poetic persona of narratorial independence of self. As such, it puts the Wordsworthian—the Romantic—sublime in a wider cultural context, showing that imagination could be addressed via a renewal of an older Augustan discourse (like Wordsworth's similar renewal in his Salisbury Plain poems of the early 1790s). In this, Bloomfield learned from Mark Akenside, Edward Young, and William Collins.

Still more important were Erasmus Darwin, whose Popean couplets and machinery the poem echoes, and Joel Barlow, whose 1787 *Vision of Columbus* surveys the American continent from the skies as "To Immagination" also does. Bloomfield's poem contains allusions to all these poets which, en masse, advertise the fact that it is almost entirely composed of lines so close to eighteenth-century verse as to risk seeming a cento. Here, allusion marks out the poet's need to be seen to possess the authority of gentlemen poets for whom it was an unproblematic sign of cultural power to adopt an abstracted, objectified, omniscient voice in which to moralize about humanity from an apparently disinterested height. It registers, then, not just assertiveness but also the underlying insecurity—a class-based anxiety—of a laborer poet turning his back on the "peasant" subjects of *The Farmer's Boy* and aspiring to the cultural position, and Latinate diction, normally reserved for the ruling classes. It is not surprising, then, that "To Immagination" has hesitancies and failings that are symptoms of the author's unease in deploying the language of authority to which his allusive method commits him. Indeed, that method might be judged, though Bloomfield never explicitly acknowledged as much, a sign of the alienation of the poet from a socially produced poetic voice that he could call his own or call the voice of his class. Allusion to past poets now was now the legacy of the despoliation of that voice by his reductive marketing as a simple peasant "warbling his wood notes wild."[8]

"To Immagination" begins with a double invocation: as Bloomfield calls on imagination to transport him he also calls up the innovations of previous poets.

> Stay sleepless guest! aieriel trav'ler stay;
> Now e'er the full invigorating ray
> Spreads from the East, where beaming glories rise;
> And dart refulgent up the vaulted skies.[9]

The scenario and vocabulary of these first lines echoes that of Darwin in *The Botanic Garden* (1799): "Aquatic Nymphs!—you lead with viewless march / The winged Vapours up the aerial arch"; and "And climbs the zenith with refulgent wheels" (Canto III, 13–14, 60). Thus, Bloomfield alerts readers to his genre and its purpose: he too will survey the activities of mankind from an imaginary aerial viewpoint. He continues with lines that allude to the hymns of the Wesley brothers, which several times include the phrase "outstretch'd wings" when invoking angels' aid.

> Whilst thus the muse her morning incence brings,
> Suspend one moment here thine outstretch'd wings
>
> (lines 5–6)[10]

Bloomfield then urges imagination to

> Mount through the regions of the whistling wind,
> Go, leave the loit'rer lightning far behind
> O'er the tall streamer'd mast on Ocean's beam
> Stretch on thy cloudless way, and lightly scim
> O'er Chili's hills, Peru's enchanting groves,
> Scenes that unfetter'd fancy dearly loves;
> O'er woodland coverts, Mountains, Floods be bold,
> Thy garb's not warlike, nor thine errand gold.
> Arising bid the haunts of Man adieu,
> Nature's magnificence invites thy view;
> O'er half-till'd regions speed thy ceaseless flight
>
> (lines 19–29)

In this passage, "Unfetter'd fancy" and "Ceaseless flight," and the aerial journey of imagination in general, refer to Edward Young's *Night Thoughts*:

> What though my soul fantastic measures trod
> O'er fairy fields; or mourn'd along the gloom
> Of pathless woods; or, down the craggy steep
> Hurl'd headlong, swam with pain the mantled pool;
> Or scaled the cliff; or danced on hollow winds,
> With antic shapes, wild natives of the brain?
> Her ceaseless flight, though devious, speaks her nature
> Of subtler essence than the trodden clod;
> Active, aërial, towering, unconfined,
> Unfetter'd with her gross companion's fall.[11]

A further allusion relates "the romantick scene" to Akenside's *The Pleasures of Imagination* where the phrase designates a "visionary landscape" summoned out of nowhere.[12]

Despite vividly imagined and powerfully involving passages, Bloomfield was chary about risking public comparison with the poets he was emulating. He was aware that his social claim upon the poem's lofty voice was slight and was acutely sensitive to the interference of his gentleman patron Lofft who, precisely because this poem was written in a gentlemanly style, felt himself still better qualified to modify it than he had been to alter *The Farmer's Boy*. Bloomfield had not the authority of experience over this poetic voice; he would never be at ease among the classically educated gentlemen, such as Lofft, for whom this voice was normal. The outcome was that, after Lofft's revisions, well-meaning though they were, Bloomfield felt alienated from his own language of the imagination. His ode fell dead in his hands and became a poem he could neither publish nor polish, written in a style he would never again attempt. Allusion to the Augustan poets had not succeeded in giving him the authority he needed to resist patronage; on the contrary, although it had allowed an escape from the confines of the "peasant poet" role, it had played into his patron's assumption of superiority. Bloomfield vented his feelings in a letter of April 1804: "Three years past I had written a long address 'to Imagination,' in what I calld Blank Verse, but my friend Mr. Lofft thinking it deficient, was for adding and explaining, and in effect perverting my meaning till I finish'd the contest by refusing to print the piece, and by ultimately destroying it."[13] The contrast with Wordsworth—whose immersion in a supportive coterie enabled him to exalt his own imagination at Tintern—was marked.

Bloomfield's need for a supportive literary coterie in which he could write and be read would not be fulfilled until the contrasting demands of patron and publisher were resolved. Matters became insupportable after 1802, when Bloomfield's second publication, *Rural Tales* was printed, at Lofft's insistence, with footnotes consisting of fulsome praise that embarrassed both author and readers. The *Anti Jacobin Review* singled them out for scorn:

> Mr. Capel Lofft has kindly anticipated our labours, by affixing his opinion to the tail of "The Miller's Maid," one of the most conspicuous articles before us, in the following words:
>
>> I believe there has been no such poem in its kind as the MILLER'S MAID, since the days of Dryden, for ease and beauty of language; concise, clear and interesting narrative; sweet and full flow of verse; happy choice of the subject, and delightful execution of it.
>
> From this decision we do not mean to dissent; though we cannot help smiling at the self-importance of the man, who, throughout the volume, has tacked his criticism to the end of each piece. But the public, perhaps, may not be dissatisfied with this; as, with the poems, they have also the annotations of the critic, by the assistance of which they will certainly be competent to form an opinion of *their own*.[14]

The booksellers responded to reviews such as this and sought the removal of these notes in the second edition; Lofft, insulted, insisted they remain. Lofft, in short, was not prepared to let Bloomfield appear before the public without a framework of interpretation designed to instruct readers how he should be read and to remind them that, as a laborer, he required patronage to appear at all. The booksellers were unwilling to let this framework stand, as public reaction suggested it held back the sale. Bloomfield, caught between patron and publisher, tried in letter after letter to negotiate with both, while maintaining his own dignity. Ultimately, to his own anguish, he failed: Lofft chose to sulk, regarding himself as betrayed, and Bloomfield lost his first supporter, despite a willingness to compromise to a degree. But he would neither simply acquiesce to Lofft's will nor toady to him: he retained his independence but at a cost that showed him forcefully that his writing was the subject of competition by others. Bloomfield was caught in (what we now know was) a transitional stage from the eighteenth-century norm of publishing under patronage, with subscribers funding the work, to the nineteenth-century convention of selling via publishers to a mass market. Stuck between patrons' expectations and booksellers' demands, he had the temerity to seek to retain possession of own writerly self, to avoid becoming alienated from his own dearest words. Clare would later experience a similar struggle when John Taylor, his editor and publisher, refused to remove from his collections the "radical" verses that his local patron, the powerful evangelical Lord Radstock, assumed the prerogative of vetoing.

Bloomfield found supportive partnership—for some years—in a literary circle of an unusual kind. The Sharp family was a philanthropic one, the best known member being Granville, the antislavery campaigner. It was, however, through the younger generation, a network of sisters and wives, that Bloomfield entered their extended circle. In 1803, the married sister, Mary Lloyd Baker, wrote to him admiringly of his poetry and soon he was invited to the family's houses in Hertfordshire, Gloucestershire, and Northants. There he was delighted to find admiring female company that made no demands upon him. The Sharp women[15] neither sought to ride on the back of his writing nor to make him perform for them. And since they were not heads of households, they did not concern themselves with money and social authority as gentlemen did. Bloomfield was freed to exercise his talent for flirtatious humor and flourished in a literary and social milieu that was a microcosm of the readership to which his rural tales appealed—female readers who valued nature writing and enjoyed verse that had little to do with classical genres, political satire, or the representation of patrons' country estates (the kind of poetry preferred by ruling-class men). The Sharp women appreciated poetry; they sketched; they toured. In writing of the rural world with their support, Bloomfield experienced it differently: it was not the countryside he met on his solitary pedestrian tours, nor the Suffolk village world of work and customs, but a feminized world of beauty disinterestedly appreciated and experienced at leisure—a feminized world that did not require the affected language of sensibility and the bowdlerization of earthy verses that Lofft had demanded. Allusion now began to feature as a mark of friendship: Bloomfield celebrated the coterie that had allowed him to escape the humiliating interference of Lofft by writing a rural poetry full of chatty references to places and phrases that had private meanings shared with the Sharps.

Bloomfield's new colloquial style came to fruition in 1807 when he took up Lloyd Baker's suggestion that he might go on a tour of the river Wye with her, her husband a local landowner, and their friends the Coopers (relatives of the radical surgeon Astley Cooper). Visiting the Wye as a laborer poet taken up by well-meaning patrons, and as a tourist temporarily socially superior to the guides, boatmen, and servants—people of his own class—Bloomfield found himself in a new and precarious position. Mostly, he enjoyed sharing the in-jokes and flights of verbal fancy that the shared experience gave rise to; he nonetheless remained aware that his viewpoint was not that of his fellow tourists. The difference is recorded in the hybrid work he composed after his return to London—*The Banks of Wye* (1811). This was a prose tour journal combined with a long poem and with many pictures. A manuscript book, its first readership was the Sharp coterie, whom its allusive private references were intended to entertain. But it had a public dimension too: Bloomfield hoped to take advantage of his popularity as a topographical poet and of the Wye's renown as a picturesque location, feeding the public's ever-increasing desire for lavishly illustrated books.

He began the making of his Wye book while still basking in the warmth of the new experience and the attention paid him by the ladies of the party. His letters show him taking his new roles as artist and tour guide very seriously, seeking sketches and verse from Mary Lloyd Baker and promising her a private view of his "whole triple-page'd Journal, Drawings, prose, and rhime" (October 2, 1807; BL 210). Once he received the sketches, Bloomfield set about recreating the tour on paper:

> I have succeeded beyond the former estimate of my own self approving vanity, and the proof that I posess that latter article, is my telling you so. They are all done by Candle light! These long winter evenings are

all in my favour, and you may figure to yourself the solid oak of my old
Table bearing on his back half the Castles in Wales, besides my two
elbows, and all the paraphernalia of drawing! Remember that though I
am in general pleased with my own performances I percieve that some
of my trees are amazingly like a pile of Cheshire Cheeses. And one in
particular, I was hamper'd with, it seem'd to have a determination to
resemble a large Oil Jar with a handle, but I cut the handle off, and, it
became as good a tree as the rest, aye and as good as some that I have
seen at Sadler's Wells.

(to T. J. Lloyd Baker, November 18, 1807; BL 211)

Mildly flirtatious language of this kind was Bloomfield's way of pro-
longing a relationship that was valuable to him: Lloyd Baker's admiration, and that of her sisters and aunt, gave him confidence without
intimidating him. He unbuttoned to them as he could not to others outside his class, knowing, all the same, that his value to them
depended upon his amusing them. He was, nonetheless, careful to
show the ladies' powerful husbands that he needed their help too,
consulting Thomas Lloyd Baker and his friend Bransby Cooper about
histories of Monmouthshire in preparation of the prose section of the
book.

Despite Bloomfield's diligent effort, his Wye book never appeared
in the intended tripartite prose/poetry/picture format. Back in
London, away from the Sharp circle, afflicted by financial difficulties and sinking into depression, he found progress slowing. It was
not until February 1811, after many months' practice at turning his
rough sketches into finished drawings and much research into local
history, that he sent the Wye book to his publishers, Vernor and
Hood, only to hear that that they were now "averse to the costly and
fashionable stile of publishing" and would produce only a smaller-
scale volume with no more than four illustrations (to Mary Lloyd
Baker, January 16, 1811; BL 250). Their decision may have been an
early indication of the financial difficulties that would bankrupt the
firm after Hood's death in 1811. At all events, it made the book they
did publish in that year a far less appealing production, containing
only Bloomfield's tour verse and a few engravings after his fellow
tourist Robert Bransby Cooper's sketches. Nevertheless, *The Banks of
Wye*, now more straightforwardly a poetry publication, was a substantial work, albeit not one for which the public was looking from a poet
whom they liked for his tales of village life.

Had the tripartite Wye book been published, Bloomfield would
have inaugurated a new kind of multiply allusive travel writing—prose,

pictures, poetry—the informal, colloquial style of which allowed him to combine the relaxed humor he shared with his tour companions with reflection on the poets and aestheticians who had preceded him along the river. Nowhere is this more evident than the opening to the manuscript tour poem, which alludes to the phrases and names shared, in conversation and letter, by the companions who had made the tour, and also to the prospect poetry of John Dyer and to the verse of Samuel Butler, whose poem *Hudibras* celebrated, tongue-in-cheek, another excursion more comic than heroic. The manuscript begins with a whimsical creation myth about a giant called Scoop, who had fashioned the hills and dales of the Gloucestershire country in which the Lloyd Bakers lived:

> When Time's young curls embower'd his brow
> And infant streams began to flow,
> Huge giant Scoop with spade in hand,
> And all the Island at command,
> With puffing breath and monstrous stride
> Came thundering on by Severn's side.
> Fancy still hears his foot rebound,
> When *Stinchcombe* trembled at the sound.
> Here Cambrian mountains caught his eye
> Towring to meet the distant sky
> Jealous he mark'd them one by one
> And dreading ~~much to be~~ sore the work out-done
> "Out-done" he cried, "'Tis true I'm warm
> But this bright prospect nerves my arm
> I too the mountain pile can rear
> Outdone, there shall be just such here."
> Then stript at once to set about it,
> (Look at the spot and who can doubt it,)
> But, at the moment he was speaking
> His limbs were stiff, his back was aching,
> For *Mendip*, and the western shore,
> The marks of recent labours bore:
> Weary he rested, full of pain,
> By *Nympsfield*, on the upland plain,
> And with a gnashing envious smile
> There stuck his spade upright the while,
> And chang'd his mind.—Then sprewing first,
> O'er Severn's Vale a cloud of dust,
> Again he pluck'd it from the ground,
> The crumbling earth flew wizzing round;
> Then dashing sternly to and fro,

He cut a casual hole or two;
In one of which (a sweet one truly)
Some modern pigmies built up Uley
And *Owlpen*, by the dark wood side,
Which none can find without a guide.
And here, the happy natives stroll
Around their green illshapen Bowl,
A Bowl all zigzagg'd round about
With one large gap to let them out.

(*Banks of Wye*, materials)

With their deliberately clunky rhymes, slangy diction, and undignified account of the country's origin as a giant's casual whim of imitating the hill country of Wales, these opening lines undercut their own pretensions to the heroic. As a beginning to a four-book landscape poem, they are highly unorthodox, a versification of the tongue-in-cheek humor of Bloomfield's correspondence with Lloyd Baker (the jokes about Uley and Owlpen are mock-insulting allusions to her home). They are playful, revealing the poet's enjoyment of his own ability to fictionalize, to tell it like it's not—and in this they reflect Bloomfield's new-found relaxed confidence because his language emerges from and plays to a circle of friends, a West Country holiday group, which allows an escape from his London cares and from his branding as a Suffolk laborer poet. Yet for all that, they do concern themselves with labor, as Bloomfield so often did: funny though they are, they show the giant working up a sweat digging. Polished, knowing and displaying a flexible deployment of Butler's hudibrastic cocktail of octosyllabic couplets, phrasal verbs, and casual diction, Bloomfield's light verses still suggest, however jokily, that the country depends on backbreaking toil—a point quietly made later in the poem when the tourists in their pleasure boat glide effortlessly past bent-backed gleaners in the fields. Bloomfield's West Country was not a holiday land for everyone.[16]

Bloomfield's lines on Scoop reveal a cultivated, accomplished, well-read poet buoyed into verse by the attention of a circle of women whose sympathy turned patronage into friendship. Invoking Butler's *Hudibras*—its comic couplets, its colloquial diction—allowed him to find a stylistic equivalent, in verse intended for a wider public, of the relaxed and humorous chat of a companionate circle; he derives from Butler's octosyllabics a relaxed yet tensile power to pattern casual observations—intensifying them so that they are at once comic and meaningful.

Meanwhile, the inevitable association of his poem with Butler's mock-heroic story (about an absurd knightly quest) gave Bloomfield the ability to laugh at, without completely undercutting, the pretensions of travel writing (and of his own little excursion in particular) to inculcate lasting truths about morals and manners. Bloomfield's style thus suggests that he was worldly enough to know that the Cotswolds were not, after all, the Andes and that describing them in pious and solemn terms would only lead to bathos. It allowed him to avoid resembling the pedantic and pompous Gilpin whose tour of the Wye in search of aesthetic principles had led to his being guyed as Dr. Syntax.

Bloomfield is not merely chatty, however: his Wye verse is also braced by a practice of literary allusion that draws attention to his ambition to follow previous West Country poets in drawing moral reflections from the experience of a hill country. The first lines, it turns out, are allusions: Bloomfield wishes his portrait of the nearby Gloucestershire hills to pay tribute to, and gain by association with, the moralizing landscape verse of a much-loved poem, Dyer's "Grongar Hill." Bloomfield thereby orientates his readers: his tour poem, written like Dyer's in rhyming octosyllabic couplets, will echo Dyer's methods and share his aim of drawing analogies between the landscape being viewed and human life in general. The allusion is prosodic and conceptual—a matter of metrical echo and thematic borrowing—as much as verbal. Dyer, describing a ruined castle on a wooded hilltop, wrote "And ancient towers crown his brow" ("Grongar Hill," line 71); Bloomfield, describing a similar hill, begins "When Time's young curls embower'd his brow." And, it turns out, he will adapt Dyer's subsequent lines on time, ruins, and mortality when he describes the ruined castle of Raglan later in the poem. Thus, the poem's opening heralds a beneficent interaction between allusions to past poets and allusions to the idiolect of Bloomfield's supportive literary circle.

The interaction proved hard to perpetuate: it came under strain as the tour became a more and more distant memory, and the flirtatious feminine circle receded from his grasp. Increasingly, Bloomfield began to worry about whether the opening was appropriate for a piece intended for public consumption. Revealingly, it was when Mary Lloyd Baker wrote to him during the course of another West Country tour she was making (of Cheddar Gorge) that, in the light of her intimate attention, he again became enthusiastic about the lines on Old Scoop, writing "He may be a personage not *altogether* to be ridiculed. I have a great mind to keep him alive" (to Mary Lloyd Baker, October 31–November 1, 1809; BL 239).

In the end, *The Banks of Wye*, to its detriment, appeared without Old Scoop: the lines fell prey to Bloomfield's anxiety (evident in the more sober main body of the poem) about his qualifications to write in the style of and from the position of a leisured gentleman—a position in which the trip put him for the first time. He internalized the perceived doubts of his patron Thomas Park, a literary gentleman who edited poetry for magazines, and consulted other friends too: it seems none of these men, arbiters of conventional taste, saw the opening as serious enough. Effectively, as another letter to Mary reveals, Bloomfield's was too feminized as well as too playful a discourse to meet male expectations about the proper language for topographical poetry:

As I advanced I began to conceive that it might even eventualy be renderd fit for publication, and this perswasion set me about a thorough examination and revision. I concieved that it was, owing to the careless and hasty manner of its early composition, much too hudibrastic, and containd a vast deal of useless matter which might give way to the superior graces of nature, or to unbridled fancy. I had finished it, as I thought, according to this plan, last summer; and I had the joint opinion of my *then* companions, Inskip, himself a poet, and a man of strong mind, and my host, Mr. Weston of Shefford, Beds,...—We read it for the purpose of criticizing closely, We all doubted the propriety of Giant Scoop in the outset of the piece, yet all agreed that the ridiculous thought was not without merit, only perhaps out of place. Previous to this I had shown it to Mr. Rogers, author of "The pleasures of memory," and he, even then, in its ruder state, said that it would probably be well recieved if published, but that it was evident that I had not taken the pains with it which might be taken. I then wrote the whole out again with great emendations, in which state Mr. Lofft gave the opinion which I very barely stated to you. I took his hints and the others in conjunction, and wrote *the whole out again*, still in the mending way with additions and curtailments, and in this new dress, without the personage above mentioned, Scoop, I submited the piece to the calm, judicious, and candid Mr. Park of Hampstead (He had seen the giant long ago and said nothing in his praise, which I know how to understand) He was decidedly of opinion that the thing would do me credit, and at the same time pencil'd his doubts and remarks. With this encouragement I *once more* wrote out the whole; gave the brat a name; and offer'd it to My Bookseller. I know of nothing which can *now* retard its ultimate appearance before the world.

(to Mary Lloyd Baker, January 16, 1811; BL 250)

Being new to the tour poem and of inferior class to his readers, Bloomfield did not dare to be facetious and mock the public's cultural expectations of such a book and of the place it described. Abandoning the lines, he left out the most characteristic and individual of his poetic voices, submitting to male arbiters of taste rather than reproduce in public the verse generated from the allusive chat he had shared with his female correspondents. The deletion was a variation of what had previously happened with his ode "To Immagination": when Lofft wanted to revise that poem to render it more properly sublime and lyrical, Bloomfield had given it over. What was lost in this new excision from *The Banks of Wye*, however, was an allusive response to the Wye valley that remade the poetic traditions in which that region had previously been compassed and that questioned the conventional pieties of the gentlemanly tour. Without this response, and lacking the prose journal and extensive illustrations intended for the tripartite publication, *The Banks of Wye* was a slighter and less original book than first planned.

The abandonment of the tripartite Wye book and the excision of Old Scoop revealed that Bloomfield was unable to go to print with writing that took comic flight away from his home ground. That home ground was both his strong resource and, by 1811, the pale within which his patrons wished to confine and define him as Suffolk poet and nothing else. In this sense, Bloomfield's Wye offered an (in the end not taken) opportunity for him to escape the category of local laboring-class writer, an opportunity to claim, as Wordsworth already had when visiting Tintern, the status of poet of innovatively voiced imagination. This lost opportunity is all the more to be regretted because *The Banks of Wye* that Bloomfield did publish contained, despite its often stilted verse, brilliant meditations on the mind's relationship to place and time. Most often, these meditations were brought about by allusion, as Bloomfield raised the energy of his verse in response to that of the past writer of whom he was reminded by the river. The process is revealed in the journal entry concerning Tintern Abbey, where, as his companions sat sketching the ruins, he "gave vent to my feelings by singing for their amusement and my own the 104th Psalm."[17] The 104th Psalm thanks the Lord for creating the earth. In the King James's version Bloomfield knew, it evokes pastoral valleys such as that in which Tintern stands. Bloomfield declared of his performance "though no 'fretted vault' remains to harmonize the sound, it soothed me into that state of mind which is most to be desired."[18] "Fretted vault" is an allusion to Gray's "Elegy Written in a Country Churchyard": "Where thro' the long-drawn aisle and fretted

vault / The pealing anthem swells the note of praise" (lines 39–40).[19]
For Bloomfield, then, the pastoral valley and ruined church call forth
a poetic act of worship, poetry being the mode that he feels to be
profound enough to express his love of nature and its creator. This
act, he knows, is over-determined: he sees the abbey and imagines his
Psalm singing as if they are allusions to Gray's portrait of the country
church as a place where the act of commemoration acquires value. He
is self-consciously following in Gray's verse steps, quietly claiming
poetry as a deeper, more pious, response to Tintern than the picturesque sketches that tourists were expected to make.

Bloomfield was ambivalent about the picturesque. His Wye book
was to feature engravings after his and his friends' sketches. His prose
journal records the party sketching at every castle they visited. In the
verse that the Tintern visit prompted, however, sketching was not a
deep enough response to place and Bloomfield offers only faint praise
of Gilpin, the aesthetician and artist who had used the Wye as a testing ground for his theories and had, famously, wished to take a mal-
let to the abbey gable's so as to render the ruins more picturesque.
Artists may learn from the Wye, Bloomfield declares, but by encountering nature's forms and rhythms rather than by applying artificial
criteria and apparatus:

> Artists, betimes your powers employ,
> And take the pilgrimage of joy;
> A thousand beauties here unfold;
> Rock, that defies the winter's storm;
> Wood, in its most imposing form,
> That climbs the mountain, bows below,
> Where deep th'unsullied waters flow.
> Here *Gilpin*'s eye, transported, scann'd
> Views by no tricks of fancy plann'd;
> *Gray* here, upon the stream reclined,
> Stored with delight his ardent mind.

(*Banks of Wye*, poem text, IV, 415–26)

The allusion is a critical one: the picturesque theorist only manages
to be "transported" when, unlike Gilpin, he looks at nature *unguided*
by fancy or predetermined ideas. Bloomfield's role model is, instead,
the poet Gray, also a Wye tour writer, who absorbs delight by letting
his ardent mind repose on the water, as if in meditation—an allusion
to the pastoral motif, derived from Virgil and adopted by Gray in
his "Ode on the Spring," of the musing poet resting by a refreshing

brook: "Beside some water's rushy brink / With me the Muse shall sit, and think / (At ease reclined in rustic state)" (lines 15–16).

How to be refreshed by the stream emerges, in fact, as the main theme of Bloomfield's poem: he expresses more directly and forcefully than ever before a new purpose for touring the Wye: not the education of taste in rules of aesthetic judgment (as in Gilpin) but the mental restorative that a holiday escape into natural beauty offered an urban middle class otherwise chained to the account book and the office.

> Wait not, (for reason's sake attend,)
> Wait not in chains till times shall mend;
> Till the clear voice, grown hoarse and gruff,
> Cries, "Now I'll go, I'm rich enough."
> Youth, and the prime of manhood, seize;
> Steal ten days absence, ten days ease;
> Bid ledgers from your minds depart;
> Let mem'ry's treasures cheer the heart;
> And when your children round you grow,
> With opening charms and manly brow,
> Talk of the Wye as some old dream,
> Call it the wild, the wizard stream;
> Sink in your broad arm-chair to rest,
> And youth shall smile to see you bless'd.
>
> (*Banks of Wye*, poem text, IV, 407–20)

The differences from Wordsworth's Wye poem are instructive. Bloomfield depicts his walker as a clerk who has to return to the job and the family: his excursion has been a once in a lifetime escape. The verse is addressed to middle-class readers who share that situation—as most of us do today—rather than to a sister and soul mate who becomes handmaid to a prophet, as Dorothy does in "Tintern Abbey." The tone is jokey rather than solemn, hudibrastic and colloquial rather than egotistical and sublime: Bloomfield's walking writing, like the local tour it celebrates, is chatty, rooted in middle-class sociability. Its prosodic and stylistic echoes of Butler's comic verse offer a poetic self-qualified by irony—one for whom humor evinces awareness of human fallibility. Thus, Bloomfield avoids the solemn self-centeredness that many saw as the vice that led Wordsworth to a pretentious over-valuing of own ordinary experiences. Yet, his poem, like Wordsworth's, is also about recollection of a past excursion. The walking tour, relived in memory, conversation and verse, revives, in an otherwise sedentary figure, a younger and livelier self. The clerk's holiday escape from the account books becomes, when recollected in later years, a blessed experience of wildness that is also a token of masculinity: the father, confined by domesticity, is cheered in himself and admired by his children because talking about his experiences of "the wizard stream" conjures into being the "manly brow" of his "prime of manhood." Walking, and recollecting walking in words, even if the excursion is brief and local and the walker gains no permanent escape from the office and family that confine and define him, becomes a preserver of imaginative vitality and of youth: the poet becomes a manly hero in his admiring children's eyes. And if this heroism is gently mocked, the humor is affectionate: in showing the walker ensconced in a cozy domesticity within which even small-scale feats seem heroic, Bloomfield celebrates family affection; if he does not rise to the prophetic role that Wordsworth claims for himself, he nevertheless eschews the pomposity and self-isolating self-regard that were Wordsworth's besetting sins. Yet, he is serious: walking, and recollecting walking, is a taste of liberty from the confinement that shapes modern man. Bloomfield here is a miniature, self-aware Wordsworth perhaps, offering a *petit bourgeois* pedestrianism that is limited but ultimately strengthened by his comic awareness of these limits and what can be achieved within them.

Bloomfield admired *Lyrical Ballads*; both he and Wordsworth revered the poetry of Dyer, sharing the Welsh poet's aim of exploring the effects on the reflective mind of recalling a spot marked out by both natural beauty and human history. In climactic verses on ruined Raglan castle, once the last stronghold of the Royalists in the Civil War, Bloomfield first evokes the triumph of nature over man's achievements, however violent and heroic they once were:

> Majestic Ragland! Harvests wave
> Where thund'ring hosts their watch-word gave,
> When cavaliers, with downcast eye,
> Struck the last flag of loyalty:
> Then, left by gallant Worc'ster's band,
> To devastation's cruel hand
> The beauteous fabric bow'd, fled all
> The splendid hours of festival.
> No smoke ascends; the busy hum
> Is heard no more; no rolling drum,
> No high-toned clarion sounds alarms,
> No banner wakes the pride of arms;
> But ivy, creeping year by year,
> Of growth enormous, triumphs here.

Each dark festoon with pride upheaves
Its glossy wilderness of leaves
On sturdy limbs, that, clasping, bow
Broad o'er the turrets' utmost brow,
Encompassing, by strength alone,
In fret-work bars, the sliding stone,
That tells how years and storms prevail,
And spreads its dust upon the gale.

(*Banks of Wye*, poem text, III, 19–40)

The ivy embraces the stone; as the castle molders, the plant prospers, until the monuments of martial valor are encased in a "wilderness of leaves" and the sounds of human life give way to the stifling constriction of the creeper. These are sophisticated verses that demonstrate how much could still be achieved in the Augustan rhyming couplet. Partly this is a matter of allusion: Bloomfield returns to the passage in Dyer's "Grongar Hill" to which he had alluded at the start of his poem. Viewing the ivy-covered ruined tower as a symbol of time's depredations, he invokes Dyer doing the same in some of the best-known lines in eighteenth-century verse:

ancient towers crown his brow,
That cast an awful look below;
Whose ragged walls the ivy creeps,
And with her arms from falling keeps;
So both a safety from the wind
In mutual dependence find.
'Tis now the raven's bleak abode;
'Tis now the apartment of the toad;
And there the fox securely feeds;
And there the pois'nous adder breeds,
Conceal'd in ruins, moss, and weeds;
While, ever and anon, there falls
Huge heap of hoary moulder'd walls.
Yet time has seen, that lifts the low,
And level lays the lofty brow,
Has seen this broken pile complete,
Big with the vanity of state;
But transient is the smile of Fate!
A little rule, a little sway,
A sunbeam in a winter's day,
Is all the proud and mighty have
Between the cradle and the grave.

(lines 71–92)[20]

And Bloomfield also invokes Milton, whose serpent Satan, bringing destruction into Eden, is not far behind the snake-like plant that "with pride upheaves" itself at the tower's expense. Recognizing these allusions, readers expect what follows to be a meditation on the inevitability of decay, loss, and mortality. This expectation in turn lends urgency to the passage's lexical vividness, rhetorical insistence, and syntactical energy: Bloomfield pressures his reader to feel awed and threatened by a nature that, in the figure of the ivy, represents the triumphant and vampiric power of death, supporting itself on the works of mankind. This is a post-Edenic fallen world, where nature is both beautiful (as in the glossiness of the leaves) and menacing because time, death, and—in Miltonic terms—sin are fundamental to its growth. It is a world, too in which nature and humanity (here represented by historical monuments to human deeds and achievements) are at odds.

Bloomfield continues with a meditation on time, history, and nature that is in productive tension with the poetry to which he is alluding—engendered by it yet contradicting what it suggests:

> The man who could unmoved survey
> What ruin, piecemeal, sweeps away;
> Works of the pow'rful and the brave,
> All sleeping in the silent grave;
> Unmoved reflect, that here were sung
> Carols of joy, by beauty's tongue,
> Is fit, where'er he deigns to roam,
> And hardly fit—to stay at home.
> Spent *here* in peace,—one solemn hour
> ('Midst legends of the Yellow Tower,
> Truth and tradition's mingled stream,
> Fear's start, and superstition's dream)
> Is pregnant with a thousand joys,
> That distance, place, nor time destroys;
> That with exhaustless stores supply
> Food for reflection till we die.

(Banks of Wye, poem text, III, 41–56)

"What ruin, piecemeal, sweeps away" echoes the lines Johnson added to Goldsmith's *Deserted Village*, "trade's proud empire hastes to swift decay / As ocean sweeps the labour'd mole away."[21] Thus Bloomfield bolsters his illustrative use of landscape imagery by calling on the magisterial self-confidence with which Johnson links social comment to natural event. Not for Bloomfield, however, Johnson's certainty about the enduring power of independence ("While self-dependent power can time defy / As rocks resist the billows and the sky" [*Deserted Village*, lines 429–30]); his meditation on time traces a more intricate, introspective route—for Bloomfield it is the encounter with nature's overwhelming of humanity's works, rather than solely with its beauty, that makes visiting the spot so endlessly educative. The surprising word is "joys": as in "Tintern Abbey" the visitor unexpectedly derives joy from a scene that should, because it reveals the passing of time, produce melancholy. This is, then, no simplistic sightseeing event, no mere touristic picturesque, but a complex response that discovers, as the paradoxical one/thousand phrasing suggests, an abundance of feelings in a brief encounter. These feelings are joys, despite the evidence of destruction that causes them, because they fertilize a human activity that turns out to be less vulnerable to time than castles and towers are—the activity of reflection that vivifies the mind and restores the past in memory and that, though it may die with us, survives in the form of "legends" and tradition—the stories, songs, and poems that we make and that others repeat after us. And these, implicitly, renew the "carols of joy" that long-dead denizens of the castle once sang with "beauty's tongue." This, of course, is an implicit poetic; Bloomfield, in the poem he is deriving from past poems, is adding another turn to the traditions, legends, and songs that allow us to redeem from oblivion the works of the past—and survive beyond ourselves. Allusion is here the result and guarantor of reflection: alluding joyfully in the poem, he retrieves the songs of yore from the ivy's clutches—demonstrating that poetry survives death even when, as in "Grongar Hill," it asserts death's all-encompassing power. This is to use the fact of allusion to counter the meaning of the words alluded to; it is also, therefore, to assert its corrective power, and Bloomfield's own redemptive power as the allusive poet—although the assertiveness is muted because Bloomfield aligns his own act of redemption with that of tradition. Verse endures—is renewed in allusion—when all else is confined to a brief span "between the cradle and the grave."

As a response to landscape, and to ruins, Bloomfield's Raglan meditation is as profound, though not as self-foregrounding, as "Tintern Abbey," which it echoes in its intimation of the ability of the human mind to overcome time's depredations when that mind, fertilized by an encounter with a temporally shaped landscape, is prompted to reflect upon itself and assert its power of song. But it remains isolated, lost in a poem of occasional brilliance that was published without its more original lines and without the prose journal and sketches that should have accompanied it. Bloomfield missed a chance, owing to his booksellers' reluctance and his own inhibiting consciousness of what was proper for a laborer visitor writing at the touring-gentry's behest. As a result, it was easy to neglect the merits of his Wye: literary criticism, although idealizing a fellow nature poet's imaginative response to the Wye valley, damned the poem with faint praise. In the twentieth century, Bloomfield's reputation dwindled to nothing. If, after Wordsworth's "Tintern Abbey," the West Country was a critical testing ground for Romantic poetry, then Bloomfield failed the test. His deleted lines on Old Scoop show us both that this failure was not of his own making and that Wordsworth's egotistical sublime was not the only way to bring into being a new and distinctive response to landscape. Bloomfield's comic sublime was also an innovative and individual discourse—his allusive chattiness, recalling the banter of the companions who made the trip down river, was a celebration of tourism as a social amusement that the sober Wordsworth could not have made, but that still allowed for meditations on nature as intense as that prompted by Dyer and Gray at Tintern and Raglan.

In later years, Bloomfield would look back on the Wye tour as the greatest experience of his life. After 1812, the year Mary Lloyd Baker died young, he would never again experience the support of so supportive a circle. In that same year, he experienced, as Scott was later to do, the risks of dependence on a highly capitalized market: his booksellers went bankrupt, depriving him, their most lucrative author, of most of his royalties and leaving his valuable copyrights in legal limbo. Whereas Wordsworth, Coleridge, and Southey, whose poetry had never sold well, had patrons and pensions to fall back upon, Bloomfield had lost his, the commercial imperatives of the publishers having alienated Lofft who had in any case provided connections rather than financial aid.[22] In the process, he lost his brother's support too. The partnership that had made *The Farmer's Boy* and *Rural Tales* such runaway successes was now utterly dissolved. In 1811, he had sought to reduce expenses by moving from London to the Bedfordshire village of Shefford, hoping to rediscover the placedness in village life that he recalled in his Suffolk youth—a placedness impossible for him to reconstitute in Suffolk because that place had become vitiated by family disputes. But in Shefford, arthritis and blindness crept upon him: his output declined and he fell from notice as Scott and Byron became the new publishing sensations. He found it hard to interest publishers in his new works while the postwar economic recession made matters worse.

It was at the nadir of Bloomfield's fortunes that one of his old gentlemen friends got in touch with him again. Mary Lloyd Baker's widower Thomas had, since her death, remarried and spent a fortune on building a new country seat for himself. He wrote in 1821, sending a banknote, but also presuming on their past membership of a companionate circle centered on his wife and her sisters to lecture Bloomfield about his conduct:

> It has been remarked that for some time past *neither yourself* nor *any of your family* have been in the habit of attending *any place of worship whatsoever.* It has also been observed that you are in the habit of reading some periodical works which are very hostile to the government of this country. Perhaps from these two circumstances coupled together has originated the idea that you have imbibed both Deistical & Republican principles. The latter tending to the subversion of that Government under which we have all lived so long free from those calamities which have befallen almost every other part of Europe—The former tending to the destruction of Christianity, & herein of *every thing most valuable* to us all (but most of all endangering the eternal welfare of those who are unhappy enough to become its Dupes) and both being so frequently united in the same persons—These considerations have induced many of your friends & patrons *upon principle* to withhold from you their accustomed protection & assistance, thinking that by doing as they had done, & as they still wish to do, they should be giving countenance to a dangerous man. I cannot think they are right. I cannot adopt such an opinion of you. In full hope that all may be explained away, & that you may again stand as high in the esteem of your friends as the religious and moral tendency of your former life & works had placed you, I take advantage of being in your neighbourhood to give you this information, & to assure you that I shall have much pleasure in making known to your former friends any answer to this letter which you may think it right to favor me with for this purpose.
>
> (T. J. Lloyd Baker to Robert Bloomfield,
> May 23, 1821; BL 351)

The language of allusion that Bloomfield had once shared with Lloyd Baker's wife could not have been more brutally destroyed. Instead of friendship, one-off aid now comes with the threat of its withdrawal if Bloomfield does not agree to have his private life monitored to ensure its compliance with Tory and Evangelical, Church and State, conservatism. Bloomfield's reply was dignified but firm, but Lloyd Baker was not satisfied. He wrote again, applying more pressure: if Bloomfield would declare he was "not hostile to the Church or Government of this country as each now exists, I am inclined to hope that something may yet be done for you" (May 29, 1821; BL 353). Bloomfield's reply to this, a vindication of his private views, was, between the lines, furious:

> I say then there is not a man or woman living who would or could say to *my face* that I have renounced the doctrines of Christ or his Miracles.—There is not a soul upon earth to say "you are an enemy to the government of your country" Fools, cannot they see that the *form* of government of a country is rather different to the administration of it? . . .
>
> [. . .]
>
> Cobbett and Hunt[23] are men whom I would not trust with power; they are too eager to obtain it.—Universal suffrage is an impracticable piece of nonscense;—Republicanism will only do in *new* establishd countrys: not in those which have been govern'd by Kings for a thousand years.—
>
> It is the natural bent and practice of *party* to go to extreems. Thus they could not let me rest even on the intermediate shelf of Scepticism but made me a Deist at once!!—I have been in the presence of great and *good* men, the Bishops Watson and Porteous,[24] but then it is equally true that I have taken snuff with Horne Tooke, and have held conversation with Hardy the Boot maker, who was tried for high treason![25]— Yea, more than all this, I had the misfortune to be born only six miles from the birthplace of Tom Paine!! This, to some ears would be horrible!—I shall go to worship again when I am well enough; and when my dear Daughter and Sons can leave me in the company of a Woman whom you know little about, they will go too.
>
> (to T. J. Lloyd Baker, May 31–June 1, 1821; BL 354)

Letters of the Lloyd Baker kind are grim evidence of the ideological strife of post-Waterloo Britain: they place in stark illumination the repression by which the ruling classes maintained their grip on power, all the while fearing revolution. Bloomfield knew he was now living through a reactionary era, in which the classes were polarized, and his public response was to create, in his final collection of poems *May Day with the Muses* (1822), a pastoral fantasy wherein the literary circle once offered him by the Sharps is reconstituted in an idealized village.

May Day is a volume built on a conceit—it is ostensibly the fruit of a poetry slam organized in a village to celebrate the traditional May Day festivities. The local squire, Bloomfield pretends, invites the villagers to recite poems about village life, accepting them in lieu of rent. Thus the landowner renews old customs, preferring poetry to money as a sign of value, and patronizes, in the best sense, rustics who are able to voice their rural experience as verse. The squire respects his tenants and they him: the ideal village, for Bloomfield, is self-policing. This was an old-fashioned and forlorn hope, perhaps, in face of the capitalization of farming and the coerciveness of squires such as Lloyd Baker, but it was one to which Wordsworth, Southey, and Gilpin also subscribed as did Cobbett: despite their political differences, their common commitment to the superiority of the remembered rural society of their youth over the capitalist one of the present led them all to romanticize a rural paternalism that was both radical and conservative in its opposition to the liberal, laissez faire ideology of "improvement" that enriched the landowning classes while impoverishing their laborers.

May Day with the Muses is an allusive tour de force. Comprising ballads and lyrics, it is effectively a conservative revisiting of *Lyrical Ballads*, with a frame narrative that, like Wordsworth's Preface (which Bloomfield had admired in 1802), was designed to outline the poems' social import and to prepare for their proper reception by the reader. Wordsworth himself had embarked on a conservative reworking of the radical *Lyrical Ballads* in his "Song at the Feast of Brougham Castle" (1807), in which the poet is imagined as a having the valued role of a bard singing of the deeds of the local Lord Clifford in the presence of that lord, his retainers, and tenants. In *May Day* not only does it seem that to be a rural poet is to be a cherished villager and vice versa, but also that poetry is a face-to-face oral activity of a united community. The benevolent squire, moreover, respects tradition and exacts no political toll for his benevolence, which he in fact regards as his duty. Meanwhile, the individual poems that the villagers recite also tell of a traditional community in which authority is vested in a single figure who can therefore be addressed, appealed to, and even, potentially, rebuked and chastised face to face.

The first poem told by a villager in *May Day* is a response to Wordsworth's transformation of the traditional ballad into a poem dealing with domestic life among modern villagers. The characters of "The Drunken Father" allude to Wordsworth's Ellen Irwin and Stephen Hill; its diction echoes "The Thorn" and "Goody Blake and Harry Gill":

> Poor Ellen married Andrew Hall,
> Who dwells beside the moor,

Where yonder rose-tree shades the wall,
And woodbines grace the door.

(lines 1–4)[26]

The story evokes "The Idiot Boy" because it features a mother wor-
rying about her young child, out on an errand at night. As in that
poem, the errand is a comic journey that might have been tragic—the
child rescues his drunken father from the alehouse and navigates him
safely home in the dark. The mother is relieved; her emotion, however, is the center of the drama. Domestic harmony is endorsed.

If the Wordsworthian "Drunken Father" imagines the traditional
rural hierarchy as being largely free of exploitation and mostly capable of healing social ills, then "The Forrester" offers a more critical view, implicitly endorsing a radical politics of nature. Bloomfield
has his narrator use the oak-tree motif that had served to legitimize
the monarchy since the time of Charles II, the motif that Cowper
and Wordsworth had developed in "Yardley Oak" and "Yew Trees"
(Cowper's *Task*, meanwhile, is directly praised in *May Day*). In
Bloomfield's poem, a mighty oak in the squire's park has fallen:

The shadowing oak, the noblest stem
  That graced the forest's ample bound,
Had cast to earth his diadem;
  His fractured limbs had delved the ground.
He lay, and still to fancy groan'd;
  He lay like Alfred when he died—
Alfred, a king by Heaven enthroned,
  His age's wonder, England's pride!
Monarch of forests, great as good,
  Wise as the sage,—thou heart of steel!
Thy name shall rouse the patriot's blood
As long as England's sons can feel.
  From every lawn, and copse, and glade,
The timid deer in squadrons came,
  And circled round their fallen shade
With all of language but its name.
  Astonishment and dread withheld
The fawn and doe of tender years,
  But soon a triple circle swell'd,
With rattling horns and twinkling ears.
  Some in his root's deep cavern housed,
  And seem'd to learn, and muse, and teach,
Or on his topmost foliage browsed,
  That had for centuries mock'd their reach.

> Winds in their wrath these limbs could crash,
> This strength, this symmetry could mar;
> A people's wrath can monarchs dash
> From bigot throne or purple car.

(lines 45–72)

The astonished deer, keen to "learn and muse" what the unexpected change means, stand in for the local rustics. They also prompt an act of political interpretation by the narrator: he reminds his audience— and us, the readers—that monarchs, however mighty, are dependent on the people. There is a hint of Jacobinism about this lesson; the royal oak can represent a "bigot" as well as a "sage" king, and bigots can be swept away. The poem concludes not with a patriotic declaration of loyalty to king and country, but by imagining nature as a leveling principle that guarantees individual liberty:

> Empires may fall, and nations groan,
> Pride be thrown down, and power decay;
> Dark bigotry may rear her throne,
> But science is the light of day.
> Yet, while so low my lot is cast,
> Through wilds and forests let me range;
> My joys shall pomp and power outlast—
> The voice of nature cannot change.

(lines 89–96)

Bloomfield's position here is close to that of Wordsworth in 1798: the wilds and forests are a reliable refuge and resource for revolutionary freedom, at least for the individual poet if not for the masses. Cowper's rural radicalism stands behind both writers, and Bloomfield honors it by borrowing the oak-tree symbol through which Cowper had most searchingly interrogated power. Thus he aligns his poetic symbolism, and the radicalism contained within his overall idealization of traditional rural society, with that of the two rural poets of recent times he most admired: allusion places him in their company; it seeks solidarity in the teeth of the destruction of rural community and literary companionship that he had suffered after 1812 and that Lloyd Baker's ideological coercion had underlined. By the time of *May Day*'s publication, allusion was one of Bloomfield's last resources: without a literary circle around him; impoverished, ill, and nearly blind, forgotten by the public, he used it as a way of summoning a poetic community—a shared language—that he could access only from the isolated margin. Cowper was long dead; Wordsworth, although an admirer of his verse, was personally unknown to him. Southey, however, recognized the poetic kinship of which allusion was a marker: he agitated for a new edition of Bloomfield's poems to relieve his poverty and helped organize a subscription for him.

CHAPTER 6

IAMB YET WHAT IAMB: ALLUSION AND DELUSION IN JOHN CLARE'S ASYLUM POEMS

"I'm John Clare now. I was Byron and Shakespeare formerly. At different times you know I'm different people—that is the same person with different names."[1] Confined in a lunatic asylum, John Clare adopted other people's voices. He told visitors he was Jack Randall, the boxer; he wrote poems as Lord Byron and as William Cowper. This adoption of other poet's voices may or may not have been related to a belief that he shared their identities. Some visitors to Northampton asylum were persuaded that Clare was deluded, yet a fellow inmate spoke of a deliberate and skilful performance: "A great knack of personating."[2] Allusion or delusion? Certainly Clare's habit of writing in language that everywhere invoked that of a favorite poet was a crafted performance; if he did believe himself to be Byron or Cowper, this belief may have been his unconscious endorsement of the success of his verse impersonation. It's more likely, however, given the strategic nature of his adoption of other poets' authorial personae, that he was perfectly conscious that he was only Byron or Cowper in the sense that his poetry was an art of his own that constantly called upon theirs, both by alluding to phrases, genres, and themes associated with them and also by imitating their style, so that even when his words were entirely his own they seemed to be echoes of *The Task* and *Don Juan*.

In what follows, I explore the "personations" Clare wrote in the asylum as a unique development of coterie language—unique in that they summon dead poets textually into Clare's writing as if they were fellow members of a circle, yet as if there were little or no difference between himself and them. Clare is not so much a son establishing his filial position by paying tribute to poetic fathers, or a friend acknowledging a language developed with his literary peers, as a man who finds his own voice in losing it—in letting his poetic identity be occupied by the language of others. This letting be, of course, is actually not a passive surrender to past poetry, but an achievement of skill and practiced artifice—Clare in fact masters other poets' style even as he seems to lose his "sole self" in theirs.[3] Part of this mastery is metrical: controlling the patterning of speech in Cowperian iambic pentameter, and the outcries of the Revelation prophet in parallelisms, bolsters Clare's identity—articulates, in other poets' rhythms, his "I am."

Imitation was fundamental to Clare's poetic vocation from the start. As a laborer living among scarcely literate villagers, Clare had to *perform* what was, in that community, the extraordinary identity of a poet—to a far greater degree than, say, Wordsworth or Coleridge, who practiced being a poet in school exercises, university coteries, and in the self-created literary partnerships of Bristol and Somerset. Clare, by contrast, lacked both social context and literary models: he had to try on poetic voices in comparative isolation, deriving them from poetry he read in newspapers, magazines and, as John Goodridge has shown, from a souvenir handkerchief on which was printed a short biography of Chatterton.[4] To master the draft of rhyme and rhythm—the deployment of iambs—meant adopting an identity for which there was no normal place among the villagers who constituted his social circle. Later, he passed his own work off as that of others—sending verse to magazines under a variety of invented identities so as to maximize his access to print and escape the "peasant poet" voice he was supposed, for marketing purposes, to adopt in his own name.

Significantly, Clare was at his happiest when part of the lower middle-class literary community of the *London Magazine*, where his vocation as poet was confirmed as his verse appeared alongside work by other writers—writers who had welcomed him socially on his trips to London. Clare became a satellite Cockney, a visiting member of a coterie that had been named after the "Lake school" of Wordsworth, Coleridge, and Southey, and that included Lamb, Keats, De Quincey, Hazlitt, Leigh Hunt, and Edward Rippingille. The *London Magazine*,  both as a metropolitan print journal and as a social circle, bolstered the confidence of one who otherwise lived on the margins of literary culture. He remembered: "As to profits—the greatest profits most congenial to my feelings were the friends it brought me and the names that it rendered familiar to my fireside—scraps of whose melodys I had heard and read in my corner—but had I only imagined for a moment that I should hold communion with such."[5] But the magazine collapsed, its publisher—Clare's editor John Taylor—unable to survive the competition in the commercial print market in 1825 and 1826. Trading conditions left Taylor suffering from "brain fever"; he withdrew not just from the magazine but also as the editor of Clare's published books, leaving Clare without the collaborator with whom he had shaped his works—both individual poems and the complete collections in which they appeared.

Lacking editorial help, Clare struggled to create a collection of his own: in 1831 he conceived *The Midsummer Cushion* as a "concept album" in manuscript, but was unable to bring it to print. Deprived of social and literary validation as a poet, he became unmanageable at home and confinement in the asylum followed. There, in notebooks, he found a way of asserting his vocation in extremis, creating planned collections of verse and prose with common themes as substitutes for the published books he had once created with Taylor and for the issues of the *London Magazine* in which his verse had appeared alongside others' contributions. The asylum notebooks, that is, sought to reproduce in their dialogic form the participation in the literary sphere on which his poetic vocation and his integrity as a person depended. Constructing them as volumes, rather than, say, a jumble of random drafts and scraps, renewed the commitment to shape whole collections he had prided himself on as a published poet. Writing in them in verse that alluded to and imitated Cowper's and Byron's acted both as a tribute to those poets and, as their words echoed in his, a means of forging a literary community of which he could be part.[6] It should be noted that Clare was not alone in this: although he took the practice to a new level, personating other poets was a not uncommon feature of Romanticism. Poets wrote in the personae of others to affirm a community of writers and readers in the face of the reading public's remoteness or neglect. Coleridge revoiced Wordsworth; Southey wrote as Coleridge; Shelley impersonated Keats; Robert Bloomfield adopted the Scots voice of Burns.

From the start of his career, Clare invoked Cowper—but not simply the popular Cowper of *The Task*. Clare's Cowper was a posthumous one, and a symbol of mental distress, because he was mediated by a number of candid accounts that appeared after his death, from Hayley's 1803 biography onward.[7] Cowper's spiritual diary was published in 1815,[8] disclosing his attempted suicide and his peculiar Calvinistic conviction that he was irreparably damned—a reprobate doomed to hell. The volumes in which Clare read Cowper's verse also told of dejection so incapacitating that it left the poet hearing voices threatening his damnation. Clare owned John Johnson's "Sketch of the Life of Cowper" (1811) which details Cowper's "mental calamity" and "extreme dejection," and shows how they were worsened by his religious beliefs.[9] He also possessed *Aikin's Select Works of the British Poets* (1820), which described how Cowper became "completely deranged" and had "little more than intervals of comfort between long paroxysms of despondency."[10] Owning several collections of his verse, Clare thus knew both the life and the poetry—the 1780s nature poetry that had made Cowper's name and the 1790s fragments of anguish that Hayley had published in 1803, including "Yardley Oak."[11]

At first, it was the nature poet who impressed Clare.[12] He wrote tributary verses that portray the poet of *The Task* as the kind of poet he wished to be—a poet for whom nature is not just a muse, but also an admiring audience that perpetuates his words.[13] Cowper, he declared, "found the muse on common ground" (line 2) and his songs "share[d] the peoples talk" (line 7). Most importantly, Cowper's nature poetry was renewed in nature:

> Birds sing his name on every bough
> Nature repeats it in the wind
> And every place the Poet trod
> And every place the Poet sung
> Are like the holy land of God
> In every Mouth on every tongue

(lines 23–28)

Here Clare imagines nature alluding to the poet who had praised it: he hears in its calls and motions invocations of Cowper's name and of his verse: the birds and winds repeat the poet's words, offering him the readership he lacks among humans. Nature is his refuge, his home, his speech community. And by implication, if Clare can hear—or imagine—the persistence of Cowper's words as the sounds of nature, then he, as Cowper's follower, can hope for the survival of his own verse.

The survival of the self in words that are both nature's and one's own became the central issue for Clare as he found his home country destroyed by landowners who were seeking greater agricultural efficiency in order to maintain profits in the postwar economic depression. Bushes were uprooted, ponds drained, hedges planted, footpaths removed, trees felled. Clare felt the loss, writing

I used to be fondly attachd to spots about the fields and there were 3 or 4 were I used to go to visit on Sundays   one of these was under an old Ivied Oak in Oxey wood were I twisted a sallow stoven into an harbour which grew into the cramped way in which I had made it   two others were under a broad oak in a field calld the Barrows and Langley Bush and all my favourites places have met with misfortunes

The old ivied tree was cut down when the wood was cut down and my bower was destroyed   the woodmen fancied it a resort for robbers...Lee Close Oak was cut down in the inclosure and Langley bush was broken up by some wanton fellows when kidding furze on the heath.[14]

In these circumstances, it is not surprising that Clare turned to Cowper's bleaker 1790s poems, for they were voicings of a desperation induced by witnessing, in the landscape, the destruction and death that affects all living things. Cowper articulated how it felt to have so close a bond with nature that its decay cut the ground from under one. What in Cowper was a natural process of loss was, however, for Clare a human one caused by the capitalization of agriculture. He described the process at work in a letter that Taylor included in the introduction to *The Village Minstrel* (1821):

My two favourite elm trees at the back of the hut are condemned to die—it shocks me to relate it, but 'tis true. The savage who owns them thinks they have done their best, and now he wants to make use of the benefits he can get from selling them. O was this country Egypt, and was I but a caliph, the owner should lose his ears for his arrogant presumption; and the first wretch that buried his axe in their roots should hang on their branches as a terror to the rest. I have been several mornings to bid them farewel.[15]

In the event, Clare's literary connection to the gentry won the trees a reprieve, but not permanently—by 1831 he was writing "They have insulted my feelings latterly very much & cut down the last Elm next the street."[16] He expressed his insulted feelings at greater length in verses titled "The Fallen Elm,"[17] in which he apostrophized the endangered trees, just as Cowper had done in "Yardley Oak." Addressing them directly, he created an individual relationship that contrasts with their relationship to their "owner." He talked to them as fellow inmates of his cottage; the owner viewed them as potential profit:

Old Elm that murmured in our chimney top
The sweetest anthem autumn ever made

And into mellow whispering calms would drop
When showers fell on thy many coloured shade
And when dark tempests mimic thunder made
While darkness came as it would strangle light
With the black tempest of a winter night
That rocked thee like a cradle to thy root
How did I love to hear the winds upbraid
Thy strength without while all within was mute
It seasoned comfort to our hearts desire
We felt thy kind protection like a friend
And pitched our chairs up closer to the fire
Enjoying comforts that was never penned

(lines 1–14)

Clare aligns his relationship to the tree with that of birds and children, the owner's with that of men who seek money and power at others' cost. The elm is made a landmark for a community: "The children sought thee in thy summer shade" (line 23). It is a bastion against the hostile world, protecting Clare's cottage "like a friend" (line 12). In a line Cowperian in its intimation of insecurity, Clare makes the elm's rooted strength a source of reassurance: "It seasoned comfort to our hearts desire" (line 11). Here *seasoned* is the crucial word: in a complex image Clare uses it as a transitive verb referring to the seasoning of food: like honey, the elm's "sweetest anthem" turned a domestic retreat into a comfort to be enjoyed. And he also suggests another more unorthodox meaning—that it was the elm's seasoned timber, strong through its growth through many seasons, that strengthened with comfort those who had known the tree through many seasons (and known themselves by dwelling in its shade).

Clare makes the tree a self-mark as well as a landmark. He describes himself in words normally applicable to it and it in words normally applicable to himself: "Thou ownd a language by which hearts are stirred / Deeper than by the attribute of words / Thine spoke a feeling known in every tongue" (lines 31–33). Here, Clare reworks Cowper in a Wordsworthian language: the poet is privileged to hear and voice nature's speech (the elms murmur, whisper, make music) whereas, at least in "Yardley Oak," the oak's failure to speak is at issue. Indeed, the terms in which Clare praised Wordsworth make it clear that it was this melding of human and nonhuman language that he valued: he called the poet a kindred spirit who "defies all art and in all the lunatic enthusiasm of nature...negligently sets down his thoughts from the tongue of his inspirer."[18] The phrasing of this tribute indicates also that Clare valued poets who risked seeming artless and excessive because of their solitary communication with landscape. Cowper was described both as an enthusiast and a lunatic in the biographies through which Clare read about him.

As Clare continues to invoke the tree, "The Fallen Elm" becomes a linguistic battle in which nature's/the poet's language (the two sounding as one) fights against the more powerful languages that threaten to overwhelm it.

> Thoust heard the knave abusing those in power
> Bawl freedom loud and then oppress the free
> Thoust sheltered hypocrites in many a shower
> That when in power would never shelter thee
> Thoust heard the knave supply his canting powers
> With wrongs illusions when he wanted friends
> That bawled for shelter when he lived in showers
>
> (lines 41–47)

Like Cowper in "Yardley Oak," Clare reveals here his sense of being trapped in corrupted speech communities: the elm, for all its strong indifference to the "wrongs illusions" that it hears, cannot survive their power to effect change; nor, therefore, can the heart-stirring language "deeper than…the attribute of words" (line 32) that the poet derives from it. And neither the cant of popular agitators nor the language of gentlemen with its self-serving justification of the tree felling can be trusted: both are inadequate to the needs of the self for a verbal source of truth and honesty. Yet, neither can be avoided. Clare's literary form aligns him willy-nilly with gentlemen patrons, his status as a rural laborer with popular agitators ("knave[s] abusing those in power"). And since the ancient trees, his chief source of a language of truth, were being felled, he no longer had a trustworthy source, no native omphalos, no piece of England whose sounds he could turn into an untainted overflow of loving speech.

He did have a tradition of radical invective at his disposal; the angry rhetoric of the poem's attack on enclosure alludes to that of the republican enemy of the monarchical constitution, Milton. Milton had urged Cromwell to "help us to save Free Conscience from the paw / Of Hireling Wolves, whose Gospel is their Maw."[19] Clare uses the same image to show that the liberty of conscience and speech that Englishmen regarded as their constitutional inheritance was being corrupted by those "Who glut their vile unsatiated maws / And freedoms birthright from the weak devours" (lines 71–72). And yet, Clare's words are imbued with the expectation of defeat by the words and deeds of men of power.[20] Neither the heart-stirring murmuring of the elm (the inarticulate language of nature) nor the Miltonic jeremiads of radical tradition will deflect the "force of might" (line 54) and the hypocritical language used to justify that force. Clare anticipates a linguistic as well as physical destruction, a mental as well as agricultural enclosure:

> Such was thy ruin music making Elm
> The rights of freedom was to injure thine
> As thou wert served so would they overwhelm
> In freedoms name the little that is mine

(line 65–68)

In face of the power of a perverted language, in which "wrong was right and right was wrong" (line 63), Clare can protest but cannot win. His own source of verbal and moral authority may remain, but it is likely to be obscured by the language of men of power—left to speak for a landscape and community that no longer exist. And how long could its speech survive the destruction of its sources? The experienced meaning of freedom will, in the poem's last grim phrase, be overwhelmed in "freedom's" name—a linguistic cancellation of self-possession ("the little that is mine" [line 68]). That way, Clare implies, silence and/or madness lies.

Throughout his meditation on the elm, Clare is speaking to the shade of Cowper. "Yardley Oak" was his model, for it dramatized death and destruction without a compensatory discovery of a remaining power and unity in the mind of the poet contemplating the ancient, broken tree. It manifested the appalling fragmentation of language and meaning that results from the destruction or corruption of an interpretable landscape on which the self is founded. Thus, at the end of Cowper's poem, the poet and the tree, crippled and vulnerably mortal, are placed in opposition to pre-lapsarian Adam. Adam, Cowper shows, was molded at once, not over a period of time. His language was not slowly and painfully learnt but instantly and exactly named the new-created world. He

> survey'd
> All creatures,...assign'd
> To each his name significant, and fill'd
> With love and wisdom, render'd back to heav'n
> In praise harmonious the first air he drew.
> He was excus'd the penalties of dull

Minority. No tutor charg'd his hand
With the thought-tracing quill, or task'd his mind
With problems; history, not wanted yet,
Lean'd on her elbow, watching Time, whose course
Eventful, should supply her with a theme

(lines 173–84; Cowper, III, 77–83, 314)

Here Eden is a place of exactitude—a paradise of language in which words not only fit things precisely but are a gift given to God in return for the gift of breath. It is a paradise too fragile to be sustained, watched by "History" and "Time"—and by Cowper, who seems to image himself as a writer-in-the-making as he identifies "the thought-tracing quill" as one of the penalties by which the fallen world is characterized. Is "task'd" even a punning allusion to his own *The Task* and the mental pain its writing cost? If so, the allusion hints at a personal, poetic fall—a fall from the timeless spiritual reciprocity of Edenic speech into writing, showing the latter to be a penalty rather than a gift, of human rather than divine origin. A canceled passage in the manuscript of the poem[21] makes the contrast more pathetic and perhaps more confessional. After the word "Minority," Cowper had originally written "no primmer with his thumb / He soil'd, no grammar with his tears, but rose / Accomplish'd in the only tongue on earth / Taught then, the tongue in which he spake with God."

After representing learning to write as one of the penalties of the fallen world, Cowper's poem fades uncompleted into silence. The text, like the oak to which it compares the poet, is shown to be acutely vulnerable to loss. Outside Eden, language, like the oak, will be felled by the consequences of the first fall—Sin, Death, and Time. The sad fate of the writer is to record this loss and thus know the inevitability of its consequences for his own—and all—writing. So too in Clare's poetic meditation on the fallen elm: here too poetry articulates its own destruction, foresees its own breakup. Clare learned from Cowper an aesthetics of loss and limit that was inseparable from the consciousness of lateness—intimations of decline, dismemberment, and oblivion rather than immortality.

Such intimations were not the whole story for Clare, even when the pressures recorded in "The Fallen Elm" led to a loss of self-possession that brought him to the madhouse. There, he became more than ever a prophet of the self-loss he saw in nature, but he also continued, fighting against that loss, to articulate nature's reparative qualities—a very Cowperian struggle. The struggle took place in a series of extraordinary notebooks that Clare compiled while a patient in Northampton lunatic asylum. These are, as Lynn Pearce termed them in a seminal essay,[22] "polyphonic," multi-generic wholes—manuscript "lodges" that resemble Coleridge's "flycatchers" in their blending of poems, translations, letters, lists, and transcriptions.[23] They reveal two especially significant writerly practices, neither of which is easily discernible in the published editions of his writing. First, they show that what the editors of his Collected Poems print as short, separate lyrics appear as parts of longer, dialogic forms, in which verse and prose of various kinds speak differently about similar concerns—and that Clare set out the pages this way. The notebook, now called Northampton MS 19, is a case in point. A slim, bound volume that Clare composed in 1845,[24] it comprises 133 pages, all covered in Clare's penciled handwriting, and written from both ends (Clare having turned the book upside down and made entries from the back as well as having proceeded from the front). Verse predominates: there are first drafts, revised drafts, and fair copies of poems. There are prose transcriptions of the Book of Revelation and versifications of these; there are letter drafts and lists. Many entries are placed consecutively; some appear to have been grouped thematically; in a few instances, Clare has squeezed a poem onto the remaining white space before and after one previously entered even if this involves working backward, leaving the new poem dispersed across several pages—for example the "Song" that appears on pp. 82 and 79–78. Second, they demonstrate that in writing in other poets' personae—Cowper, Byron, the prophet of Revelation—Clare inscribed a struggle between visions of nature as shelter and refuge on the one hand, and alienation and destruction on the other.[25]

If imitation developed, in the asylum, into impersonation of the poet imitated, the causes were Clare's need for partners in rhyme, and his loneliness in the asylum. Yet, he was not wholly without people interested in his writing while at Northampton; indeed, the notebooks are testaments to the concern of William Knight, house steward in the asylum from 1845 to 1850. Though essentially Clare's keeper, and so a man with institutional power and far from an equal partner, Knight encouraged Clare's writing, in 1848 planning to edit a volume of poems that he and others had transcribed—plans that come to nought owing to the death of Clare's son and Knight's transfer to another institution. Nonetheless, for five years, Knight was the nearest thing to Taylor—a constantly involved reader and editor prepared to labor on Clare's manuscripts—and Clare wrote prolifically for him, as he recorded in a letter:

Thus John keeps joging on from theme to theme—from passion to calm nature—from solitude to bustling life—I have not yet seen him this morning but I have no doubt he has something for me—early as it is—for he is up most mornings at six o'clock—and his mind must be employed in writing poetry or Clare will be Clare no longer.[26]

The need to write to retain self-knowledge and self-possession is evident throughout Notebook 19, not least when, paradoxically, it involves not just invoking another writer's style but also adopting his persona: writing *as* Byron or Burns, for instance. Clare asserted his virtuosity and his membership of a sustaining circle of poets by direct personation, but also by stylistic allusions, in Clare's own persona, that treat the scenes—the named landscapes—of another's poem as if Clare were responding directly to them—as he does to Cowper's *The Task*. Allusion also subtended the transformation of a text from prose to verse, so that Clare the poet came to take over the authority and voice, if not the name, of the original writer—as he did to the prophet of Revelation. The notebook juxtaposes these means of transformation; they cross-fertilize each other and form dialogues with letter drafts, memoranda, and names, creating a book that has some affinities with the heteroglossic pages of a printed magazine. Thus, it includes a poem that Clare begins with a line of Coleridge's; it also contains verse in Burns's manner and many new versions of traditional love songs.[27] But the voices of Cowper, Byron, and the Revelation prophet dominate, forming a dialogue between rival envisonings of space and time, the rhythm of which is lost in the Oxford Poems edition.

The epigraph from Cowper is a case in point. It appears on the first notebook page thus:

> John Clare
> Northborough
> ~~xxx~~ 1845

> "Oh for a lodge in some vast wilderness,
> Some boundless contiguity of shade,
> Where rumour of oppression and deceit,
> Of unsuccessful or successful war,
> Might never reach me more." Cowper[28]

Immediately after it, Clare writes, in rough iambics:

> & in the maple bush there hides the style
> & then the gate the awthorn stands before
> Till close upon't you cannot see't the while

> Tis like to Ivy creeping oer a door
> & green as spring nor gap is seen before
> & still the path leads on—till neath your hand
> The gate waits to be opened—& then claps—the sower
> Scatters the seeds of spring beneath his hand
> & then the footpath tracks the elting land.[29]

The manuscript suggests that these lines are a continuation of Cowper's words, making the quotation Clare's own starting point. They develop the Cowperian need for refuge into the disclosure of a hidden path, shielded by nature from all but the observant, shared by poet and reader, leading to a pastoral world in which labor is unalienated—the sower's hand and the elting land match in rhythm and rhyme; Clare moves into verse through Cowper's—a process that the notebook will repeat again and again. Thus on p. 46 a simple tribute to Cowper identifies the "charm" of his poetry with the power of the sun to "gild" the landscape:

> Verses on Onley
> A charm is thrown oer Olney plains
> By Cowper's rural muse
> While sunshine gilds the river Ouse
> In morning's meadow dews.[30]

In context, this tribute endorses the nature description immediately preceding it, in which Clare delineates with exactitude the transforming effect of the sun on normally unnoticed weeds, the first signs of spring.

The opening epigraph from Cowper prepares for such endorsements of the unnoticed. To begin a book written in a lunatic asylum with the words of a mad poet would be poignant. To begin it with that poet's yearning for an asylum is grimly ironic. After all, in a letter written in 1848 Clare called the asylum, "The Land of sodom where all the peoples brains are turned the wrong way . . . the purgatoriall hell & French Bastile of English liberty."[31] In this context, his epigraph from Cowper indicates that he needed an asylum from the asylum—a place of rural seclusion and peace; and that he would seek one by calling on others' poetic voices—particularly Cowper's because he knew that Cowper, a poet on the edge of darkness, had fashioned such an asylum for himself on paper—in the imagined nature of his verse. Clare would harness that verse, as well as invoke Cowper as a sponsor, in an effort to make the notebook a lodge—a place wherein his poetic voices could be secreted from the babel of the madhouse.

Jonathan Bate has suggested that we "should not rule out the possibility that [Clare's] own derangement was partially shaped by his reading about the mental sufferings of other writers";[32] reading of Cowper's madness did not so much teach Clare how to be mad, however, as how to both articulate and find a refuge from distress in writing about nature. Clare admired Cowper because his sense of nature's healing power was so hard won—the "lodge" it offered the solitary poet was indeed surrounded by a "vast wilderness" of anxiety in which he could find no resting place for himself, since "rumour of oppression and deceit, / Of unsuccessful or successful war" inevitably blighted his rural retreat. But Cowper did not succumb to or luxuriate in a despair that rendered all of nature a wasteland, as Byron seemed to do in "Darkness." Clare would again and again personate Cowper's struggle to find in nature a refuge rather than a wasteland that was a correlative for a devastated self.

Imprisoned, unable to get his family to release him, Clare chose to mark out Notebook 19 as a Cowperian book—one that used *The Task* to find an internalized exile from the asylum prison to an imaginary shelter he had chosen—Cowper's lodge in the wilderness but also the shelter of Cowper-like verse, a more peaceful poetry to rewrite than Byron-like verse. Thus on p. 68, between lyrics that lovingly observe, as Cowper does, the minutiae of plants and trees, he writes an inscription that identifies the notebook itself—its paper and ink—as the place wherein Cowper's visionary nature exists. The named spots of Cowper's Buckinghamshire are transposed to the verse that Clare writes in tribute to Cowper, and to the book that contains that verse. This is not just a tribute but also a relocation of Cowper's landscape to Clare's—of poeticized place to poetry, that generates new writing from an already-written reality. Thus, after a stanza describing the arum sprouting in spring, Clare continues,

> Here is the scenes the rural poet made
> So famous in his songs—the very scenes
> He painted in his words that warm & shade
> In winters wild waste & springs young vivid greens
> Alcove & shrubbery—& the tree that leans
> With its overweight of Ivy—Yardley oak
> The peasants nest & fields of blossomed beans
> The bridge & avenue of thick set oak
> The wilde ness—here Cowpers spirit spoke.[33]

The Oxford editors print these lines as a separate short lyric on the grounds that "it is not clear from the MS whether this stanza goes with the preceding one or is separate from it."[34] One sympathizes with their dilemma: the manuscript is not clear. Nevertheless, the separation that the scholarly apparatus imposes (they sever the lines from the preceding stanza by a headnote and white space) dislocates the manuscript writing, undermining the self-reflexivity that is a vital part of Clare's procedure. When he writes "Here is the scenes," he is commenting on the notebook itself, and the ability of the lines inscribed in it to allow secret access to the world of nature presented in Cowper's, and his own, words. And when he writes "The very scenes / He painted" and "Cowper's spirit spoke" he envisions a translation from print to manuscript and then to speech and song—visual and read to oral and heard. Apparently, poetry mediates nature both by word pictures (on paper) and voicing (as song and speech)—the trajectory being that Clare rewrites Cowper's word pictures that he has encountered in books, reinscribes them on paper as if seeing for himself the actual scenes Cowper described: he takes possession of the literal literally. This reinscription of printed pictures into the more intimate, personal, and bodily form of handwriting makes Cowper's spirit "speak" in/as Clare's own words: it liberates the silent, inferred speech present in a printed poem into manuscript and then to audible words. Nature here escapes the page by transcription—Clare personates not just Cowper's verse but also the scenes that verse describes by tracing print out on paper. It then becomes so immediate and present that it becomes voice rather than description, just as the poet's page transcends its silent materiality: in one gesture, nature and spirit come to being in the poet's voice as writing moves from print to manuscript. The effect is self-reflexive in its deixis: Cowper's spirit spoke not just at Yardley oak and the peasant's nest but also in Clare's verse, which rewords *The Task* and in the process renews Clare's own nature poetry in the voice of another. Given Cowper's fragile identity and Clare's physical location when he wrote these lines, it is implicit that it is the sensitive poet, the writer whose ego boundaries are abnormally low and who is therefore labeled eccentric or mad, who can best bring nature and himself to speech in his writing. Cowper's lambs articulate Clare's "I am."

Nature does not always speak peacefully through the poet in Notebook 19. If Clare envisions rurality as refuge in Cowper's words, he also envisions it as desolation in Byron's and in the Bible's. These (re)visions are in fact starkly opposed, their difference emphasized by their juxtaposition on the notebook pages. On pp. 11–15 Clare copies out, from the King James Bible, Revelation 6. 1–17. On pp. 15–16 he then reworks the transcribed passage in verse, using a highly repetitive rhyme scheme to produce a poetry whose form gives it prophetic authority as it patterns destruction into a series of sonic echoes:

> I saw the lamb who opened the first seal
> & heard a voice like thunder "Come & see"
> From one of the four beast—then did reveal
> The heaven a portion of its mystery...
>
> The second seal was opened & I heard
> The second beast say "Come & see" aloud
> Another horse went out ~~& like~~ red as a pard
> & power was given him to stir the crowd
> & take peace from the earth & whom was bowed
> & hell cried havoc falling while the crowd below like a flood
> <bursting like a flood>
> With a hugh sword to murder & to slay
> ~~Till warm blood flowed like water in the~~
> ~~frig~~ Rushed headlong hurrying from <the hellish brood>
> While citys <burned> to flame & earth itself ~~to~~ <wept> blood.[35]

Clare, in fact, acquires a prophetic voice, a language of scriptorial/scriptural power, by first alluding to and then impersonating the Revelation prophet, transforming the prose of the King James Bible into verse. Here he envisions a nature that is not a refuge of peace but a place of destruction; although the vision is grim, its rhyme and rhythm establishes the poet's authority: he knows the future, sees into the end of time. Prosody ensures vision is here anything but a disregarded discourse and the poet, by association, is not a babbling asylum inmate but a revered biblical seer.

Immediately following, and clearly, from the evidence of the penciled emendations in both texts, composed or revised at the same sitting, is a nature poem whose imagery is influenced by the Revelation passage but that counters its vision and its metrical irregularity with a more even iambic pentameter. In other words, it was written and should be read as part of a continuous sequence of envisionings of nature: first the Bible transcription, then the versification of the transcription, then the nature poem.

> Now evenings rosey streaks—a ribbond sky
> Spreads in the golden ~~streaks~~ <light> of the far west
> & mighty rocks are pillowed <dark &> ~~on the sky~~ high
> The image & the prototype of rest
> The heavens prophesy where peace is blest—
> A stillness soft as fall of silent dews

> Is felt around—the very dusk looks blest
> As is the maiden while her heart pursues
> Her evening walk oer fields in silent dews
>
> ———
>
> Ave Maria tis the hour of love
> When sighs & pains & tears on beautys breast
> Are whispered into blessings from above
> Ave Maria tis the hour of rest
> For man & woaman & the weary beast
> & parents love the miniature delights
> That blesses all ~~with slumber Ave Maria~~ with sleep & quiet rest
> Ave Maria tis the hour of night
> Like to an Indian maiden dressed in white.[36]

Here, Clare draws upon the authoritative language of Catholic prayer, via allusion to Byron's *Don Juan*,[37] to oppose the apocalyptic prophecy of his Revelation persona with an evening voluntary in which the heavens prophesy peace rather than destruction—and do so in familiar, regular meter. Juxtaposition of opposing voices is a typical procedure in the notebook, much of which is taken up with transcriptions of Revelation and with prose and poetry derived from them. Page 130, for example, contains poetry that envisions a nature in which time, regulated by the circling sun, is a round of error and misdeeds, a nature infected, as is the case in Revelation, by "death's diseases."

> False time what is it but a rogues account
> Of books wrong kept—times keystone is the sun
> True natures wronged—& what is the amount
> But deaths diseases—that their circuit run
> Through error & through deeds that faith has done...[38]

Here, nature ends without restoration of past losses, without justice. Clare, it seems, cannot regard the apocalypse that is heralded in Revelation as the prelude to a divine millennium. More desperate and less Christian, he finds in its language a way of dramatizing, as an universal predicament, a personal experience of time as error—error because he is, in the slang of convicts, "doing time"—time being governed by the asylum keepers and the priests who provide the ideological justification for his captivity. His own notebook functions as a book of resistance to and refuge from the "books wrong kept" by the "rogues" who falsify his time.

Having impersonated the Revelation prophet in verse transcriptions, then written his own verse in their style, Clare finds the

Revelation vision engenders other discourses. Thus he writes, immediately after this poem on p. 129, a letter to his wife on the subject
of lost time, on his family growing up without him while he remains
under the rule of cant in the asylum.[39]

> My dear Wife
>
> I have wrote some few times to enquire about yourself & the Family &
> thought about yourself & them a thousand othe[r] things that I use to
> think of the children—Freddy when I led him by the hand in his child-
> hood—I see him now in his little pink frock-sealskin cap—& gold
> band—with his little face as round as a apple & as red as a rose—&
> now a stout Man both strangers to each other the father a prisoner
> under a bad government so bad in fact that its no government at all
> but prison disapline where every body is forced to act contrary to their
> own wishes "the mother against the daughter in law & the daugh-
> ter against the mother in law" "the father against the son & the son
> against the Father"—in fact I am in Prison because I wont leave my
> family & tell a falsehood—this is the English Bastile a government
> Prison where harmless people are trapped & tortured till they die—
> English priestcraft & english bondage more severe then the slavery of
> Egypt & Affrica while the son is tyed up in his manhood from all the
> best thoughts of his childhood bye lying & falsehood—not dareing to
> show love or remembrance for Home or home affections living in the
> world as a prison estranged from all his friends still Truth is the best
> companion for it levels all distinctions in pretentions Truth wether it
> enters the Ring or the Hall of justice shows a plain Man that is not
> to be scared at shadows or big words full of fury & meaning nothing
> when done & said with them truth is truth & the rights of manage of
> reason & common sense are sentences full of meaning & the best com-
> ment of its truth is themselves—an honest man makes priestcraft an
> odious lyar & coward & a filthy disgrace to Christianity—that coward
> I hate & detest—the Revelations has a placard in capitals about "The
> Whore of Babylon & the mother of Harlots" does it mean Priestcraft
> I think it must—this rubbish of cant must soon die—like all others—I
> began a letter & ended a Sermon—& the paper too
>
> I am dear Wife yours ever John Clare

Here the implicit accusation is that time has been stolen from him—
the madhouse inmate is (in what may be a telling metaphor since
physical restraint was used at the Northampton asylum) "tied up"
from recalling his childhood because to do so is too painful, given
his imprisonment and his consequent inability to return home. He is
instead fed the false consolation—"cant"—of priest craft—perhaps
a reference to the Church of England cleric who led worship at the

asylum—against which he fights by citing the Book of Revelation. It turns out, then, that the notebook entries are a sequence: the biblical transcriptions and versifications grant Clare a visionary voice in which he can both articulate the hidden dynamics of the asylum and extrapolate from his own experience to a prophetic view of time and space. And this is vital for the later Clare, because, unable to revisit his family, he feels plagued by his past. His envisioning of that past is tantalizing, reminding him of a present that is a living sepulcher—a death in life. Writing of time's destruction liberates him from this, albeit negatively, recouping power as he allies himself to the culturally authoritative discourse of biblical prophecy, in which time and space are both subject to the power of the visionary's words. The letter, then, is intimately related to the biblical transcriptions and versifications, and to the poems they stimulate; all of these prophetic texts contrast, however, with the Cowperian nature verse and the love lyrics that fill the surrounding pages. The notebook has a textual dynamic—based on a struggle over the envisioning of nature, and self-as-nature—that is central to Clare's performance of the role of poet.

The dynamic places Clare's Cowperian persona next to a Byronic one, as well as to his biblical voice. On p. 30 is a fragment that alludes to Cowper's description, in *The Task*, of his domestic walks:

> A Favourite Place
> Beautiful gravel walks overgrown
> With moss & grass little places where
> The poet sat to write.[40]

Are these Cowper's words—another quotation—or Clare's? There is an identification here of poetic voice and persona and of notebook and nature: the "little places" in which the "poet sat to write" are both outside, on the moss and grass, and inside the notebook itself. Writing—the process of inscribing words on paper—meanwhile, is the process of which we are now reading the product. The notebook inscribes, as a therapeutic activity, the translation of nature onto the page of which it is the evidence.

No sooner has it done so than it switches to a darker writing and grimmer thematization of writing. Immediately following "A Favourite Place" on the same page, and clearly, to judge from the pencil marks, inscribed on the same occasion, is a Byronic poem, "Song Last Day." Clare had assumed the persona of Byron before: as Philip Martin, Anne Barton, and Simon Kövesi have shown,[41] he wrote his own versions of "Childe Harold" and "Don Juan," asserting his poetic virility, satiric energy, and class resentment. Notebook 19 creates a version of Byron so far ignored by critics, as Clare responds to Byron's apocalyptic poem about entropic nature, "Darkness." "Song Last Day" alludes to "Darkness" but takes an inward turn that Byron eschews, so that the imploding natural world is clearly a correlative for mental anguish.

> Song Last Day
> There is a day a dreadfull day
> Still following the past
> When sun & moon are past away
> & mingle with the blast
> There is a vision in my eye
> A vacuum oer my mind
> Sometimes as on the sea I lye
> Mid roaring waves & wind
>
> When valleys rise to mountain waves
> & mountains sink to seas
> When towns & cities temples graves
> All vanish like a breeze
> The skyes that was are past & oer
> That almanack of days
> Mary Ann Peasgood
> Year chronicles are kept no more
> Oblivions ruin pays
>
> Pays in destruction shades & hell
> Sin goes in darkness down
> & therein sulphurs shadows dwell
> Worth wins & wears the crown
> The very shore if shore I see
> All shrivelled to a scroll
> The Heavens rend away from me
> & thunders sulphurs roll
>
> Black as the deadly thunder cloud
> The stars shall turn to dun
> & heaven by that darkness bowed
> Shall make days light be done
> When stars & skys shall all decay
> & earth no more shall be
> When heaven itself shall pass away
> Then thou'lt remember me.[42]

If one compares this with "Darkness," the increased emotional intensity is at once obvious: it is both more confessional and more powerfully evocative of flux—a world becoming unhinged, as mountains and sea turn into each other and as nature veers from being an observed externality to a stage for the poet's mental drama. Meanwhile the woman's name, "Mary Ann Peasgood" inscribed at the page foot beneath "that almanack of days," but aligned with the other lines of the stanza, creates interference, forcing the reader to wonder whether it is part of the poem, a marginal comment, or whether no meaningful relationship to the verse was intended. The effect is, however, to make the reader question whether s/he is to refer the name to a particular day of the almanac—a first meeting? a love tryst?—and whether the poem is addressed to or a reflection upon Mary Ann. The question is not decidable, but the relationship of personal and prophetic inscriptions is brought into play: poetry's textuality is highlighted as the reader is forced to recognize the materiality of the manuscript inscription—and this in a poem in which textuality is a theme (the almanac is "kept no more" and nature, in an allusion to Revelation, is "shrivelled to a scroll").

Clare's Byronic voice fixes again and again on the issue of writing and authority. Entropic nature is a book compiled by death, rather than by the poet (though the poet vicariously shares in death's bookkeeping power by writing of it):

> Infants are but cradles for the grave
> & death the nurse as soon as life begins
> Time keeps account books for him & they save
> Expences for his funeral out of sins....[43]

In another fragment, the measuring line with which sailors' fathom the sea's depth becomes an internal abyss that poetic lines cannot bridge: measures, whether nautical or poetic, prove unable to gain purchase on a "darkness" that is both within and without. Metaphors transmute alarmingly as they try to articulate, and thereby to steady, unstable thoughts: thus, darkness becomes "day at midnight," an image not of Christian light in darkness but of paradoxical nonentity:

> There is a chasm in the heart of man
> That nothing fathoms like a gulph at sea
> A depth of darkness lines may never span
> A shade unsunned in dark eternity
> Thoughts without shadows—that eye can see
> Or thought imagine tis unknown to fame

> Like day at midnight such its youth to me
> At ten years old it boyhoods secret came
> Now manhoods forty past tis just the same.[44]

These stanzas are not just more internalized than their Byronic source but also more inscriptionalized. They thematize writing as a means to order and power in the world—the external world and the emotional world—as if in response to their own status as handwritten entries on the paper of a notebook that will not reach print. Clare, that is, reflects the activity of handwriting in the poetry he enters in his notebook: it is, to an extent, a commentary on itself and constructs its writer not as an author but a manuscriber.

In the end, it's clear that Clare writes like Cowper not simply because doing so validates the healing nature of pastoral poetry, but because Cowper offers him a way to battle an alienation that he too expresses in terms of darkness and destruction. Clare as Cowper is not the opposite of Clare as Byron, but the antidote made from his venom. "The Wreck of the Emelie" is a key poem in this respect, for it comes toward the end of the notebook, as Clare's Cowperian rewrite of the apocalyptic nature he had voiced in Byronic and biblical terms. "The Wreck" is a response to Cowper's "The Castaway." Both pieces tell of drowning at sea; Clare's adapts the ballad meter of Cowper's and, at the end, even borrows its rhyming sounds. But Cowper's ends with the sailor drowning in full view of his helpless shipmates and the famous inward turn of:

> No voice divine the storm allay'd,
>   No light propitious shone;
> When, snatch'd from all effectual aid,
>   We perish'd, each alone:
> But I beneath a rougher sea,
> And whelm'd in deeper gulphs than he.

> (lines 61–66; Cowper, III, 214)

Clare's concludes on a note of fragile hope:

> Above them glomed the angry sky
> & through the pitch black rock
> Of clouds the splintered lightnings flye
> None could resist the shock
> Down & in a moment gone
> Nine men plunged in the wave
> & all the seamen lost but one

> There met a watery grave
> One still survived that fatal wreck
> By billows washed ashore
> Though all had hopes that stood on deck
> That now can feel no more
> He through the boiling waves did beat
> Al in the boiling sea
> & on the beach upon his feet
> Viewed the shipwrecked Emelie.[45]

Imagining a survivor, rather than empathizing with the drowned man, Clare finds, from Cowper's scenario, a tentative refuge that neither "The Castaway" nor "Darkness" allow for. Sailing is perilous; most are drowned, but one at least escapes the boiling sea to stand on his feet, even if left lonely on the shore looking at the wreck of his vessel and the deaths of his comrades. It is as if the allusive relationship to Cowper's poem gives Clare a talisman against the despair that poem expresses: one poet draws upon another to discover that neither perishes "each alone." It's significant that this poem comes near the end of the notebook entries, for it holds together, if it does not resolve, the envisionings of nature that have been in struggle throughout—Byronic and biblical as well as Cowperian. Here, for a moment, the Cowperian and the Byronic voices sound as one.

Calling up others' voices in Notebook 19, Clare renews a literary community in which he had once participated via printed collections and magazines. But he makes this community more immediate, mediating typography toward speech via the bodily act of handwriting that he construes as the intensification of print's visuality to such a pitch that it metamorphoses into still more present orality. In doing so, he creates what we should see as a new form of book—a manuscript that substitutes both for speech and print composed in an institution where speech seemed mad and print unattainable. It is an experimental notebook, like Blake's, like Coleridge's, like Dickinson's, featuring long form lyrics that combine verse and prose and make their meanings by their visual layout on the page. Romantic in its experimental modes, its confessional intimacy, its rural themes, Clare's notebook shows him doing what he could not do in print and, thereby, asserting his vocation. Collecting himself there, he appears, not as the self-consumer of his woes but the self-producer of his writing—a writing, however, only possible because it is also that of an imagined poetic partnership (substituting for the lack of a real literary circle) that he summons to the page.

PART III

THE LINGO OF LONDONERS: THE "COCKNEY SCHOOL"

CHAPTER 7

—◦◦◦◦—

ROMANTICISM LITE: TALKING, WALKING, AND NAME-DROPPING IN THE COCKNEY ESSAY

It is "an age of personality," wrote Coleridge in 1809 (*Friend*, II, 286–87), discomfited by the appetite of readers for details of the private lives of public figures and literary men. In this chapter, I investigate the role of allusion in fueling this appetite, focusing on the particular uses to which it was put in the new genre that, more than any other, characterized the age—the magazine essay. Shorter, lighter, less demanding than poetry, the essay was also more amusing and popular. In the hands of the coterie who wrote for the *London Magazine*, it was also informal, colloquial, spontaneous, intimate— celebrating the ordinary pleasures and bemoaning the routine pains of the metropolitan life that the essayists shared with their readers. These authors—disparagingly termed "Cockneys"—voiced with a new focus and zest the middlebrow perspective of London "cits"— shopmen and office workers. No deep learning or classical education was needed to enjoy their prose: although it shared some of the values defined in Wordsworth's *Excursion* and Coleridge's *Biographia*, readers did not have to grapple with Miltonic inversions or allusions to Schelling: the essay was user friendly.

Allusion of a particular kind became one of the essayists' chief *modus operandi*. Their innovation was to supplement and even to replace the literary allusion to past poets, requiring as it did readerly knowledge of poetic tradition, with an old motif made new—the dropped, or almost dropped, name. Hinting at names had been a vital part of Pope's satirical method in *The Dunciad*: he had used it to draw together, as a group who shared standards, readers sufficiently clever, or sufficiently "in the know," to fill in the blank names of the men he saw as dunces—his enemies and the enemies of literature. The Cockney essayists, however, filled their pages with hints at the names of friends—each other, and well-known writers of their acquaintance. By this means they teased readers into a vicarious extended coterie: if readers were sufficiently "in the know" to find the name from the hint, then they could congratulate themselves on their privileged position of sharing restricted knowledge, of being within the circle, no longer part of a reading public but a participant of private talk: an eavesdropper at worst; at best a trusted confidante, aware enough to put names to Mr. L—, Mr. H—, and Mr. C—. The coteries thus accessed, moreover, were not just a matter of dropped names or allusions to each other's writings as among the 1790s' poets. The essayists also revealed intimate details concerning the people whose names they dropped: thus they drew readers into a relationship of pseudo-intimacy, creating the illusion of knowing literary figures off guard in private. It was this tendency that Coleridge saw as a deplorable trait of a new age of personality, for it substituted celebrity gossip for the reading of writers' works.[1] Why struggle though Coleridge's *Sibylline Leaves* when you could eavesdrop on how awe inspiring it had been to walk alongside the inspired Mr. C— in 1798? Romanticism lite, allusion trite.

Lite and trite sometimes led to an unexpected seriousness and even to a lasting redefinition of Romantic aesthetics. Walking was a popular scenario in the Cockney school's writing for the same reason that (almost) name-dropping abounded there: the authors wanted to suggest that their writing was the spontaneous overflow of companionable conversation and social activity, recollected in tranquility, rather than the labor of years of solitary scholarship. By walking, talking, and name-hinting, the essayists renewed, in more relaxed and sociable form, the coterie aesthetics expressed in Coleridge's 1790s' conversation poems: readers could feel reassured that the essay they were reading had sprung from the kind of sociable pastime they themselves enjoyed, a rural stroll with friends, rather than from a poet's years of scholarly toil at his desk or from his wandering lonely as a cloud through sublime mountain ranges.

Considerable scholarly attention has been paid to the *London Magazine* writers since the 1990s. The poetry of Keats and Hunt has been revalued as the work of a "Cockney school"; the prose of Hazlitt and Lamb has been reexamined as part of a discourse pioneered, with

other lesser writers, in the literary magazine; John Clare's connections with the Cockneys have also been explored.[2] The rise of the
magazine and its effects on Romantic motifs and the literary marketplace have also been carefully documented. Here, I want to send
this scholarly revival in a new direction by tracing the characteristics
and influence of a genre that, I think, has not been properly credited to the Cockneys who pioneered it—the essay on walking.[3] It
is this genre, I argue, that is the Cockneys' most striking innovation and significant legacy: nothing like its gossipy, namey evocation
of rambling existed previously and its descendants still feature today
in newspapers, books, magazines, and TV—fueling a huge leisure
industry that sees thousands of hikers, every weekend, heading off
from city to country to wander a valley or climb a hill. The Cockney
walkers—and among them I number writers not previously included
by scholars in the circle—were among the most influential Romantics
and also the most percipient, for, at its most intense, the name-hinting essay ramble was an articulation of a structure of feeling, then
new but still powerful now, conditioned by the new regimentation
of men's labor in the bourgeois urban workplace of garret, mill, and
counting house—by the kinds of work and work discipline produced
by the capitalist society we still inhabit.

Wordsworth and Southey had criticized this work discipline and
worried about its social and moral effects; but they had withdrawn
from the city in disgust. It was their Cockney admirers, writing as
Londoners, who adapted, for people who could not withdraw from
the metropolis, their Romantic idealizations of wandering free among
nature's healing powers. The essayists wrote for the increasing mul-
titudes of clerks who, from circa 1810, had to spend their weekday
lives confined in the office and segregated from women: these men
sought leisure together at the weekend and walked out to the country, a new form of homosociality. And they read the new magazines
that technological changes in printing made possible for them to
afford. The walking essay spoke to their experience: it was noticeably
masculine—the walker and his partner or addressee are male. It was
suburban, a discourse of the Sunday, the weekend, the annual holiday week—a new pastoralism, shuttling from city to idealized country in the imaginary company of famous men. In effect, it valued
companionable walking as an escape from the destructive effects of
the nine-to-five—clock discipline and office regimen—on the city
worker's mental health. Its name-hinting bonhomie and aimless wandering was strong in proportion to its fear of the colonization of the
self by the task-driven discipline of the job. Thus, it was double-sided,

featuring conviviality, joviality, comedy, and even self-mockery but also anguish, anxiety, and alienation.

Perhaps the first Cockney writing to articulate this double-sided celebration of escape from clerkdom was Robert Bloomfield. In 1800, as we saw in chapter 5, Bloomfield's Georgic poem *The Farmer's Boy* became a hit. The poem changed Bloomfield's life: previously a poor artisan, he now became a clerk when his patron found him a job endorsing legal contracts and charters in the busy Seal Office. Bloomfield's letter on the subject (to his brother George, February 29, 1803)—a cry of desperation—reads as if written by the narrator of Blake's "London" imprisoned by "each chartered street," for it highlights the mental toll taken by the binding of self to bureaucratic institutions:

> On Friday, the day after the Holidays, I expected a busy day at the Seal Office; and so I found it with a vengeance. I had eat no breakfast, and the Mob of Lawyers made me perfectly savage: at One o'clock we shut the Office, but shut in between 40 and 50 people, and did not get through the Work for 3 quarters of an hour after one. I then grew faint, and knew if I walkd home to the City Road that my Wind and indigestion would get the upper hand of my Stomach, and should eat no dinner; so I put into the Cook's in Salsbury Court and eat heartily. by this time there was no time to go home and then to Temple Bar again by 4; so I sulkd away the time in St George's Fields, and then took another 3 hours' Mobbing at the Office, having seald during the day nearly 1100 Writs! by far the busiest day (if Mr. A is to be credited) that have occurrd for eight years past. Returnd to my sick house, tired and insufferably disgusted.—This I shall call Black Friday—my cough plagues me, and I have no time to write down my Rhimes, I have enough on my mind to craze a saint, but I feel my soul soar above it all—I know that I shall triumph—and that "Spring will come and Nature smile again."[4]

> (BL 103)

Here, Bloomfield highlights what are still the stresses and strains of the modern world of the office—new at the time as the bureaucratic state was rapidly expanding. It's a world of separate spheres: there are no women at work, and there's no time to go home to them between shifts. What plagues Bloomfield is the lack of privacy and self-command, the need to prepare a public face, the slavery to the new discipline of clock time and office hours, the reduction of human interaction to overworked clerk, unyielding boss, and demanding client. His final quotation—alluding to the last line of own "Autumn" from *The Farmer's Boy*—reassures him by reminding him and his correspondent that, despite the present menial drudgery, he has been a poet. It evidences his true vocation, in the midst of depressing circumstances, and it reconfigures the present experience of London's chaotic crowds with a vision of the seasonal order of the rural world that is to be taken metaphorically, as a proverb, reassuring Bloomfield and his brother that things will improve.

In "Autumn" the line is realistic as well as metaphorical, sounding a note of hope amidst the description of the cold and scarcity suffered by the rural poor in winter:

> Then wellcome, Cold; wellcome, ye snowy nights!
> Heav'n midst your rage shall mingle pure delights,
> And confidence of hope the soul sustain,
> While devastation sweeps along the plain:
> Nor shall the child of poverty despair,
> But bless the power that rules the changing year;
> Assur'd,—though horrors round his cottage reign,...
> That Spring will come, and Nature smile again.
>
> (*The Farmer's Boy*, "Autumn," 353–60)[5]

Invoking this nature description, the allusion in the letter implies that the new greenery of spring will be a more than metaphorical savior, for nature's seasonal rhythm will supersede the unchanging clock-watching of the office: nature is here a yearned-for and sensual antidote to the impersonal discipline of the city workday.

Bloomfield's allusion has the function of reassuring its reader: it shows his brother that his poetic spirit has not been entirely smothered by the effects on his mind of the office grind. It counters, by its very allusiveness as well as by its proverbial optimism, the desperation of the rest of the letter. And it also harks back to life in the country: before taking the job at the Seal Office, Bloomfield had worked where he lived, among his family, writing poems, tending his garden, in the suburbs—on the City Road, among the smallholdings and orchards, next to the Shepherd and Shepherdess Inn. The office job alienated him from this domestic productivity, dividing him between work and leisure, office and home, colleagues (male) and family (mixed), center and outskirts. London's geography became colonized by the effect of the work world on his soul because he took the job home with him (unlike Dickens's Wemmick, who fights off this colonization by turning his suburban house into a mini-castle with drawbridge). Effectively, Bloomfield's mental geography was overwhelmed, as was his temporality: office hours dominated his waking, sleeping, and thinking patterns; the job colonized his selfhood.

Depressed by this colonization, Bloomfield took to making walking tours, refreshing himself with a leisured consumption of nature in which he was, for a few days, his own master, his time and space his own, rather than "sulking about St. George's Fields." These tours were holiday escapes to the rural from the urban—brief recreation won from the commercial round. They were a reaction against his lack of a stable place in which independence, self-respect, and rural community could be sustained, when even his suburban retreat on the City Road became prey to the pressure of business. So Bloomfield walked away for a while—not to France, the Alps, or the Lakes, because he hadn't enough time off. He was not like Wordsworth, free from a job, remote from the city, able to tour sublime landscapes and to recuperate them in hymns to his own imagination—he walked only to Dover and to Dorking, recording his trips in intimate and informal letters rather than epic poetry. These letters, however, constitute a new kind of tour journalism reflecting a new social practice: the middle-class holiday excursion, the London "cit" down in the country for a week away from his clerking. This kind of walking, and walking narrative, is necessarily small scale: it produces not the introverted epic of Wordsworth's Alpine tour in the *Prelude*, but self-deprecating comedy that acknowledges its own limited range and paradoxical nature. After all, Bloomfield was an urbanite visiting a countryside to which he felt emotionally connected by virtue of his rural upbringing but in which he had no present-day social or economic place. He was conscious of this anomalous status, and was ready to record the funny side of being out of place wherever he visited. As such, he was an unwitting pioneer of a practice of nature writing—informal, informational, conversational, humorous—that began to feature and still features in magazines, newspapers, travel books, and TV. We go on holiday rambles in the countryside still, and, once back in our suburban routines, we watch others do so via print or video.

The description Bloomfield made of his 1803 escape from the Seal Office to Surrey pioneers the features that became typical of the genre—unexpected encounters, mistaken paths, hill country, romantic views, assertions about nature's restorative powers, a welcoming pub, an intimate correspondent. George, the addressee, was Bloomfield's elder brother and father figure—the man who had given him a home, and work as a shoemaker, and who had found a patron and publisher for his manuscript. A fellow poet, he was someone with whom Bloomfield shared viewpoints and values, and work rhythms and holiday excursions. There was a preexisting sympathy of feeling on which the letter relies and which it renews.

Having been harrassd by too much thinking and too many trivial engagements, and an employment that I shall never like, I determined that I would respire one mouthfull of real country air if possible and I know at the same time that pollution of smoke reaches ten miles round the Metropolis. I had heard much of Leithe Hills and of Box Hill in the neighbourhood of Dorking. This was the time to see them. I started from the Spread Eagle, GraceChurch Stt. at 3 in the afternoon of Monday and soon rode away from the gay Bonnets and red faces that made a perfect current towards Greenwich. The road is like all others within ten miles of town, much too spruce and too full of inhabitants for my fancy. Epsom is a pretty little town and the country round it open and flat; but 3 or four miles beyond it assumes a quite different aspect, becoming more hilly than I had ever before seen. Remember that I am no Welshman, therefore to me these Hills are Cader Idris's and Snowdens.—

Evening drew on as we approached the old town of Dorking, and the prospect to me was delightful; but to prove that enjoyment is often dashd with a strange and unexpected kind of naucia, we had behind us on the Coach two Lasses, the one going to join the Thunderer[6] on her arrival at Portsmouth from Chatham, and the other to meet a party of Marines passing through Dorking; they drank Brandy all the way, and then work'd off the fumes by songs of a description which were new to me, so that you see that the school of poetry has many stages. I supt and insured a lodging for two nights at the 3 Tons where the Coach put up, and on Tuesday morning set off with a determination to reach Leith Hill; but though I had a good map of the County in my pocket I took the wrong rout, and as the place of my destination was about 6 miles and my attention and inclination drawn to other and nearer objects I made for the top of a Hill which is planted with about 8 or ten Fir Trees which are very conspicuous at a great distance; this Hill the inhabitants denominate with no small share of pride "Dorking's Glory." It affords certainly a most delightfull view on every side; here I could discover that had I kept on nearly in the direction in which I started that I might have passd over Boar Hills to Leith Hills which here appear eminently conspicuous, having a square tower on one summit and being much higher and of greater extant than any other in sight. Being alone and in the pure unadulterated spirit of Idleness and Gratitude mix'd, I cut on an oak bench

> "From the smoke of London free
> I bless thee, Rural Liberty."

Box Hill which I had passd the foregoing evening in the way from town lay southward from "Dorkings Glory" and made a noble appearance but it did not appear to me to be higher than that on which I stood;———…At the sign of the Cock a little country pot house at the foot of the Hill on the London road I was tempted by a bench that invited me kindly to sit down, I did so, and drank a pint of Ale. Somthing was rudely painted by way of inscription across the window shutter—I was much pleased to find it contained the following lines which certainly possess some humour, and suited me, and my random expidition to a nicety.

> "probonopublico"
> "To those who cannot summer's thirst endure
> Clark's brown Elixa is a certain cure
> In winter too some doses are supplied
> Which may be taken at this fire side;
> And when the symptoms are not very bad
> Relieve for twopence only may be had."

(BL 106)

Real ale, perhaps, is Bloomfield's "something far more deeply interfused." His inscriptions are not very Wordsworthian in tone but their comedy celebrates the countryside as a place of liberty and self-restoration, for men at least, if not for a man and his female companion, as in Wordsworth. Bloomfield debunks his poetic seriousness too: he carves his verse into the scene, to make the place permanently record the feeling of freedom that rural walking brings, only to find his inscription superseded by that on the window shutter, which defines the country's relief of a visitor's ills as the satisfaction of more basic physical desires. Both inscriptions, however, are welcome as indications of freedom from the soon-to-be-resumed mechanical labor of mind and body. Wordsworth, of course, rejected the life of the urban worker for that of the rural bard and in the Preface to *Lyrical Ballads* declared that such urban work corrupts the workers: confined all day and all week, they want more and more outrageous and sensational forms of entertainment in their time off. Bloomfield's walking expedition suggests that Wordsworth was off the mark—unduly alarmist—for it is not random: it has a restorative purpose, but its free wanderings are made in the consciousness that he cannot avoid the world of work discipline and clock time for long. The holiday ramble is an invention of leisure, a refreshing small-scale aimlessness to contrast with the new world of regular hours in the office. It's a ludic escape but it is not escapist, because what it offers is restorative of a real self that has no outlet in the world of regimented labor—the playful, humorous self able to spontaneously embrace the possibilities of the moment. Bloomfield is up for it, and the bawdy and drunken women he meets on the coach are emblems of his excursion, although he will be less coarsely hedonistic than they. There may not be sex, but there will be cakes and ale.

Bloomfield's pedestrianism was an early example of a discourse expressing a new, suburban sensibility that became associated chiefly with the circle of poets and journalists around another bourgeois Londoner, the former clerk Leigh Hunt, who was accused by conservative critics of fostering a Cockney school—a kind of writing that smacked of the lower-middle-class attitudes and colloquialisms of London tradesmen. The Cockney school was typified by the ornamented verse of Keats and Hunt himself and also, as a number of critics have shown,[7] by the new commercial literary format of the magazine essay. What has been less observed is that Cockneyism was also epitomized by a certain kind of decidedly masculine walking narrative, of which Bloomfield—himself criticized for "cockneyisms"[8]—was the forerunner. A prime example is Hunt's essay "A Rustic Walk and Dinner," which appeared in *The Monthly Magazine* in 1842—a piece celebrating the jokes and pleasures of two men who ramble out of London to the countryside for the day.

"A Rustic Walk" is formally unusual, a magazine essay in what Leigh Hunt called "intentionally unelevated" blank verse—literally "sermo pedestris—poetry on foot"—a verse that rambles to the rhythm of a wandering walker. The purpose is companionable pleasure, the mode is the miniature picaresque—a comic ramble of unexpected discoveries:

> How fine to walk to dinner, not too far,
> Through a green country, on a summer's day,
> The dinner at an inn, the time our own,
> The roads not dusty, yet the fields not wet,
> The grass *lie-down-uponable.*

> (lines 1–5)[9]

The companion, it turns out, is the reader: Hunt takes us with him, as a town gent going rustic for the day:

> The reader and I,
> Who tow'rds our inn thus far have come from town,
> Now loose, now arm-linked,—first by suburb-garden,...
> ...—and the turnpike,

> With pocket-apron'd man, jingling his cash,—
> And the high road, with its dry ditch dock-leaved,—
> And ever-met horseman, and waggoner
> Slouching, and jockey-capp'd postilion trim,
> Interminable of dance on horse's back,—
> And then by field-paths, and more flowery ditch
> White-starred, and red, and azure,—and through all
> Those heaps of buttercups, that smear the land
> With splendour, nearly extinguishing the daisies;—
> And hill, and dale, and stile on which we sat
> Cooling our brows under the airy trees,
> And heard the brook low down. . . .

> (lines 46–62)

The listing of detail establishes the tone: the poem proceeds by no stronger a narrative structure than "And then"—noticing everything that the walker happens upon in its individuality. It's not, in other words, a poem that is going anywhere important—or directly—but a digressive wander that emerges from conversation. Both the colloquial diction of "jingling," "slouching," and "smear," and the awkward phrasing ("heaps of buttercups," "extinguish the daisies") keep the verse as close to casual, in-the-moment speech as possible. Likewise, the poem digresses as the author surprises himself with a reminiscence triggered by association:

> and found that hunk
> Of bread so exquisite, to the very crumbs
> That shared a pocket-corner with its halfpence.—
> (O Shelley! 'twas a bond 'twixt thee and me,
> That power to eat the sweet crust out of doors!
> You laughed with loving eyes, wrinkled with mirth,
> And cried, high breathing, "What! can you do *that?*
> I thought that no one dared a thing so strange
> And primitive, but myself."—And so we loved
> Ever the more, and found our love increase
> Most by such simple abidings with boy-wisdom.)

> (lines 62–72)

Biting mouthfuls off a grubby hunk of bread found in his pocket, Hunt relives, with the reader, what he had once done with Shelley— dropping the famous name to give the reader the thrill of vicariously following in the celebrity's footsteps. In an "age of personality," the poem ramble sells the illusion to the mass public reading the magazine that each of them is up close: walking if not with the star then with one who has often walked with him. Thus, Leigh Hunt offers not just pastoral pleasure unworried by propriety, decorum, and civilization, but also privileged access to intimate details of the life of the famous pastoral poet. Recalling boyish high spirits by means of direct, informal, speech, Hunt is both less solemn and high-minded, and more youthful and male, than Wordsworth addressing Dorothy in "Tintern Abbey." His "rustic walk" is a shrewdly marketed spontaneous overflow of brotherly feeling recollected in hilarity.

The world in which Hunt wants to situate romance is one of mobility, found by wandering out of the city world of convention, business, and work into a bucolic world of plenty. It's also one of celebrity—the reader talks/walks with a minor poet and hears about a major one, as if at a pro-am golf tournament. It's the ramble, the ramblers, and their words, rather than the countryside itself, that are poetic and Romantic, for Hunt knows that his is a pleasure that depends upon imagination and illusion: a private friendship is relived in verse for the public, as if it were still private. Thus, Shelley's tastes and habits are revealed—celebrity gossip—so as to license Hunt's own overflow of joy at escaping the town: his land of milk, ham, and eggs is the idealization of a suburbanite.

> *Reader*: What a land for meals!
> Look in the dell here, in this steep hill-shade,
> Under the trees,—look at the colour'd cattle.
> They're milking them. There's pretty breakfast for you;
> There, and in yonder corn-field, past the hedge.
> Red with the poppies; you just see the skirts of it.
> Upon this other side clusters the farm,
> As full of eggs, and flitches, and all sorts
> Of eatables, as eggs are full of meat,
> And with its homesteads making you feel at home,
> Although a stranger. Farms are all men's homes
> A sort of homely golden age in fancy;
> Often in fact, did but the inmates know it.
>
> (lines 302–14)

This knowing, self-amusing pastoralism, dedicated to pleasuring the appetites, alludes to Falstaff's and Aguecheek's visions of sensual satisfaction in rural plenty. Farmers, Hunt notes, "grow fat and ruddy, / And live on ales and creams, and scent new hay, / And kiss the dairymaid. Who would be miners?" (lines 318–20). The country is jokily portrayed as a fertile, sexual Eden made to satisfy male desires.

For miners, confined to toil underground in the dark, Hunt might just as well have written "clerks," for his rustic walk leads the reader away from the town and the office, rather than the pit. His readers in the *Monthly Magazine*, that is to say, were more likely to be in trade than in collieries, living in the suburbs and able to identify with the walk to the country inn. It is at an inn that the rustic walk ends—just as Bloomfield's did—and the inn offers men an attainable substitute for the life of fleshly pleasure that farmers are imagined to enjoy.[10]

> Now our pleasures are,
> Not a beef-steak, (as our last Canto's line
> Might have prefigured,) but, with the month being June,
> A lamb chop and a salad, with cold tart
> Of gooseberry (youngest fruit-cry of the year,
> Bringing the little boys about their mothers)
> And such good drink as pewter makes still better,—
> Liquidest freshness become solid bliss,—
> Pure quench, and heart's ease, and swill'd bosom-joy,
> Follow'd with a king's "Hah!" Whales, gasping southward,
> And coming on a fairy sea of *malt*,
> Would gulf it in, and count it Fishes' Paradise.
>   Lo! the white table-cloth—lo! knives and forks—
> Lo! glasses—lo! the salt—lo! covers—lo! the salad—
> Lo! table drawn to the open window—lo!
> Two chairs drawn too—lo! prospect out and in;—
> Lo! we.
>   The door is shut; the fresh malt coming.
> Now sticketh fork in flesh, and the chops vanish:—
> Now, by the gods! We speak not for five seconds;—
> Now meat is hot, and the crisp salad cold
> And it's in basins;—deep;—we fork it up,
> Like haycocks; and the first attempted words
> Are mums and mutterings, stifled in the bliss;
> Beautiful, ill-bred smotherments of munch.
> The clear good utterance at length leaps forth;—
> "Fine!"
>   "Is not this the thing?"
>   "The right one."
>   "Hah!—
> Nothing like hunger, ease, and an inn-room.
> But you *eat nothing*."
>   "Oh!—excuse me there;
> 'Tis *you* eat nothing."
>   "Pardon me;—you *lie*."

(lines 394–423)

The verse no more stands on ceremony than the inn—it is slangy, humorous, immediate, jesty, unexpectedly breaking into direct exclamations. It is deliberately mock-heroic too, with ridiculous apostrophes and incongruous comparisons—whales swimming in a beery fishes' paradise. Hunt's verbal and formal playfulness expresses good humor, tipsiness, conviviality: in style and substance this is a report from a pub meant to epitomize everything that is good about England and Englishness—pastoral pleasure accessible from the town, a resort of enjoyment, goodwill and love of one's fellow men. Of course, it is only men in practice, even if women are included in the bonhomie— for the pub was the domain of men in Hunt's time, and the conversation is that of boys being boys, free from the decorum required when conversing with gentlewomen, their wits quickened and their mood heightened, on a tide of ale.

"A Rustic Walk" builds to its climax with a parade of unlikely allusions to ancient authors of rustic verse. Or rather, not allusions to topoi or phrases in Latin and Greek poetry—for these would demand learning and speak only to a readership of classically educated gentlemen—but the dropped names of poets. The rural view from the inn window, Hunt declares,

> brings up Horace,
> An author made to sip of, half for love
> And half for custom; whom we soon displace
> For hearty draughts out of Theocritus,
> Th' Elizabethan men, and the old jovial
> Hero (for he himself's a hero) Homer,—
> Carver of men and gods, and chines, and verses.

(lines 428–34)

Here, classical verse is no more demanding than drinking: it's another form of sensual pleasure shared, like quaffed beer, in pub conversation. Readers vicariously partake the atmosphere of poetic and scholarly (albeit tipsy) concourse without having to know any particular poem. Such allusion as there is, is comic: in Hunt's zeugma, Homer is a carver not only of verses but also of chines (joints of meat cut around the backbone) because there are so many descriptions in his epics of the slaughter of sacrificial lambs. And in the next sentence the inn companions are Homer's fellow carvers, as they carve the joints of lamb set on the table in front of them. Thus, the seriousness of poetic writing and the exclusivity of literary learning is undercut: allusion is a joke.

Hunt ends the poem with a tribute to a special form of jokey allusion—the pun—and to his fellow Cockney essayist, Charles Lamb:

> Hail, Paranomasia!
> Humanest Punning! Every body's pow'r!
> Common as laughter; no more evil deem'd
> By wisest lips, from Homer to Charles Lamb.
> "One touch of *punning* makes the whole world kin."
> *Reader.* Vide the punster who wrote Lear and Hamlet!

(lines 487–92)

Wittily misquoting Shakespeare's *Troilus and Criseyede*, Hunt reproduces a boozy pub conversation. But he has a heartfelt point too—that puns are common rather than elite: after all, everyone can pun; puns are not the province of the educated classes. Hunt celebrates them as peace bringers that heal social and national divisions. He drops the name of a present-day punster, his fellow Cockney essayist Charles Lamb, making him the inheritor of the great tradition of Homer and Shakespeare. But the great tradition is revalued: it is no longer the lofty tradition of epic and dramatic poetry but the common province of wordplay. This is a tongue-in-cheek democratization of the literary past that tipsily wrests it from the grasp of guardians of taste. The anxiety of influence under the influence. In Hunt's beerily benign vision of the world from the inn, one does not need Greek to share past literature's significance—every man renews the genius of Homer and Shakespeare when his punful playfulness brings love and understanding through laughter. The allusion to Lamb democratizes wit and places the reader vicariously there in the pub almost within reach of the living embodiment of a literary tradition. This is Hunt's philosophy of inn-spiration, as it were—the good cheer of literary friends renewed in an example of the genre to which that good cheer had given rise—the self-referential, name-dropping magazine essay.

It was his democratization and personalization of literature that conservative critics most disliked about Hunt. They saw it as pandering to the poorly educated, as dumbing down high culture, and as being dangerously radical in its implicit liberalism. The writing of the Cockney coterie smacked of the ignorant commercialism of lower-class London shopkeepers and clerks. While the politics of language in the Cockney dispute have been extensively discussed, the significance of pedestrianism has not. Hazlitt, a member of the circle, saw pedestrian rambles to the suburban inn as typically Cockney, but understood their social function as an escape and praised the act of imagination they involved (while acknowledging its limits). In his essay "On Londoners and Country People" he portrayed the Cockney as "a lawyer's clerk at half-a-guinea a week" or "a shopman, and nailed all day behind the counter" who nevertheless also "lives in a world of romance—a fairy-land of his own," one location for which is the pub on the rural fringes of the city, to which he walks on a summer Sunday:

> This kind of suburban retreat is a most agreeable relief to the close and confined air of a city life. The imagination, long pent up behind a counter or between brick walls, with noisome smells, and dingy objects, cannot bear at once to launch into the boundless expanse of the country, but "shorter excursions tries", coveting something between the two, and finding it at White-Conduit House, or the Rosemary Branch, or Bagnigge Wells....The benches are ranged in rows, the fields and hedge-rows spread out their verdure; Hampstead and Highgate are seen in the back-ground, and contain the imagination within gentle limits—here the holiday people are playing ball; here they are playing bowls—here they are quaffing ale, there sipping tea—here the loud wager is heard, there the political debate.[11]

In "On Going a Journey," Hazlitt considers the country walk in detail.[12] He begins by sounding an unusual note for the Cockney essayists, claiming that he preferred to go for walks alone as "I like to have it all my own way; and this is impossible unless you are alone, or in such company as I do not covet." This is a paradox, of course, since by publishing the essay on his solitary walks he shares them, at least after the event, with thousands of readers. He also incorporates quotations from unnamed poets throughout, not merely to illustrate ideas he has just expressed, but to articulate his thoughts in the first place: he thinks in other men's words. In effect, this compositional method is allusion transcending itself: so direct are the references and so organically absorbed into his prose that locating their sources seems beside the point. Hazlitt alludes not in order to display knowledge or flatter readers who identify his authorities (many of which are anyway so obscure as to be unidentifiable by his readers), but to represent the stream of consciousness, the internal conversation, that fills his mind when he walks alone. The quotations and allusions are the voices of company he does covet—and company he keeps—the company of past writers who inform his thoughts. Rather than the disagreeable interruptions of a real companion, he prefers these voices—others *as* himself—because, being internal and unwilled, they do not cut across his flow but form it—they let him "have it all my own way." For the reader, meanwhile, they give an overall impression that Hazlitt the essayist is a conversationalist conferring culture upon one: even if one does not pick up all or any of the references, it seems glamorous to gain access to the literary through him. And the glamour is increased when, like Hunt, he offers another kind of allusion—not the quotation from past works but the hinted name of a famous poet, offering privileged glimpses of his private life. Hinting at Coleridge's name, Hazlitt proffers enough biographical detail about walking with him for readers to guess his identity:

> We must "give it an understanding, but no tongue." My old friend C—, however, could do both. He could go on in the most delightful explanatory way over hill and dale, a summer's day, and convert a landscape into a didactic poem or a Pindaric ode. "He talked far above singing." If I could so clothe my ideas in sounding and flowing words, I might perhaps wish to have some one with me to admire the swelling theme; or I could be more content, were it possible for me still to bear his echoing voice in the woods of All-Foxden. They had "that fine madness in them which our first poets had"; and if they could have been caught by some rare instrument, would have breathed such strains as the following
>
>> Here be woods as green
>> As any, air likewise as fresh and sweet
>> As when smooth Zephyrus plays on the fleet
>> Face of the curled streams, with flow'rs as many
>> As the young spring gives, and as choice as any;
>> Here be all new delights, cool streams and wells,
>> Arbours o'ergrown with woodbines, caves and dells:
>> Choose where thou wilt, whilst I sit by and sing,
>> Or gather rushes to make many a ring
>> For thy long fingers; tell thee tales of love,
>> How the pale Phoebe, hunting in a grove,
>> First saw the boy Endymion, from whose eyes
>> She took eternal fire that never dies;
>> How she convey'd him softly in a sleep,
>> His temples bound with poppy, to the steep
>> Head of old Latmos, where she stoops each night,
>> Gilding the mountain with her brother's light,
>> To kiss her sweetest.—"Faithful Shepherdess."
>
> Had I words and images at command like these, I would attempt to wake the thoughts that lie slumbering on golden ridges in the evening clouds: but at the sight of nature, my fancy, poor as it is, droops and closes up its leaves, like flowers at sunset. I can make nothing out on the spot: I must have time to collect myself.

The quotation from the unidentified poem by the unnamed (and little-known) Keats illustrates and intensifies the power of speech that Coleridge had at his command at Alfoxden; in turn it is itself glamorized by being inserted into a biographical anecdote that is studded with other quotations from the unnamed Shakespeare, Beaumont, and Fletcher, and Drayton (the quotation from Drayton is doubly allusive—it praises Coleridge by citing a passage in which Drayton is praising Marlowe). The overall effect is to make Hazlitt the companion of poets and a conduit to poetry, which is revealed to be a more inspired and transformative response to rural walking than he or the reader by themselves can achieve. The obscure and unnamed verse of the past does not just live on in Hazlitt's thought but is embodied, given a local habitation and a name, in C— its living representative. Name-hinting and allusive quotation here work side by side to position writer and reader as both adoring fan and privileged intimate of men who speak and write a discourse—verse—of which the prose essay is a record but to which the essayist cannot aspire.

For Hazlitt, poets are a cut above his fellow essayists: the witticisms of Lamb, he hints, do not elevate a walk, but distract from its enjoyment:

> In general, a good thing spoils out-of-door prospects: it should be reserved for Table-talk. L— is for this reason, I take it, the worst company in the world out of doors; because he is the best within.

This kind of allusion flatters the reader, treating him as a confidante of a gossipy private judgment made about an equal—familiarity rather than the fandom displayed toward Coleridge and Keats. But it still peddles the illusion of special access, if the reader can guess the name, to a literary circle while acting as a kind of cross-reference to essays by Lamb through which the reader could also access personal tidbits. Company, vicariously shared, is the prize: even if Hazlitt is a solitary walker, he is, nonetheless, a convivial writer, inducting the reader into the free and easy company of men made to seem just like him.

Charles Lamb was, like Hunt and Hazlitt, singled out as a "Cockney Scribbler"[13] and, like his fellow essayists, he did indeed pose as the reader's friend in his own walking essays, which are expressions of male sociability. Like Hunt and Hazlitt, Lamb celebrates suburban rambles, yet he also lays bare the relationship of the holiday walk to the workday confinement in even starker terms than Bloomfield had. A clerk for the East India Company for 36 years, Lamb understood the psychological cost of clerkdom—a colonization of the self that in his case could not be easily escaped even when wandering down rural lanes: in a letter of 1805, he declared "Pen & Ink & Clerks, & desks" to be inventions of Satan.[14] As a result, his walking writing has an undercurrent of anxiety, which he explores in "The Superannuated Man," the essay he published after he was allowed to retire early on grounds of stress. First, the essay describes the effect of work on Lamb's experience of time:

> Each day used to be individually felt by me in its reference to the foreign post days; in its distance from, or propinquity to, the next Sunday. I had my Wednesday feelings, my Saturday nights' sensations. The genius of each day was upon me distinctly during the whole of it, affecting my appetite, spirits, &c. The phantom of the next day, with the dreary five to follow, sate as a load upon my poor Sabbath recreations.[15]

This is one of the earliest expressions of that internalization of bureaucratic discipline that Melville, in *Bartleby*, and Kafka, in *The Castle*, would identify as the imprisoned soul of modernity. It is not just that Lamb works to the rhythm of an external order; it is also that this order becomes what he is. Grimmer than Bloomfield, Lamb shows that brief holidays cannot lift the burden of this commodified self: his annual leave was "a series of seven uneasy days, spent in restless pursuit of pleasure, and wearisome anxiety to find out how to make the most of them" (p. 715). A note of desperation enters as he tries to walk off his confinement in the counting house by a pedestrian marathon—exhausting himself as he tries to outpace his work self: "If Time hung heavy upon me, I could walk it away;...thirty miles a day" (p. 715). Idleness is impossible: time hangs heavy without the regimentation of the office, so he must labor to dissipate it. It was the creeping colonization of the self by this regimentation that Bloomfield was dispelling by his walking tour: turning oneself out of doors for aimless wandering equated to freedom. But it was, it seems, too late for Lamb: once the clerk is a clerk in body and soul, there is no effective escape from work by its opposite, holiday walking. Or rather, he is given purpose, willy-nilly, on his days off by his days on. He cannot rest: liberation from office work takes the haunted form of a different kind of work—bodily motion, mental creativity instead of drudgery.

This opposition applied to Lamb's writing as well as his walking: for years he had written ledgers and accounts all day and all week, and humorous essays of Elia in the evenings and Sundays: the work of office writing had conditioned the literary writing as a mode of liberation—liberation in that it was a scriptorial labor under Lamb's own control rather than the East India Company's, and in his resolute avoidance of didactic purpose in what he wrote. Comic inventiveness—the expression of the self through ironic personae rather than the promulgation of truths—enacted a freed, elusive self opposed to the self who had to enter true facts and accurate figures at an office desk all week. Both were labor: Elia/A liar was shaped by the clerk's bondage, the clerk was renewed by his Elian liberty. The two writerly selves fed each other as the two pedestrian selves did—the man who walked the same way to work every weekday for years versus the Sunday and holiday 30-miles-a-day man walking where he willed at pace.

Lamb dispelled the anxiety with the same walking aid that Hunt and Hazlitt so enjoyed—the pub. On Sundays, Lamb came to measure out his life not in coffee spoons but in tankards:

> "Scott," says Cunningham, "was a stout walker: Lamb was a porter one. He calculated distances, not by long measure, but by ale and beer measure. 'Now I have walked a pint.' Many a time I have accompanied him in these matches against Meux,[16] not without sharing in the stake, and then, what cheerful and profitable talk! For instance, he once delivered to me orally the substance of the 'Essay on the Defect of Imagination in Modern Artists,' subsequently printed in the *Athenaeum*. But besides the criticism, there were snatches of old poems, golden lines, and sentences culled from old books, and anecdotes of men of note. Marry, it was like going a ramble with gentle Izaak Walton, minus the fishing."[17]

The anecdote comes from another Cockney essayist, Thomas Hood. He drops names of coterie members—John Scott, Allan Cunningham, Lamb—to place the impressed reader at the scene of famous men's creativity: if the essay is a testament to the origins of writing in men's intimate and convivial conversation, it seeks to replicate that intimacy and conviviality in the relationship it creates with the reader. Its mode, therefore, is not the learned literary allusion that demands an educated knowledge of old poetry, but the casual mention of a public figure's private life.

The pub not the peaks: here Lamb, like Bloomfield, is not so much a Wordsworthian prophet of nature, as an oracle of ale. But it's not just a rambling pub crawl—it's a model of peripatetic conviviality, like Hunt's rustic walk and Bloomfield visiting Dorking. The beer and the bodily motion bring forth a flow of conversation that is amusing, learned, and creative, a spontaneous overflow of sociable feelings that then floods into Lamb's conversational writings. His intimate essay style, that is to say, is founded on the wandering but continual progress of the enlivened—or tipsy—man who talks as he walks, even when walking is nowhere mentioned in the essay (as it is not in "The Defect of Imagination in Modern Artists"). This is walking not just as suburban relaxation but also as companionable inspiration, and the references to the green lane and to Izaak Walton suggest that it is deeply rural and English—a means by which the lower middle classes claim for themselves a version of pastoral that is both traditionalist and nationalist. At the same time, in giving the reader a glimpse of the private lives that led to essays such as the one they were presently reading, Hood made writing emerge from a social activity that writer and, vicariously, readers shared—the reveries of a companionable walker who, the dropped name revealed, was not just any pedestrian but a famous literary rambler whose essays they might already have read.

Walking was not always companionable and creative for Lamb. Retirement from his job interfered with the restless but productive opposition of office and ramble. He did not know how to live with his free time, save to stay tipsy for longer and to ramble more often. He expresses, for the first time in literature, the bewilderment of the retiree who doesn't know what to do with himself or how to do it, so much has he become an office man. And he expresses it by discussing walking, appealing to the very paving stones that have felt his daily tread:

> Stones of old Mincing-lane, which I have worn with my daily pilgrimage for six and thirty years, to the footsteps of what toil-worn clerk are your everlasting flints now vocal? I indent the gayer flags of Pall Mall. It is Change time, and I am strangely among the Elgin marbles. It was no hyperbole when I ventured to compare the change in my condition to a passing into another world. Time stands still in a manner to me. I have lost all distinction of season. I do not know the day of the week, or of the month.

("Superannuated Man," p. 718)

Cast adrift from his work discipline and clock time, Lamb rambles rather than treads: he no longer measures his pace or counts the miles. A different walker, he is an altered person, relaxed but also empty, perhaps depressed: "I am already come to be known by my vacant face and careless gesture, perambulating at no fixed pace, nor with any settled purpose. I walk about; not to and from" (p. 719). What saved his errant self was a dog, as his friend P. G. Patmore recalled—a large

and very handsome dog, of a rather curious and singularly sagacious breed, which had belonged to Thomas Hood, and at the time I speak of, and to oblige both dog and master, had been transferred to the Lambs—who made a great pet of him, to the entire disturbance and discomfiture, as it appeared, of all Lamb's habits of life, but especially of that most favorite and salutary of all, his long and heretofore solitary suburban walks: for Dash (that was the dog's name) would never allow Lamb to quit the house without him, and, when out, would never go anywhere but precisely where it pleased himself. The consequence was that Lamb made himself a perfect slave to this dog—who was always half a mile off from his companion, either before or behind, scouring the fields and roads in all directions, up and down "all manner of streets," and keeping his attendant in a perfect fever of anxiety and irritation, from his fear of losing him on the one hand, and his reluctance to put the needful restraint upon him on the other. Dash perfectly well knew his host's amiable weakness in this respect, and took a due doglike advantage of it. In the Regent's Park in particular, Dash had his quasi-master completely at his mercy; for the moment they got within the Ring, he used to squeeze himself through the railing, and disappear for half an hour together in the enclosed and thickly planted greensward, knowing perfectly well that Lamb did not dare to move from the spot where he (Dash) had disappeared till he thought proper to show himself again. And they used to take this walk oftener than any other, precisely because Dash liked it and Lamb did not.[18]

Writing in 1854, 27 years after the events, Patmore drops the names of the *London Magazine* essayists who had themselves dropped his name. The aim is that of celebrity gossip on the one hand, giving the reader the illusion of inclusion in the intimate lives of a famous literary circle; on the other, it is to memorialize that circle—Lamb was long dead—and even perpetuate it after its demise, by adding another chatty essay to the chatty essays it had produced in the 1820s. Patmore thus positions himself as a last survivor of the group and therefore its true interpreter and memorialist, important because he alone can give present-day readers access to the literary lions of yesteryear.

What Patmore remembers presents Lamb as an endearingly harmless figure: a writer's life becomes evidence of the cozy whimsicality that the Victorians were led to value in his works. Walking the dog—or being walked by him—turns a pedestrian exercise into a comic drama, keeping a superannuated man in the moment, subordinating his directionlessness to Dash's dashing qualities. Dash replaces the office; Lamb is the dog's slave: he has a master again, giving him purposeful work. But it is a comic slavery because it is unpredictable, erratic, picaresque: the pair resemble Don Quixote in pursuit of

Sancho's donkey. A suburban ramble becomes an event of suspense and surprise, a comic peregrination—not so much the internalization as the canine-ization of the quest romance.

Eventually, Lamb gave Dash to Patmore to look after, and moved to a suburban village, Enfield, whence he wrote Patmore on the subject of his lost walking companion. His original letter is more intense and subversive than Patmore's later memorialization: beneath its wit, a complex of emotions is discernible:

> Dear Patmore—Excuse my anxiety—but how is Dash? (I should have asked if Mrs. Patmore kept her rules and was improving—but Dash came uppermost. The order of our thoughts should be the order of our writing.) Goes he muzzled, or *aperto ore*? Are his intellects sound, or does he wander a little in his conversation? You cannot be too careful to watch the first symptoms of incoherence. The first illogical snarl he makes, to St. Luke's with him. All the dogs here are going mad, if you believe the overseers; but I protest they seem to me very rational and collected. But nothing is so deceitful as mad people to those who are not used to them. Try him with hot water. If he won't lick it up, it is a sign he does not like it. Does his tail wag horizontally or perpendicularly? That has decided the fate of many dogs at Enfield. Is his general deportment cheerful? I mean when he is pleased—for otherwise there is no judging. You can't be too careful. Has he bit any of the children yet? If, he has, have them shot, and keep him for curiosity, to see if it was the hydrophobia.... If the slightest suspicion arises in your breast that all is not right with him (Dash), muzzle him, and lead him in a string (common packthread will do; he don't care for twist) to Hood's, his quondam master, and he'll take him in at any time. You may mention your suspicions or not, as you like, or as you may think it will wound or not Mr. H's feelings. Hood, I know, will wink at a few follies in Dash, in consideration of his former sense. Besides, Hood is deaf, and if you hinted anything, ten to one he would not hear you. Besides, you will have discharged your conscience, and laid the child at the right door, as they say.[19]

Despite the faux naivety, Lamb misses the dog and feels too distant from town. Making excursions to villages on the fringes was rather different from living in one of those villages. Lamb's walks became melancholy; the retiree found that his pedestrian self, once a pacy strider-out working off the pent-up energies produced by the working week's confinement, was purposeless. Suburban rambling had gone sour, spoilt by the prior colonization of self by work's regulation of time and space—the office hours, the clerk's desk. Lamb's tipsy pedestrianism articulated an undercurrent of a peculiarly modern desperation beneath its surface bonhomie and beneath the jokiness of the circle of walkers and writers. The urban world of regimented work, with its commodification of body and soul, is the specter raised by the Cockney coterie, a specter that ensures that its shared language replays the language of the Bristol and Lakes poets with an unsettling undercurrent of absurdity and anxiety. Lamb, invoked by name in Coleridge's celebration of companionable walking and verse making, "This Lime-Tree Bower My Prison," revisits his pedestrian role in that poem, but rural liberty is now contaminated by city culture: his Cockney essay replays, only to undercut, the Romantic idealism of the West Country circle of which he had once been part. In this respect, his prose is prophetic: like him, but unlike the Lake poets, our lives are confined by the office or the business, the time clock or the schedule. We hope, moreover, but do not always succeed, to leave behind the anxiety and regimentation that come with our jobs: in this respect, whether pushing on for mile after mile, or taking two or three pints too many, we are the heirs of Bloomfield and of Lamb.

CHAPTER 8

ALLUSIONS OF GRANDEUR:
PROPHETIC AUTHORITY AND
THE ROMANTIC CITY

My last chapter again explores the alienation under the surface of the *London Magazine* essay as written by a member of the Cockney school who was also a participant in the Lakes coterie. Thomas De Quincey was a disciple of Coleridge and Wordsworth who had lived in Wordsworth's former cottage in Grasmere. Like Lamb, he produced a distinctive Romanticism by replaying Lake coterie motifs—ruralism, imagination, confession, prophecy—in the context of the Cockney essay, product of a commercial London by which the Lake poets were both fascinated and repelled. In the process, he asked whether Romantic poetry could lyricize the city, when the city destroyed the communal relationships, the coterie languages, on which Romantic poetry depended—when to write from the city was to write from an experience of commodification, isolation, and alienation. His answer to his question was to oppose country to city and poetry to prose, precipitating a lasting polarization, inscribed into the very discourse that he defined—"English literature."

De Quincey's reworking of the Lake poets' motifs hinged on the nature of prophetic writing, as produced in Grasmere and as produced in London. I begin by exploring the latter, investigating a number of Cockney millenarians for whom prophecy was not their own, subjective act of figuration—a rhetorical construction relating present to past and future—but a verbal record of an actual historical relationship that they merely observed, or literally embodied.

As we saw in chapter 1, in the 1780s, William Cowper first delineated the new capitalism and its effects on the metropolis, recently enriched by the profits of empire. Cowper detected corruption beneath the city's glittering surfaces, and reached for a biblical allusion to indict it:

> ...where has commerce such a mart,
> So rich, so throng'd, so drain'd, and so supplied,
> As London, opulent, enlarg'd and still
> Increasing London? Babylon of old
> Not more the glory of the earth, than she
> A more accomplish'd world's chief glory now.

(Task, I, 715–24; Cowper, II, 135)

Cowper likened London to the Babylon that featured in the Book of Revelation because its wealth stemmed in great measure from the Oriental colonies that had, since Lord Clive's conquests in India, been pouring money into the coffers of the East India Company. According to Cowper, this Oriental wealth was responsible for a rise in consumption not only of goods but also of other people. Appalled by imperial greed, Cowper left London for rural retirement, as Wordsworth also did—satirizing it, and all it stood for, from a moral distance. He invoked the Book of Revelation for millenarian reasons too: his allusion to the biblical city of evil implied that the last days foretold by the prophet of Apocalypse were being fulfilled in the new imperial metropolis. He himself, meanwhile, borrowed scriptural authority via the allusion, using it to lend urgency to his indictments of immorality.

Cowper influenced Clare's apocalyptic rhetoric, as we saw in chapter 6. Others adopted similar language: millenarianism sprang up all over town in the last decades of the eighteenth century and the first decade of the nineteenth. The 1780s began with the religious riots whipped up by the prophet George Gordon using allusions to Revelation; later the Swedenborgians attracted hundreds to their New Jerusalem Church. In the 1790s, Londoners of all classes—respectable Anglican clergymen, members of Parliament, veteran scientists, servant girls from the West Country, half pay navy officers, artisan engravers—invoked biblical prophets to make sense of their city. They were joined by outsiders responding to the French Revolution and its aftermath. Dissenting minster Joseph Priestley announced that the violence of the French war was fulfilling Daniel's prophecies that a fifth monarchy, ruled by the Son of Man, would shortly supersede all others. Bishop Samuel Horsley alluded to the Antichrist of John's epistles and the Beast of Revelation to prophesy that the French Revolution heralded "a dissolution of the whole fabric of the external world."[1] And G. S. Faber, Fellow of Lincoln College Oxford, also turned to Revelation, claiming that Britain would alone be saved like "a column in the midst of the surrounding ruins [w]hile mighty empires totter to their base, and while Antichrist advances with rapid strides to his predicted sovereignty over the inslaved kings."[2]

Many historians make a distinction between the "respectable" pre-millenialism of middle-class writers such as Priestley, Cowper, Faber, and Coleridge and the postmillenialism of artisans and laborers.[3] The former, the argument runs, prophesied the millennium's arrival but did not claim to know when it would occur; the latter claimed privileged knowledge of its imminent arrival. The former interpreted the Bible text; the latter claimed to see visions. The former remained within Christian orthodoxy; the latter did not. The problem with this schematic presentation, however, is that it ignores the ambiguity attendant upon the allusiveness at the heart of prophetic discourse. Priestley and Coleridge occasionally offered disclaimers denying that their prophecies of apocalypse and millennium referred to any particular imminent time, or depended on privileged knowledge; nevertheless, their allusions made biblical prophecy refer to the present day—so that both imminence and privileged knowledge were implicitly part of the figurality they employed. In "Religious Musings," for instance, Coleridge wields the prophetic authority deriving from Biblical allusion—he imagines the French Revolution as the opening of the fifth seal; he envisions an elect which prepares for millennium—before climbing down and disclaiming the authority to know. He has his manna and eats it. Priestley is also equivocal about the specificity of his prophecy—denying elsewhere what his allusive interpretation of the revolution could not help but suggest.[4]

It was another dissenting minister—the Rev. Richard Price—who most stridently made the capital the seat of prophecy. On November 4, 1789, in the Old Jewry Presbyterian Meeting House in the heart of the City of London, Price, an economics expert and financial adviser to government as well as a preacher, delivered a sermon "On the love of our country." Price built his sermon up to a prophetic peroration, hailing the French Revolution by means of a biblical allusion:

> What an eventful period is this! I am thankful that I have lived to see it, and I could almost say, *Lord, now lettest thou thy servant depart in peace, for mine eyes have seen thy salvation.* I have lived to see a diffusion

of knowledge which has undermined superstition and error. I have lived to see the rights of men better understood than ever, and nations panting for liberty, which seemed to have lost the idea of it. I have lived to see thirty millions of people, indignant and resolute, spurning at slavery, and demanding liberty with an irresistible voice, their king led in triumph, and an arbitrary monarch surrendering himself to his subjects. After sharing in the benefits of one Revolution, I have been spared to be a witness to two other Revolutions, both glorious. And now, methinks, I see the ardor for liberty catching and spreading, a general amendment beginning in human affairs, the dominion of kings changed for the dominion of laws, and the dominion of priests giving way to the dominion of reason and conscience. [...] Tremble all ye oppressors of the world! Take warning all ye supporters of slavish governments and slavish hierarchies! Call no more (absurdly and wickedly) reformation, innovation. You cannot now hold the world in darkness. Struggle no longer against increasing light and liberality. Restore to mankind their rights and consent to the correction of abuses, before they and you are destroyed together.[5]

The function of the quotation (from Luke 22.29–30) was to give Price the rhetorical authority to write as a prophet, to greet the spread of liberty and inveigh against tyrants. But precisely what Price was prophesying was left implicit. The gospel text continues, beyond the words Price quotes, with phrases normally taken to signify the prophesied millennium—the return of Christ's kingdom on earth: "Mine eyes have seen thy salvation. Which thou hast prepared before the face of all people; A light to lighten the Gentiles, and the glory of thy people Israel." Price alludes to these phrases by the words he does cite, but leaves them unsaid: he thus suggests, without actually stating it, that the French Revolution heralds the imminent return to earth of Christ in majesty.

Price's equivocal use of allusion provoked the wrath of Edmund Burke. Burke's famous *Reflections on the Revolution in France* (1790) was not simply a reply to Price's optimism, but an attack on his— and other dissenters'[6]—prophetic discourse. Burke portrayed this discourse as a dangerous habit: interpreting contemporary events by allusion to the Bible led to the justification of revolutionary violence as merely a necessary stage in the prophesied millennial return. Price, Burke wrote, was both intoxicated and blinded by the allure of prophecy—by "the fumes of his oracular tripod."[7] He profaned "the beautiful and prophetic ejaculation, commonly called 'nunc dimittis,' made on the first presentation of our Saviour in the temple, [by] applying it, with an inhuman and unnatural rapture, to the most horrid, atrocious, and afflicting spectacle, that perhaps ever was exhibited to the pity and indignation of mankind."[8]

Burke's *Reflections* provoked immediate controversy but also became a book of lasting influence, largely for its defense of custom and tradition. Its critique of contemporary prophecy has received less comment, yet was central to its account of its times. Burke did not just discredit millenarian prophecy and biblical allusion as valid means of historical and political interpretation—itself an influential move that contributed to the destruction of a prophetic tradition dating back several hundred years—he also, in the process, defined that tradition as the product of a particular class of people in a particular place—sketching out an incisive social, rather than religious, analysis of it. Prophecy, he suggested, was the expression of the vanity of London dissenters who were mostly men of commerce. It was politically naïve, because these men were inexperienced beyond the world of finance. It displayed their will to power—their wish to triumph over the traditional social order in which they were subordinate to the landed aristocracy and the monarch.[9] It signaled, in its callow, self-congratulatory rhetoric, the triumph of a mercantile mentality that was disastrous for European civilization: "The age of chivalry is gone," Burke lamented, and "that of sophisters, economists, and calculators, has succeeded; and the glory of Europe is extinguished for ever" (p. 113). Notably, it was a discourse of London—the London not of Westminster but of the City, not of palace and townhouse but of workshop, merchant hall and exchange—the Cockney London of artisans, tradesmen, and businessmen rather than the West End London of lords, gentry, and servants.

It was biblical allusion's very potency that made it attractive to Eastenders. A pattern emerged: the more socially disadvantaged the prophet, the more literally he drew on the Bible. Allusion allowed the last to be first; it converted insignificance to authority. Thus, the more the prophet spoke from the city's crowded alleys, courts, and garrets, the more Britain, and, at its center, London, was seen as a sinful sign of God's wrath[10] and the more apocalypse and millennium were confidently predicted to be at hand. Millenarian allusion was particularly attractive to poor artisans struggling to make a living from their trade and able, by virtue of chapel preaching and debating societies, to view their struggles as part of a larger pattern. Politicized by their religion, by the successful revolution in France and by their experience of the city, London artisans such as "laborious mechanic"[11] Richard "Citizen" Lee banded together, sharing a discourse that combined prophecy and republicanism. Lee published "Babylon's Fall" in 1795, imagining the destruction of the monarchical city of Babylon in the present tense:

> Babylon the Great is fallen!
> All her Pomp descends to Hell;
> How the Kings of Earth are wailing!
> How they trembled when she fell![12]

Lee's regicide handbill *King Killing*, as Jon Mee shows, imagined the death of George III by invoking Daniel's prophecy (4:33) about King Nebuchadnezzar being brought down to "eat grass as oxen"—a prophecy illustrated by Blake in *The Marriage of Heaven and Hell* (1790) and again in 1795.

Daniel empowered revolutionaries to write; the biblical status of his antimonarchical rhetoric lent the republicans who alluded to him the verbal authority to counter the massive and intimidating discourses of legitimacy that surrounded Church and King.[13] He also gave them an interpretative key to decode the city in which they worked and published. Together, they fashioned a common discourse, political and religious—the prophetic discourse of autodidact artisans, many of whom worked in the book trade. For example, Daniel stood behind the allusive discourse of Garnett Terry, a commercially unsuccessful engraver and bookseller who became a political radical and a millenarian illustrator. Terry described Daniel's Babylon as the London of his experience: it was a place "to make merchandize of men, and to sell them by kingdoms, bishopricks, parishes, or parcels."[14] His fellow London bookseller Thomas Spence, as Michael Scrivener has shown, invoked Isaiah, Leviticus, and Revelation when he imagined the redistribution of land and the destruction of private ownership as the triumph of the captive Israelites over Babylon:

> Welcome that day draws near,
> For then our rents we share,
> Earth's rightful lords we are
>   Ordain'd for this.
>
> How hath the oppressor ceas'd,
> And all the world releas'd
>   From misery!
> The fir-trees all rejoice,
> And cedars lift their voice,
> Ceas'd now the Feller's noise,
>   Long rais'd by thee.

The scepter now is broke
Which with continual stroke
The nations smote![15]

Spence clearly expected the purchasers of his verse to take strength and
comfort as they recognized his allusions to the forthcoming destruction of tyrants. The land reform for which he was, in fact, arguing,
could thus be believed to be the fulfillment of biblical prophecy.

Spence was jailed on a treason charge in 1794: his allusions too
clearly referred to the death of the monarch. Those of Blake, like
Terry an engraver and like Spence a seller of books, were less direct.
As Mee has shown, Blake invoked Jeremiah and Lamentations when,
in *Europe* (1794), he alluded, through the figure of the grieving
"shadowy female," to Jerusalem as a city destroyed by its king's determination to make war. The contemporary relevance of this figure was
implicit: although it did not imagine George III's death, it nevertheless alluded to London, capital of a Georgian nation making war on
France.

Revolutionary France was the destination of another engraver,
William Bryan, who in 1789 travelled to Avignon with his friend
John Wright to join the society of prophets there. On his return, he
lived at 51 Upper Mary-le-bone Street, neighbored by the Painite
radical Thomas Clio Rickman and the Swedenborgian Carl Bernhard
Wadstrom.[16] His prophecies, issued in London in 1795, expected the
divine destruction of the capital city. "Here is the time," he wrote,
"in which God will break the laws made by the children of the earth.
Here is the time wherein he will reprove the science of men, and here
is the time of his justice. This is the time that we must believe all
those who announce the new reign of the Lord."[17] Bryan became a
follower of Richard Brothers, the self-styled "King of the Hebrews,"
who in 1795 declared London to be the "SPIRITUAL BABYLON"
of Daniel and Revelation 18: it would be destroyed in retribution for
its commercialism, whereby all things, even human beings, were for
sale: "Beasts, Sheep, and Horses,... *and Slaves*, and *Souls of Men*."[18]
George III, as monarch of Babylon, would be struck down by the
Lord and die unless he gave up his throne.

Brothers galvanized Londoners: from 1794, in the space of little
more than a year, he attracted thousands of followers. Yet, neither he
nor his supporters were simply energized by revolutionary politics or
the republic in France. Brothers had become a prophet after living
in penury on London's streets and in its workhouses; his followers
had initially been attracted by his habit of giving out small sums of

money. London poverty—the lived experience of its social environment, its commercial capitalism—motivated prophecy. It was because
the city seemed at once so powerful and so dreadful in its reduction of
everything to an item for sale that it demanded the allusion to biblical
Babylon: it was uncategorizable in natural terms. Thus, the Scottish
moralist Robert Mudie, writing in 1825, termed the city "the Great
Babylon" because it presented an "unthreadable labyrinth," producing
a "total insignificance of single persons and single objects."[19] The figure of Babylon gave London's endless dizzying parade, so overwhelming in its relentless trivialization and commodification, meaning where
it seemed meaningless. The city became an example of sin, set aside for
God's wrath. There was a divine plan to its alienating chaos.

It was because London was categorizable as Babylon that it was
possible, and necessary, to make it the New Jerusalem: so appalling
was its destruction of authenticity that it was imperative to transform
it to its opposite to reassert the human values that would otherwise be
denied. Its assault on human sympathy and therefore on the imagination—encapsulated by Wordsworth's "The face of every one / That
passes by me is a mystery" and Blake's "Mark in every face I meet /
Marks of weakness, marks of woe"—demanded, of those who felt it,
a reassertion, an alternative London, created by the imagination, in
which meaning value and justice recolonize the streets, shops, and
squares (*Prelude*, 1805, VII, 596–97; "London," in *Songs*).

Within the framework provided by biblical allusion, this imagination
often took literal and material form: many of the visionaries were sure
that a coming apocalypse would see London replaced by a real millennial city, a new, rectilinear and salubrious Jerusalem of spacious squares
and symmetrical buildings. They transformed the teeming chaos of
Babylon into neoclassical order in an effort to delineate a redeemed
polis in which laws, ethics, and human relationships are right and true.
They exercised, that is to say, their architectural imagination in order to
prophesy the setting in stone of a society again governed by the sympathy and empathy that present-day "chartered" London had eroded.

In 1801, Brothers set out a detailed architectural plan of the New
Jerusalem in which he tried to unite the visions of Ezekiel with modern town planning: his city is all garden squares, good ventilation, and
Corinthian columns.[20] Jerusalem, it turns out, is rather like the new
area of London then being named after the reformist Whig magnates
who called themselves "friends of the people": as in Bloomsbury's
Bedford and Russell Squares, symmetry of design and a hint of the
pastoral characterize the redeemed city, replacing the dense, crowded,
crooked narrow streets of the medieval town.

As John Barrell has shown, imagination was a politicized issue in the mid-1790s, as a repressive government, alarmed that agitators would bring about a revolution akin to that occurring in France, arrested radicals on a charge of "imagining the king's death."[21] Imagination, became, in the ministry's eyes, a reason to try radicals for treason whether or not any action had been taken to kill the monarch. But it was not imagination alone, but imagination invoking biblical prophecy that the government, like Burke attacking Price, regarded as dangerous—because it literalized allusion: if Brothers, invoking a text nearly everyone knew and regarded as God's word, persuaded people of the literal truth of the relationship that his allusions mobilized between past and present, then he might produce fanatical belief on a mass scale. Convinced that the biblical words he heard in dreams and saw in visions would come about—including the death of George III as the fulfillment of Revelation prophecies of the death of kings—Brothers was, at the very least, accustoming his supporters to the idea that the overturning of monarchs was inevitable and right. To ministers, this raised the specter of disorder and revolution. In 1795, they had Brothers arrested, interrogated, and committed to a madhouse. It was time for visionaries to be careful about what they imagined and how they alluded. Richard Lee fled arrest, disguised as a woman, and went to America. William Blake, having printed nine prophecies since 1789, now began to develop a complex mythology that could not easily be referred to present-day events and that would not be printed for another 15 years.

When Blake's prophecy of the New Jerusalem did appear, after 1820, it contained residues of the literalism of millenarian prophecy from the 1790s. He imagined "London blind & age-bent begging thro the Streets / Of Babylon, led by a child" (*Jerusalem*, plate 84) and echoed Brothers in invoking Revelation 21.10–27 to show the redeemed city as an architectural superimposition on the sinful one, a new Eden where all had access to green fields:

> The fields from Islington to Marybone,
> To Primrose Hill and Saint Johns Wood:
> Were builded over with pillars of gold,
> And there Jerusalems pillars stood.

> (*Jerusalem*, plate 27)

As Morton D. Paley pointed out in 1973, the difference between Blake's poetic imagination and the literal imaginations of Brothers, Bryan, and Joanna Southcott is that Blake knew his visionary city was symbolic of the liberation of human imagination from the repression that flourished in the real city—an alternative, mental reality in which "the stones are pity, and the bricks, well-wrought affections / Enamel'd with love & kindness & the tiles engraven gold" (*Jerusalem*, lines 31–32 of plate 12). Designed to make people question what they thought was true—to bring about "mental fight"—Blake's Jerusalem was similar to Coleridge's Xanadu, of which he says "I would build that dome in air" ("Kubla Khan," 46). The reality of imagination's vision is mental—a castle in the air—but no less valid and no less communal, when shared through published words and images, than was the material city that the millenarian prophet envisioned. Brothers, on the other hand, represented the extreme of the practice of which Burke had accused Price. Vainly certain he was right, he saw the relationship of present to past—and both to future, not as the rhetorical product of his linguistic act of allusion; rather, allusion simply marked up a relationship that was displayed by historical events. Certain the city of his dreams would take material form, he declared himself to be the Prince of the Hebrews, whose return to earth was predicted in the Bible. But by thus claiming to embody the biblical figure to which he was alluding, he only demonstrated its figurality, for when the day announced for apocalyptic destruction passed with nothing worse than a storm, prophecy was shown to be a subjective, even perverse act of personal interpretation. Many of his disappointed followers now deserted him and transferred their interpretative desire to Joanna Southcott, only for her claim to be literally bearing the returning Shiloh to be revealed, in 1814, as a figural, rather than bodily, relationship: she neither gave birth to the Messiah nor, when examined after her death, turned out to have been pregnant. The literalization of biblical allusion had proved its undoing.

After this, various of Southcott's followers jostled to be her successor: none attracted a large following in the city. The Cockney culture of millenarian prophecy withered. When John Wroe established a cult in the 1820s and 1830s, it was in rapidly industrializing Yorkshire towns where handloom weavers were experiencing unemployment and poverty. But Wroe was unsuccessful in London, where no prophets achieved a mass following for their vision of a metropolitan millennium. Biblical allusion retained a powerful critical charge however, if not a millenarian one, because the city still seemed to many a wen of human exploitation and alienation as well as a commercial powerhouse at the center of empire. Thus, the painter John Martin exhibited his vast canvases *The Fall of Babylon* (1819) and *Belshazzar's Feast* (1820), portraying the capital as a vast array of classical architecture in the face of which its people were reduced to insignificance. But it was easier to imagine London as Babylon on the eve of destruction, than, transformed, as the New Jerusalem. In 1825, the *London Magazine* published "The Bricks of the Modern Babylon"—an article foreseeing the new architecture of Regent Street in terminal decay: "Its skin will peel off, like the bark of a rotten tree, and the hide will hang in rags and tatters about the rotting carcass."[22] Martin also offered no millenarian visions of the remade city but published, instead, a series of detailed practical plans for the gradual amelioration of London's sewage collection and fresh water provision.[23] These plans involved hiding the necessary tunnels and pipes under arrays of neoclassical buildings: Martin's imagination was visual and architectural but he envisaged change occurring by the adoption of empirical measures, the case for which had been made by rational argument.

Martin's pictures of Babylon and schemes for improvement were symptomatic. After the Southcott debacle, much of prophecy's imaginative energy was displaced into discourses that accepted their own fictional status and highlighted the figurality of allusion, offering their imaginative visions as rational or emotional responses to the city rather than as divinely or biblically given. If Blake's *Jerusalem* was a case in point, Coleridge, as we saw in chapter 3, derived authority over the political sphere from a rationalized version of biblical prophecy that aligned it with philosophy. In *The Statesman's Manual* (1816) he "present[ed] himself as a vehicle for divine vision, and the foresight he afford[ed] the statesman corresponds to and consists in the hindsight of correctly reading the prophets whose truths, he insist[ed], are for a thousand generations."[24] Prophecy, on this model, is valid because it is philosophy—an expression of the self-evident principles on which historical change is based and therefore true for once and always. This redefinition allowed Coleridge to take a vantage point above the political fray—to bolster his authority as a commentator—without seeming to be an enthusiast. However, it so revised prophecy that its oracular quality, its gnomic strangeness, and its application to specific events was removed.

After 1816, Coleridge, in Carlyle's words, sat on Highgate Hill, "looking down on London and its smoke-tumult like a sage escaped from the inanity of life's battle."[25] His former disciple Thomas De Quincey wrote from below, as one trapped in the dirty mazes of the city. His *Confessions of an English Opium Eater* was a vision of London as hell. Published in the September and October 1821 numbers of *The London Magazine*, *Confessions of an English Opium Eater* became the most popular contribution to a periodical that aimed to convey a view of "the very 'image, form, and pressure' of that '*mighty heart*' whose vast pulsations circulate life, strength, and spirits, throughout this great Empire."[26] Elsewhere in the October number, Charles Lamb described his city dreams as pleasurable experiences, as if to present London life as a delightful as well as civilizing influence on the mind. De Quincey, however, stands out against this urban and urbane context: he not only imagines London as a labyrinth of "Babylonian confusion," but also makes the city resonate with biblical symbols of guilt, sin, and punishment.[27]

It is his experience of having been a runaway child sleeping rough that first brings De Quincey into contact with the grim London experienced by the socially disadvantaged. He uses the street child he met then, the lost child prostitute Ann, as a Magdalen figure of the city's commodification of bodies—and of his inability to remedy the process. He lost Ann in the teeming crowds and could never again find her to restore her tainted innocence. Seared by this experience, he configures London as a place of alienation that he is unable to redeem, not least because of its effects on his own body and mind: "The calamities of my novitiate in London," he writes "had struck root so deeply in my bodily constitution, that afterwards they shot up and flourished afresh, and grew into a noxious umbrage that has over-shadowed and darkened my later years" (*Confessions*; DeQ, II, 39–40).[28] Led by his pain into addiction to London's principal Oriental commodity and source of wealth—opium, he dreams of the city presided over by the biblical and Miltonic figure of Sin, the "stony hearted stepmother" of Oxford Street, who forbids redemption and consumes her own children. For De Quincey, vision is experienced as constraint, for it is the unwilled eruption, in the forms of dreams, of an imagination already malformed by drug addiction. His opium dreams offer a theater that is the visionary and the prophetic shrunk and subjectivized, an avowed internalization of the city, which is replayed in symbolic form in the head. They diagnose urban experience as dependence and loss of identity and are at the same time symptoms of it—involuntary haunting.[29] Thus, he writes that his dreams "haunted me so much, that I feared lest some dropsical state or tendency of the brain might thus be making itself...*objective*; and that the sentient organ might be projecting itself as its own object" (*Confessions*; DeQ, II, 69). Here, he offers himself as an enmind-ment as well as embodiment of addiction: his imagination as well as his brain is diseased by opium and by the city where he buys his opium—its most lucrative commodity. He is, he implies, thoroughly commodified.

Unable to redeem the city in his own imagination, De Quincey still wants, like the millenarians, to build an imaginary London, a symbolic city that can repair, for those who dream it or read his dream narratives, the real London. Precisely because he recognizes himself as a guilty embodiment of the perverse pleasures and pains of the city of capital / capital city, his aim is to convert addiction and alienation into redemption and forgiveness. But he cannot do this by himself, of his own volition, or by literalization of allusion as prophecy, or by adopting the jocular coterie language of the Cockney contributors to the *London Magazine*. One of the circle of *London*ers, De Quincey nevertheless stood on its circumference. If he resembled Lamb and Hazlitt in exposing the alienation that lurked in city experience, and in contrasting that experience with the ruralism epitomized by the Lake school, he was nevertheless singular in admiring that ruralism so unequivocally. De Quincey's New Jerusalem was envisioned in a Cockney school essay but depended on an allusion to the allusive vision of a partner prophet who was critical of London and its culture. That partner was Wordsworth, whose still-unpublished *Prelude* rejection of London's dazzling but ultimately degrading allure De Quincey was one of the few to have heard.

Wordsworth appears in *The Confessions of an English Opium Eater* when De Quincey, attempting to find a language adequate to the description of his strange, haunting, opium dreams of city architecture, quotes from *The Excursion*:

> From a great modern poet I cite the part of a passage which describes, as an appearance actually beheld in the clouds, what in many, of its circumstances I saw frequently in sleep:
>
>> The appearance, instantaneously disclosed,
>> Was of a mighty city—boldly say
>> A wilderness of building, sinking far
>> And self-withdrawn into a wondrous depth.
>> Far sinking into splendour without end!
>> Fabric it seem'd of diamond and of gold,
>> With alabaster domes and silver spires,
>> And blazing terrace upon terrace, high
>> Uplifted; here, serene pavilions bright,
>> In avenues disposed; there towers begirt
>> With battlements that on their restless fronts
>> Bore stars—illumination of all gems!
>> By earthly nature had the effect been wrought
>> Upon the dark materials of the storm
>> Now pacified; on them, and on the coves,

And mountain-steeps and summits whereunto
The vapours had receded—taking there
Their station under a cerulean sky.

The sublime circumstance—"that on their *restless* fronts bore stars"—
might have been copied from my own architectural dreams, so often
did it occur.

(*Confessions*; DeQ, II, 69)

In its original context in *The Excursion* the poetic passage is offered
as a modern equivalent to biblical prophecy: the buildings seen in the
clouds are "such as by Hebrew Prophets were beheld / In vision"
and the whole passage alludes to Ezekiel's vision of a heavenly city
(*Excursion*, II, 869–86).[30] Nevertheless, it is the capacity to see
visions, rather than the truth of the visions as fulfillments of biblical
prophecy, that excites the poet—and De Quincey too, as his comment
indicates. "Restless fronts bore stars" is the phrase in the passage that
points up the seer's awareness that the buildings he visualizes are
actually fluttering shapes in the night sky—creations of his imagination but not about to become miraculously existent material realities.
The phrase ensures that the vision is offered as a demonstration of
imagination's power to conjure something from nothing, rather than
a divinely communicated reality. It is, therefore, an internalization
and secularization of prophecy that highlights the figurality of the
allusive relationship on which it depends. In *The Prelude*, Wordsworth
denominates himself a "prophet of nature" (*Prelude*, 1805, XIII,
442), one whose poetic imagination is so fostered by the rural world
that he can see beyond its material form into its spiritual life (and that
of the people who live in it), as Ezekiel and Isaiah once did. But he
does not offer to predict the future: he does not, unlike Ezekiel and
Daniel, or for that matter Dobbs and Brothers, literally believe in the
advent of the millennium. Rather, he seeks to inherit the role that,
according to the revisionist accounts of the biblical scholars Robert
Lowth and Johann Michaelis, the Hebrew prophets played—the role
of expressing the spiritual yearnings and needs of their people in the
language available to them in that place and time.[31] They were proto-
poets, rather than passive receptors of God's dictated word. And, as
such, Wordsworth makes himself their heir.

A significant element in De Quincey's citation of Wordsworth's
passage is its apparent individuality: he terms the Jerusalem vision
Wordsworth's own. Yet, this is not quite accurate, for in its original context the passage is that of an individual who speaks, as De
Quincey was unable to do, from a rural community. It is a rural vision

of a heavenly city, seen not by the poet in his own person but by the character whom he calls the Solitary—a man who has retreated from the disappointments of revolutionary politics to a self-isolated life of contemplation in one of the Lake District's loneliest valleys. The Solitary experiences the vision alone, when he steps aside from the party bearing home from the fells the body of an old man (a fellow tenant of the Solitary's rural cottage) who has been lulled by hypothermia into a state of semiconsciousness after becoming lost in a snowstorm. The old man is left enraptured by his near-death experience of mountain exposure but it is the Solitary, an educated fellow who knows his Ezekiel and Revelation, who turns fellside rapture into an allusive vision that aligns his own experience with biblical prophecies. And, as a further displacement, the poet then tells out the Solitary's vision in the poem called *The Excursion*: there's a chain of substitutions through which dumb rapture becomes more and more articulate, so that Wordsworth's metrical blank-verse rendition of the New Jerusalem becomes the most sophisticated version of a condition that begins with the silent rustic. The Solitary's vision and, by self-referential implication, Wordsworth's own poetry, become an articulation—a telling out in prophetic words—of what the inarticulate rustic feels but cannot / does not say. As such, they are both personal and solitary (a formulation of a lonely insight) and communal (derived from and a displacement of others' solitary responses to the fells), as if Wordsworth is dramatizing the contradictory affiliations of his own muse to, on one hand, the rural community and, on the other, to separate solitary encounters with landscape. Here, then, Wordsworth identifies visionary power as something both intensely personal and derived from the experience of people who maintain traditional ways of interacting with nature. If he turns prophecy into imagination, biblical allusion into poetic scene, he does not turn it into a power vouchsafed to himself only. Nevertheless, he confidently places himself at the apex of all those who live in harmony with nature, assuming the authority to speak what they know but cannot say. Also, of course, he takes vision outside the city: for Wordsworth the New Jerusalem cannot be imagined in London but only in the parts of the countryside still immune from the commodifying processes of capitalism and corrupting mass culture of urban life.

The function of the passage in the *Confessions of an English Opium Eater* is complex: by quoting it and alluding to its author as a great modern poet, De Quincey supplements his prose with another's poetry, and describes his dream in another's words. This is a different process from Wordsworth's own: whereas the poet, at the articulate end of a chain of substitutions of which the dumb rustic is the beginning, positions himself as the spokesman for a community of which he is part, De Quincey imports another writer's words. If Wordsworth's vision is both his own and that of a community, De Quincey, borrowing it for his own text, can speak neither by himself nor for others. The redemptive holy city is never wholly his own: his dreams defer to another's poem. Moreover, Wordsworth's vision comes from out of town, from the countryside, rather than the city in which De Quincey is stuck. Here, there is a deference to the rural and communal as the location for redemptive vision that is still more apparent in a passage in which De Quincey identifies the Wordsworthian Lakes as a region of spirituality he cannot discover in London:

> Amongst these attractions that drew me so strongly to the Lakes, here had also by that time arisen in this lovely region the deep deep magnet (as to me only in all this world it then was) of William Wordsworth. Inevitably this close connexion of the poetry which most of all had moved me with the particular region and scenery that most of all had fastened upon my affections, and led captive my imagination, was calculated, under ordinary circumstances, to impress upon my fluctuating deliberations a summary and decisive bias. But the very depth of the impressions which had been made upon me, either as regarded the poetry or the scenery, was too solemn and (unaffectedly I may say it) too spiritual, to clothe itself in, any hasty or chance movement as at all adequately expressing its strength, or reflecting its hallowed character. If you, reader, were a devout Mahometan, throwing gazes of mystical awe daily towards Mecca, or were a Christian devotee looking with the same rapt adoration to St. Peter's at Rome, or to El Kodah, the Holy City of Jerusalem (so called even amongst the Arabs, who hate both Christian and Jews) how painfully would it jar upon your sensibilities if some friend, sweeping past you upon a high road, with a train (according to the circumstances) of dromedaries or of wheel carriages, should suddenly pull up, and say, "Come, old fellow, jump up alongside of me; I'm off for the Red Sea, and here's a spare dromedary," or "Off for Rome, and here's a well-cushioned barouche." Seasonable and convenient it might happen that the invitation were; but still it would shock you that a journey which, with or without your consent, could not but assume the character eventually of a saintly pilgrimage, should arise and take its initial movement upon a casual summons, or upon a vulgar opening of momentary convenience. In the present case, under no circumstances should I have dreamed of presenting myself to Wordsworth. The principle of "veneration" (to speak phrenologically) was by many degrees too strong in me for any such overture on my part.
>
> (*Confessions* [1856 text]; DeQ, II, 147)

The Bible again: De Quincey's holy land is Cumbria because it is there that Wordsworth prophesies, demonstrating the capacity of the poetic imagination to form spiritual visions when nourished by nature. The Lakes' circle provides what the Cockney school cannot, a ground on which redemptive vision can flourish because humanity has not been alienated from itself by city life. All at sea in the capital, De Quincey has already yearned to escape thence: "During my first mournful abode in London," he says, "my consolation was (if such it could be thought) to gaze from Oxford Street up every avenue in succession which pierces northwards through the heart of Marylebone to the field and the woods; for *that* said I, travelling with my eyes up the long vistas which lay part in light and part in shade—'*that* is the road to the north and, therefore, to Grasmere'... 'and if I had the wings of a dove, *that* way I would fly for rest'" (*Confessions*; DeQ, II, 40). Here the allusion to the dove positions Grasmere as Ararat, a haven for overwhelmed exiles, and De Quincey as an arkite refugee from God's destruction of sinful cities. Grasmere is a biblical promised land.

If Grasmere is the promised land, London is Babylon—a Babylon that De Quincey, without Wordsworth's aid, cannot transform to the New Jerusalem. It is after Wordsworth's *Excursion* vision that he relates his own Jerusalem dream in the Lake District. From Grasmere churchyard he sees

> The domes and cupolas of a great city—an image or faint abstraction, caught perhaps in childhood from some picture of Jerusalem. And not a bow-shot from me, upon a stone, and shaded by Judean palms, there sat a woman; and I looked; and it was—Ann! She fixed her eyes upon me earnestly; and I said to her at length: "so then I have found you at last."
>
> (*Confessions*; DeQ, II, 73)

It is in a Wordsworthian mountain vision that he refinds the lost innocent; only after this rural redemption does he finally dream of being "in Oxford Street, walking again with Ann" and thus repairing his urban alienation and guilt. But the dream slips away; visions alluding to Milton's "caves of hell" and "incestuous mother" Sin return; he slips back into tormented addiction (*Confessions*; DeQ, II, 74).

De Quincey is not Blake, not even Brothers, Bryan, or Edward Irving—the charismatic preacher who began to draw large London congregations to his millennial church in the 1820s. He cannot redeem the city, much as he wants to, so great is the burden of guilt that it, and the opium habit it sponsors, lays upon him; instead, allusion takes it back to hell. This not least because it has its sinful pleasures as well as pains: the city and the drug (the city as drug) produce a theater in which De Quincey vicariously experiences delights, whether as a solitary walker in London's night-time streets, or as an opium dreamer. And so, stimulated by and addicted to the city's pleasures and pains, a solitary and damaged product of its culture, he imports Wordsworth's rural vision of the heavenly city to substitute for a redeeming vision and an imaginative community that neither he, nor anyone else for whom he can speak in the London of exploited and commodified Cockneys, can form. He does, however, claim, having quoted Wordsworth's vision and thus made his dreams secondary to it, that it is secondary to his own—it "might have been copied from my own architectural dreams." But this is a brief and half-hearted gesture, an attempt to prioritize the redeeming power of his own imagination that he cannot sustain. Ultimately the redemptive consolation of biblical prophecy is lost to De Quincey's city self; it is available only by allusion to a poetic import from the sole remaining land in which he can imagine the purity necessary for a healthy imagination to exist—the uncorrupted Lake District. It will not be formulated in his London-based prose, and he cannot aspire to the transcendence possible for Wordsworth in the medium of verse. Nor, he imagines, can anyone else: De Quincey undermines prophetic London, doubting the ability of the city dwellers to generate visions of renewal as well as hell, for to be a Cockney is to be vitiated by alienation, abjection, and guilt, or, like Leigh Hunt, to be satisfied with the commercial and trivial, while such visions demand what he terms "power." By the same token, he identifies poetic imagination as the medium for redemptive vision, terming "power" the defining characteristic of true literature and deriving it from a heightened language that is to be found in verse rather than in the prose that befits urban life. He borrows this key term, and that of the "creative," from Wordsworth and Coleridge, and then makes it the criterion for "literature"—now defined in opposition to writing that seeks only to communicate knowledge. In effect, as Jonathan Bate has shown,[32] this definition was enormously influential: it inaugurated "English literature" as a cultural field, producing for the first time the "subject" that would be studied in schools and universities—and characterized in terms of "creativity," "imagination," and "power." De Quinceyan by origin, it depended on his borrowing ideas from, and alluding to the verse of, his Romantic forebears. Thus, to illustrate the literature of power and creativity, De Quincey adduces the poetry of Wordsworth, Shakespeare, and Milton, declaring of the latter (in a phrase allusive to Wordsworth's discussion of poetic imagination) that it acts as "a vital agent on the human mind."[33] It is poetry's dense figurality that gives it vitality and power, and this is epitomized by Wordsworth's vision of Jerusalem, Shakespeare's verbal conjuring of the storm in and outside of Lear's mind, and Milton's allegorical characters Sin and Death. This figurality, reflected by the figure of allusion that everywhere permeates De Quincey's prose, becomes the hallmark of true literature, conceived as a coherent body of texts superior to factual writing—one capable of raising people above the commodified and demeaning modern world epitomized by London. Allusion, it follows, is a figure simultaneously demonstrating De Quincey's authority as a critic and inadequacy by comparison with the poets in whose circle he had been: it invokes their figurality but remains deferential and dependent, producing no original or independent power of De Quincey's own.

Prose writer rather than poet, buying in words and substances from outside, De Quincey presents, for the first time in history, a self-portrait of the artist as commodity, a product of the Cockney culture that he and Wordsworth bemoaned. Exiled from the Lakes and from Wordsworth, he has no supportive rural coterie, but nor can he participate in the now-exploded Cockney culture of millenarian prophecy. Isolated, he is unable of his own free will to see visions: his dreams, fuelled by opium, are involuntary and internal—the dark inverts of Wordsworth's fellside epiphanies and Blake's city prophecies. They are Romantic allusion's perverted urban other, the doppelganger of the rural, lyric imagination that characterizes "real" literature. Racked by dreams he cannot control, De Quincey appears as a new phenomenon, the perverse guide—in prose—to a self crippled by the city experience that speaks through him but that he cannot transcend. A definer of Romanticism who brings it into being conceptually because, he assures us, he knows its costs, in body and soul, for the city dweller. And of course this urbanite—the alienated hollow man in romantic agony—is an inaugural figure of modernity: he would be enormously powerful, through Baudelaire, Poe, Stevenson, Conan Doyle, Conrad, and Eliot and into today's popular culture, partly as a result of De Quincey's direct influence.[34]

Crippled by and addicted to the city, De Quincey could not be Blake and imagine its renewal from within: neither poetic imagination nor the artisan culture of millenarian prophecy would succeed in redeeming urban experience. Nor would the jovial embrace of suburban pleasures made by the other essayists of the Cockney school: redemption would not be found in recounting companionable rambles and celebrating beery sociability. And in this he was, iron-ically enough, prophetic: his borrowed Jerusalem signaled a pivotal moment in English culture, for it gave a new direction to a split between the rural and the urban that would not be overcome—effec-tively the retreat of poetic vision from the city (a retreat that the next 200 years of English lyric poetry would follow as it sought transcen-dence and visionary insight but found them among the cliffs, hills, and hedges rather than on the streets). The causes of this develop-ment were seen clearly by De Quincey's successor as commentator on the psyche of London—Mudie—when he noted that "the very igno-rance and consequent indifference which each has toward all whom he meets, together with the politeness which is necessary to render a heartless society bearable, throw the gates of experiences as wide as any man can wish; and thus, though London may not be the place in which one may best study the poetry of one species, it is the one in which to study the prose."[35] Urban dwellers were prosaic and iso-lated: they were bombarded with new experiences but lacked deeper relationships. Poetry, the medium for such relationships, ebbed from the city: as it largely gave up its traditional narrative function and concentrated on briefer lyrical forms,[36] it would henceforth be the worldly, disenchanted prose of the magazine essay and the satirical novel that would envision the pleasures and pains of London. And what this prose saw there was, more often than not, a city of dread-ful night.[37] As for poetry, Jerusalem would increasingly be invoked from the rural fringes as a figure of allusion's figurality—as a mark of allusion's empowerment-by-association of the imagination that calls upon it. Jerusalem would echo anew among the poetic circles that gathered at Tintagel, in Adlestrop, in Little Gidding, and in Fern Hill: it would no longer be seen in Paddington, in St. Pancras, and along the Old Kent Road.

NOTES

INTRODUCTION

1. Pioneering scholarly exceptions to this relegation include the "Cool World of S. T. Coleridge" series of articles contributed to *The Wordsworth Circle* in the early 1970s by Paul Zall.

2. See, among others, Elizabeth Fay, *Becoming Wordsworthian* (Amherst, MA: University of Massachusetts Press, 1995); *Romantic Sociability: Social Networks and Literary Culture in Britain, 1770–1840*, ed. Clara Tuite and Gillian Russell (Cambridge: Cambridge University Press, 2002); Michelle Levy, *Family Authorship and Romantic Print Culture* (New York and Basingstoke, UK: Palgrave Macmillan, 2008); Scott Krawczyk, *Romantic Literary Families* (New York: Palgrave Macmillan, 2009); Jon Mee, *Conversable Worlds: Literature, Contention, and Community 1762 to 1830* (Oxford: Oxford University Press, 2011); Nicola Healey, *Dorothy Wordsworth and Hartley Coleridge: The Poetics of Relationship* (Basingstoke, UK and New York: Palgrave Macmillan, 2012).

3. Cf. *Literary Couplings: Writing Couples, Collaborators, and the Construction of Authorship*, ed. Marjorie Stone and Judith Thompson (Madison, WI: University of Wisconsin Press, 2006).

4. Jeffrey Cox, *Poetry and Politics in the Cockney School: Keats, Shelley, Hunt and Their Circle* (Cambridge: Cambridge University Press, 1998); Greg Kucich, "'The Wit in the Dungeon': Leigh Hunt and the Insolent Politics of Cockney Coteries," *European Romantic Review*, 10 (1999), 242–53 and "Cockney Chivalry: Hunt, Keats and the Aesthetics of Excess," in *Leigh Hunt: Life, Poetics, Politics*, ed. Nicholas Roe (London: Routledge, 2003), pp. 118–34; Gregory Dart, *Metropolitan Art and Literature, 1810–1840: Cockney Adventures* (Cambridge: Cambridge University Press, 2012).

5. Clare was so called by Charles Elton in "The Idler's Epistle to John Clare," *The London Magazine* (August 1824), 143–45. On Clare's participation in a Cockney coterie centered on J. H. Reynolds, see Simon Kövesi, "John Hamilton Reynolds, John Clare and the *London Magazine*," *The Wordsworth Circle*, 42.3 (2011), 226–35.

6. See David Stewart, *Romantic Magazines and Metropolitan Literary Culture* (Basingstoke, UK: Palgrave Macmillan, 2011); William Christie, *The Edinburgh Review in the Literary Culture of Romantic Britain: Mammoth and Megalonyx* (London: Pickering and Chatto, 2009); Mark Schoenfield, *British Periodicals and Romantic Identity*

(New York and Basingstoke, UK: Palgrave Macmillan, 2009); Richard Cronin, *Paper Pellets: British Literary Culture after Waterloo* (Oxford: Oxford University Press, 2010).

7. Jon Klancher, *The Making of English Reading Audiences 1790–1832* (Madison: University of Wisconsin Press, 1987).

8. Lee Erickson, *The Economy of Literary Form: English Literature and the Industrialization of Publishing, 1800–1850* (Baltimore: Johns Hopkins University Press, 1996).

9. Andrew Franta, *Romanticism and the Rise of the Mass Public* (Cambridge: Cambridge University Press, 2007).

10. On this aspect of Byron's writing see Tom Mole, *Byron's Romantic Celebrity: Industrial Culture and the Hermeneutic of Intimacy* (Basingstoke, UK and New York: Palgrave Macmillan, 2007).

11. See Kevin Gilmartin, *Print Politics: The Press and Radical Opposition in Early Nineteenth-Century England* (Cambridge: Cambridge University Press, 1996); Paul Keen, *The Crisis of Literature in the 1790s: Print Culture and the Public Sphere* (Cambridge: Cambridge University Press, 1999).

12. By the 1820s there was a new prestige in becoming a writer of essays for popular magazines or a reviewer for journals: such a writer was no longer necessarily seen as a hack but was, prospectively at least, an author—while an epic poet, traditionally the most high-status author, might find himself viewed as out-of-date and out-of-touch. See Erickson, *The Economy of Literary Form*.

13. A term retrospectively applied in *The Antijacobin Review and True Churchman's Magazine*, 50 (1816), 825.

14. Jack Stillinger, *Multiple Authorship and the Myth of Solitary Genius* (Oxford: Oxford University Press, 1991).

15. For example Coleridge/Southey's *Joan of Arc*, "Vision of the Maid of Orleans," "Destiny of Nations," "Mohammed," "The Devil's Thoughts," as well as a series of jointly written sonnets. Wordsworth/Coleridge's "Barberry Tree," and "Solitude of Binnorie."

16. Margaret J. M. Ezell, *Social Authorship and the Advent of Print* (Baltimore: Johns Hopkins University Press, 1999).

17. Lucy Newlyn, *Reading, Writing and Romanticism: The Anxiety of Reception* (Oxford: Oxford University Press, 2000), and "Dorothy Wordsworth's Experimental Style," *Essays in Criticism*, 57.4 (2007), 325–49.

18. Wolfson, *Romantic Interactions: Social Being and the Turns of Literary Action* (Baltimore: Johns Hopkins University Press, 2010).

19. Wolfson, *Romantic Interactions*, p. 2: "distinctive instances where a Romantic 'author' gets created, as a literary consciousness, in a web of reciprocally transforming and transformative creative subjects—in what I term *interaction*."

20. Ashley Cross, "Robert Southey and Mary Robinson in Dialogue," *The Wordsworth Circle*, 42.1 (2011), 10–17.

21. Sally Bushell, *Text as Process: Creative Composition in Wordsworth, Tennyson, and Dickinson* (Charlottesville and London: University of Virginia Press, 2009).

22. On the Wordsworth/Coleridge poetic relationship see Lucy Newlyn, *Coleridge, Wordsworth and the Language of Allusion*, 2nd edn. (Oxford: Oxford University Press, 2001); Stephen Prickett, *Coleridge and Wordsworth: The Poetry of Growth* (Cambridge: Cambridge University Press, 1980); Gene W. Ruoff, *Wordsworth and Coleridge: The Making of the Major Lyrics 1802–1804* (London: Harvester Wheatsheaf, 1989); Paul Magnuson, *Coleridge and Wordsworth: A Lyrical Dialogue* (Princeton: Princeton University Press, 1988).

23. Allusion: "An expression designed to call something to mind without mentioning it explicitly; an indirect or passing reference: mid 16th century (denoting a pun, metaphor, or parable)." Allude: "late 15th century (in the sense 'hint at, suggest'): from Latin *allus-*, *alludere*, from *ad-* 'towards' + *ludere* 'to play'" (OED). For a clear discussion of recent theorizations, including allusion's difference from intertextuality, see Gregory Machacek, "Allusion," *PMLA*, 122 (2007), 522–36 (pp. 523–24); and Stephen Hinds, *Allusion and Intertext: Dynamics of Appropriation in Roman Poetry* (Cambridge: Cambridge University Press, 1998).

24. I take it that allusion is normally a more self-dramatizing figure than borrowing and echo: it plays upon another text (literary or nonliterary—on a name, for example) in such a way that the playing text and that played upon are brought visibly into relation and the allusion is seen as the figure effecting that relation. As Christopher Ricks puts it, it incarnates relationship, even if the poet is not aware he is alluding: "Paradoxically it is often by courtesy of another, with the aid of allusion, that a poet becomes himself. Allusion calls into play 'the production of another person,' 'something given to him,' something 'scarcely his own'" (*Allusion to the Poets* [Oxford: Oxford University Press, 2003], p. 161). Likewise, Jonathan Bate argues in *Shakespeare and the English Romantic Imagination* (Oxford: Oxford University Press, 1986), p. 36: "Unconscious allusion shows that the precursor-text has literally penetrated the recesses of the later writer's mind; it enables him to derive support from that text without becoming a plagiarist or ape, to speak words that are both his own and another's."

25. Even if allusions are normally more self-dramatizing than borrowings, nevertheless, there is no absolute distinction to be made between quieter allusions and the most obvious borrowings, although typically the latter, like echoes, are not self-dramatizingly foregrounded and may even be unwitting. Yet, even if borrowings do not comment on the text being invoked so strongly as do allusions, they do create conjunction between texts: two (or more) are called to the readers' mind as he reads one, ensuring that it is seen as using dialogic, or shared, language.

26. For a theorization of echo see John Hollander, *The Figure of Echo: A Mode of Allusion in Milton and After* (Berkeley and Los Angeles: University of California Press, 1981), for whom echo is distinguished from allusions that expect recognition by the reader: it is unconscious. Hollander's rehabilitation of echo is helpful; in order to establish it as a separate object of enquiry; however, he creates multiple distinct categories of allusion and borrowing that attempt to tie down allusion's playfulness. As Bate shows, in practice the categories bleed into each other: *Shakespeare and the English Romantic Imagination*, pp. 32–33.

27. Ricks, *Allusion to the Poets*, p. 157. Ricks's emphasis on allusion as a form of play that operates a flexible relationship (as in the play between wheel and axle)—does away with the insistence that allusions must be conscious on the alluder's part (for which see William Irwin, "What Is an Allusion," *The Journal of Aesthetics and Art Criticism*, 59.3 [2001], 287–97). It also supersedes arguments that attempt to pin allusion down as a mode of oblique reference to another text that must include a "marker" that an unknown reader can be expected to recognize—for example, Carmela Perri, "On Alluding," *International Review for the Theory of Literature*, 7.3 (1978), 289–307. As M. H. Abrams points out, many allusions appeal not to an unknown reader's expectations but to a private, coterie audience of the author's acquaintance. "Allusion," *A Glossary of Literary Terms*, 6th edn. (Fort Worth, TX: Harcourt Brace College, 1993), p. 8.

28. Keats, Letter to George and Georgiana Keats, October 14, 1818. *The Letters of John Keats 1814–1821*, ed. Hyder A. Rollins (Cambridge, MA: Harvard University Press, 1958), I, 394.

29. On this, see Newlyn, *Coleridge, Wordsworth and the Language of Allusion*.

30. A few examples among many studies of satirical allusions in post-revolutionary politics are David V. Erdman, *Prophet against Empire: A Poet's Interpretation of the History of His Own Times* (Princeton: Princeton University Press, 1954); Carl Woodring, *Politics in English Romantic Poetry* (Cambridge, MA: Harvard University Press, 1970); John Barrell, *Imagining the King's Death: Figurative Treason, Fantasies of Regicide, 1793–1796* (Oxford: Oxford University Press, 2000); Vic Gatrell, *City of Laughter: Sex and Satire in Eighteenth-Century London* (London: Atlantic Books, 2006).

31. The prevalence of allusion as a Romantic compositional method has been demonstrated, with regard to Shakespeare, by Bate, in *Shakespeare and the English Romantic Imagination*, with regard to Milton, by Lucy Newlyn, in *Paradise Lost and the Romantic Reader* (Oxford: Oxford University Press, 1993), and with regard to eighteenth-century poets, by Ricks, in *Allusion to the Poets*. Also, Edwin Stein, *Wordsworth's Art of Allusion* (University Park: Pennsylvania State University Press, 1988).

32. Edward W. Said, *Orientalism: Western Conceptions of the Orient* (London and New York: Penguin, 1978); Nigel Leask, *British Romantic Writers and the East: Anxieties of Empire* (Cambridge: Cambridge University Press, 1993); Javed Majeed, *Ungoverned Imaginings. James Mill's the History of British India and Orientalism* (Oxford: Oxford University Press, 1992); Saree Makdisi, *Romantic Imperialism: Universal Empire and the Culture of Modernity* (Cambridge: Cambridge University Press, 1998).

33. Stuart Curran, "Mary Robinson's *Lyrical Tales* in Context," in *Re-Visioning Romanticism: British Women Writers, 1776–1837*, ed. Carol Shiner Wilson and Joel Haefner (Philadelphia: Pennsylvania University Press, 1994), pp. 17–35; Marilyn Butler, *Literature as a Heritage, or, Reading Other Ways* (Cambridge: Cambridge University Press, 1988); Lynda Pratt, "Introduction," *Robert Southey: Poetical Works 1793–1810*, gen. ed. Lynda Pratt, 5 vols. (London: Pickering and Chatto, 2004), V.

34. On the social nature of allusion, see Susan Stewart, "The Pickpocket: A Study in Tradition and Allusion," *Modern Language Notes*, 95 (1980), 1127–54; Eleanor Cook, *Against Coercion: Games Poets Play* (Stanford, CA: Stanford University Press, 1998).

35. Felicity James, *Charles Lamb, Coleridge, and Wordsworth: Reading Friendship in the 1790s* (Basingstoke, UK and New York: Palgrave Macmillan, 2008), p. 3. See also Levy, *Family Authorship and Romantic Print Culture*, pp. 45–69.

36. David Fairer, *Organising Poetry: The Coleridge Circle, 1790–1798* (Oxford: Oxford University Press, 2009), pp. 212–13.

37. Part of this term's pejorative force was its reference to the market-driven ethos of London's lower middle-class shopkeepers, tradesmen, and artisans.

38. Thus, we see allusion indicating affinity and mutuality but also, as Lucy Newlyn notes, "register[ing], on a more submerged level, disparity, aggression, and unease." Newlyn, *Coleridge, Wordsworth and the Language of Allusion*, p. xv.

39. See the work on patronage and professionalization of Dustin Griffin, *Literary Patronage in England, 1650–1800* (Cambridge: Cambridge University Press, 1996); and Scott Hess, *Authoring the Self: Self-Representation, Authorship and the Print Market* (London and New York: Routledge, 2004).

40. On this for Clare see Jonathan Bate, *John Clare: A Biography* (London: Picador, 2003), pp. 198–203.

41. See *The Letters of Robert Bloomfield and His Circle*, ed. Tim Fulford and Lynda Pratt, Romantic Circles Editions. http://www.rc.umd.edu/editions/bloomfield_letters/

42. The title of his first London collection.

43. Bate, *Clare: A Biography*, pp. 204–8, 221–22.

1 THE POLITICIZATION OF ALLUSION IN EARLY ROMANTICISM: MARY ROBINSON AND THE BRISTOL POETS

1. See Colin Campbell, *The Romantic Ethic and the Spirit of Modern Consumerism* (Oxford: Blackwell, 1987). Also, Daniela Garofalo, *Women, Love, and Commodity Culture in British Romanticism* (Farnham, UK and Burlington, VT: Ashgate, 2012).
2. Coleridge, *Opus Maximum*, ed. Thomas McFarland (London and Princeton: Princeton University Press, 2002), p. 126.
3. Quoted in John Barrell, *Imagining the King's Death: Death: Figurative Treason, Fantasies of Regicide 1793–1796* (Oxford: Oxford University Press, 2000), p. 213.
4. In his *Imagining the King's Death* Barrell cites, from 1794, many regicidal allusions to the death and execution of kings, most of which refer not to George III himself, but to "kings" or "tyrants"—though Baxter's mock playbill "LA GUILLOTINE; or GEORGE'S HEAD IN THE BASKET" did name the king, but took the form of a parody of a dramatic entertainment rather than a statement of intent (pp. 213–15). See also Michael Scrivener, *Seditious Allegories: John Thelwall and Jacobin Writing* (University Park: Pennsylvania State University Press, 2001), pp. 102–5.
5. "Reflections on Having Left a Place of Retirement," published in the *Monthly Magazine* for October 1796 and Coleridge's *Poems* (1797); lines 11–13 (CPW, I, i, 262).
6. Quoted in Neil Rennie, *Far-Fetched Facts: The Literature of Travel and the Idea of the South Seas* (Oxford: Oxford University Press, 1998), p. 101.
7. Line 2 of the sonnet "The world is too much with us; late and soon."
8. Ibid., line 4.
9. Benedict Anderson, *Imagined Communities: Reflections on the Origin and Spread of Nationalism* (London: Verso, 1983).
10. On Katterfelto and Cowper's attack on advertising, see John Strachan, *Advertising and Satirical Culture in the Romantic Period* (Cambridge: Cambridge University Press, 2007), p. 112; Paul Keen, *Literature, Commerce, and the Spectacle of Modernity, 1750–1800* (Cambridge: Cambridge University Press, 2012), p. 189.
11. On this see Paula Byrne, *Perdita: The Life of Mary Robinson* (London: Harper Collins, 2004), p. 192. Also, Judith Pascoe, *Romantic Theatricality: Gender, Poetry and Spectatorship* (Ithaca: Cornell University Press, 1997), p. 158.
12. Michael Gamer and Terry F. Robinson, "Mary Robinson and the Dramatic Art of the Comeback," *SiR*, 48.2 (2009), 219–56.
13. In this respect, Robinson was attempting to direct to her own benefit what Laura Brown has argued was a popular motif of the time—in

which the figure of Lady Credit imaged the speculative financial system as a stereotypical woman (given to unpredictable fluctuation and contradiction). *Fables of Modernity: Literature and Culture in the English Eighteenth Century* (Ithaca: Cornell University Press, 2001), pp. 96–97.

14. Della Cruscanism was "a commercial democratisation and eroticisation of the ideal of sociability" according to Jon Mee, "'Reciprocal expressions of kindness': Robert Merry, Della Cruscanism and the Limits of Sociability," in *Romantic Sociability: Social Networks and Literary Culture in Britain 1770–1840*, ed. Gillian Russell and Clara Tuite (Cambridge: Cambridge University Press, 2002), pp. 104–22 (p. 108).

15. William Gifford, *The Maeviad*, line 103. In *The Baviad and Maeviad* (London, 1827).

16. *The Baviad*, lines 27–28.

17. Quoted in Byrne, *Perdita*, p. 273.

18. Quoted in E. P. Thompson, *The Romantics: England in a Revolutionary Age* (New York: The New Press, 1997), p. 302.

19. Quoted in Thompson, *The Romantics*, p. 44.

20. *The Tribune: A Periodical Publication, Consisting Chiefly of the Political Lectures of John Thelwall* (London, 1795), pp. 285–86.

21. Thompson, *The Romantics*, p. 44.

22. Coleridge, *Lectures 1795, on Politics and Religion*, ed. Lewis Patton and Peter Mann (London and Princeton: Princeton University Press, 1971), p. xxxiii.

23. Anne Frances Randall, *A Letter to the Women of England on the Injustice of Mental Subordination* (London, 1799), pp. 76–77.

24. On this see Adriana Craciun, *Fatal Women of Romanticism* (Cambridge: Cambridge University Press, 2003), pp. 66–67.

25. *Angelina*, p. 121, vol. III, ed. Sharon M. Setzer, of MRW.

26. *The Beauties of the Anti-Jacobin* (1799), p. 306.

27. On this fashion see David Dabydeen, *Hogarth's Blacks: Images of Blacks in Eighteenth Century English Art* (Manchester: Manchester University Press, 1987).

28. Timothy Morton, "Blood Sugar," in *Romanticism and Colonialism: Writing and Empire, 1780–1830*, ed. Tim Fulford and Peter J. Kitson (Cambridge: Cambridge University Press, 1998), pp. 87–106.

29. *Watchman*, pp. 90–91. On Coleridge's engagement with Wollstonecraft's feminism, see Anya Taylor, "Coleridge, Wollstonecraft and the Rights of Women," in *Coleridge's Visionary Languages: Essays in Honour of J. B. Beer*, ed. Tim Fulford and Morton D. Paley (Cambridge: D. S. Brewer, 1993), pp. 83–98.

30. See Ashley J. Cross, "Robert Southey and Mary Robinson in Dialogue," *The Wordsworth Circle*, 42.1 (2011), 10–17.

31. The imagery of plumes, leafless boughs, loftier flights, and soft glances echoes that beloved of Robinson in her Della Cruscan, flowery, highly emotive phase.

32. Coleridge's poem and its companion piece (for which see CI, I, 312, 316; CPW, II, i, 339–45) draw upon Burns's "Now Westlin Winds" in their use of bird imagery to make lyric statements that are applicable to humankind.

33. Vol. I, ed. Daniel Robinson, of MRW.

34. This context is detailed by Ashley Cross, "Coleridge and Robinson: Harping on Lyrical Exchange," in *Fellow Romantics: Male and Female British Writers, 1790–1835*, ed. Beth Lau (Farnham, UK and Burlington, VT: Ashgate, 2009), pp. 39–70.

35. On these explanations see Susan Luther, "A Stranger Minstrel: Coleridge's Mrs. Robinson," *SiR*, 33.3 (1994), 391–409.

36. *The Morning Post*, February 12, 1798.

37. On the language of friendship see David Fairer, *Organising Poetry: The Coleridge Circle, 1790–1798* (Oxford: Oxford University Press, 2009), p. 213: "poetic organisation...is the medium through which friendship operates." See also Raimonda Modiano, "Coleridge and Wordsworth: The Ethics of Gift Exchange and Literary Ownership," *The Wordsworth Circle*, 20.2 (1999), 113–20. On Lamb's resentment that Coleridge revised his allusive verse, see Felicity James, *Charles Lamb, Coleridge and Wordsworth: Reading Friendship in the 1790s* (Basingstoke, UK and New York: Palgrave Macmillan, 2008), pp. 59–62.

38. On their poetics of friendship see, as well as Fairer, *Organising Poetry*; James, *Reading Friendship*; Michelle Levy, *Family Authorship and Romantic Print Culture* (Basingstoke, UK and New York: Palgrave Macmillan, 2007); Gurion Taussig, *Coleridge and the Idea of Friendship, 1789–1804* (London and Cranbury, NJ: Associated University Presses, 2002).

39. Lamb's seventh sonnet in *Poems* (1797) has these bathetic lines: "My lov'd companion dropt a tear, and fled / And hid in deepest shades her awful head" (lines 9–10; p. 223).

40. *Poems* (1797), lines 20–31, pp. 111–15; CPW, I, i, 276.

41. See Lloyd's "Christmas," lines 23, and "Stanzas Written after a Journey into North Wales," line 13, *Poems* (1797), pp. 183 and 271.

42. "Religious Musings," line 366, p. 144; "Songs of the Pixies," VI, line 1, p. 37; "On the Christening of a Friend's Child," line 11, p. 264.

43. Robinson uses it in "To the Poet Coleridge" line 10, and "The Haunted Beach" line 77 (MRW, I); Robert Merry used it to refer to the "mystic strain" of "extatic Poetry," which is female and accompanies genius. "Genius in Diversity. A Poem" (London, 1788), lines 51, 33 (pp. 14, 13).

44. On the renewal of the Lamb, Lloyd, Coleridge axis around Southey, and the politics of friendship therein, see James, *Reading Friendship*, p. 123; Harriet Guest, in *Unbounded Attachment: Sentiment and Politics in the Age of the French Revolution* (Oxford: Oxford University

Press, 2013), pp. 103–6, assesses Lloyd's extension of friendship to Mary Wollstonecraft.

45. Lamb's letter to Robert Lloyd, November 13, 1798, *The Letters of Charles and Mary Lamb*, ed. Edwin J. Marrs (Ithaca and London: Cornell University Press, 1975), I, 144.

46. Cross, "Robert Southey and Mary Robinson in Dialogue," 15.

47. SL 462. Southey to Coleridge, December 15, 1799.

48. See Nicola Trott, "Poemets and Poemlings: Robert Southey's Minority Interest," *Robert Southey and the Contexts of English Romanticism*, ed. Lynda Pratt (Aldershot, UK and Burlington, VT: Ashgate, 2006), pp. 69–86 (p. 82): "It provided for maximum diversity of personae with minimum risk of exposure. [It was] at once self-promoting and self-protective."

49. Southey, Cross shows, marked it out as such in the advertisement for the first, 1799, volume, which likened it to the literary almanacs in which the fashionable ballads of Schiller and Burger had appeared. See also Barbara Benedict, "The Paradox of the Anthology: Collecting and *Différance* in Eighteenth-Century Britain," *New Literary History*, 34 (2003), 231–56.

50. *Monthly Magazine*, 9 (1801), 32; *Anti-Jacobin*, 8 (1800), 412.

51. The phrase, from the introduction that Coleridge wrote for Robinson's "The Solitude of Binnorie" when it was published in the *Morning Post*, is quoted in EOT, III, 291.

52. I quote the seventh stanza, lines 55–63, from the text included in *Annual Anthology*, 2 (1800), 256. Cf. Mary Robinson, *Lyrical Tales* (London, 1800; facsimile rpt. Oxford: Woodstock Books, 1989), pp. 72–77.

53. Exceptions include Trott, "Poemets" and Cross, "Robert Southey and Mary Robinson in Dialogue."

54. Luther, "A Stranger Minstrel," 408.

55. Cited in SPW, V, xxv.

56. In the *Anti-Jacobin* of December 1797, Southey's "The Soldier's Wife" was parodied.

57. *The Morning Post*, October 14, 1800.

58. On this collection see Ashley J. Cross, "From Lyrical Ballads to Lyrical Tales: Mary Robinson's Reputation and the Problem of Literary Debt," *SiR*, 40 (2001), 571–605, esp. 583.

59. See Stuart Curran, "Mary Robinson's *Lyrical Tales* in Context," in *Re-visioning Romanticism: British Women Writers, 1776–1837*, ed. Carol Shiner Wilson and Joel Haefner (Philadelphia: University of Pennsylvania Press, 1994), pp. 17–35.

60. On this see Daniel Robinson, *The Poetry of Mary Robinson: Form and Fame* (Basingstoke, UK and New York: Palgrave Macmillan, 2011), pp. 164–67.

61. See Stuart Curran, "Mary Robinson's *Lyrical Tales* in Context," 22–23, where Curran points out that Robinson's interlocutor in *Lyrical Tales* is more Southey than Wordsworth. On *Lyrical Tales*,

also see Lisa Vargo, "Tabitha Bramble and the *Lyrical Tales*," *Women's Writing*, 9.1 (2002), 37–52.

62. Line 179 of "The Female Vagrant" (WLB, p. 56).

63. Line 1 of Book I of the 1798–1799 two-book *Prelude*.

64. See Simon Bainbridge, "'Was it for this [...]?': The Poetic Histories of Southey and Wordsworth," *RaVon*, 32–33 (November 2003/ February 2004). http://www.erudit.org/revue/ron/2003/v/n32-33/009258ar.html. Bainbridge notes this allusion to Ariosto, *Orlando Furioso*, III, 475—Orlando is rebuked for becoming a lover rather than the warrior hero that he had been educated to be, renouncing his expected historical role "Was it for this, thy infancy I bred." See *The Orlando of Ariosto Reduced to XXIV Books*, trans. John Hoole, 2 vols. (London, 1791). In *The Aeneid*, IV, 895 "Was it for this" is the anguished question asked by Dido's sister as she realizes the queen has killed herself, grief stricken by Aeneas's abandonment. For its implicit historical and political import in *The Prelude*, see H. H. Erskine-Hill, *Poetry of Opposition and Revolution: Dryden to Wordsworth* (Oxford: Oxford University Press, 1996), p. 184, who shows that it is linked with the discussion of "this time / Of dereliction and dismay" in the second book of the poem (*Prelude*, 1798–1799, II, 486–87).

2　Brothers in Lore: Fraternity and Priority in *Thalaba*, "Christabel," and "Kubla Khan"

1. Charles H. Parry, in a journal-letter headed "Göttingen May 4, 1799," Bodleian MS Eng. misc.d.608 f 181^r.

2. In *Poems, consisting chiefly of Translations from the Asiatic Languages. To which are added, two Essays, I. On the Poetry of the Eastern Nations. II. On the Arts, Commonly Called Imitative* (Oxford, 1772). On Jones's influence see Michael J. Franklin, *Sir William Jones: Selected Poetical and Prose Works* (Cardiff: University of Wales Press, 1995).

3. Edward Said, *Orientalism: Western Conceptions of the Orient* (London and New York: Penguin, 1978).

4. See Javed Majeed, *James Mill's the History of British India and Orientalism* (Oxford: Oxford University Press, 1992); Nigel J. Leask, *Romantic Writers and the East: Anxieties of Empire* (Cambridge: Cambridge University Press, 1993). Also, Diego Saglia, "Words and Things: Southey's East and the Materiality of Oriental Discourse," in *Robert Southey and the Contexts of English Romanticism*, ed. Lynda Pratt (Aldershot, UK: Ashgate, 2006), pp. 167–86.

5. See Harold Bloom, "The Internalisation of the Quest Romance," *Romanticism and Consciousness: Essays in Criticism*, ed. Harold Bloom (New York: W. W. Norton, 1970), pp. 3–23.

6. See Southey's letter of October 18, 1799 to Humphry Davy, "At Exeter the advantage of a good library induced me to employ my time in laying in materials, a magazine of information, winter-stores for this country, where there is a dearth of books. So I travelled into Egypt & the Levant & Persia & the East Indies with every traveller whom I could find going that way—Fryer—Olearius—Mandelslo—De la Roque—the lying Lucas—Chardin the Jeweller who is worth them all," SL 447.

7. Elizabeth Schneider, *Coleridge, Opium and "Kubla Khan"* (Chicago: University of Chicago Press, 1953; rpt. New York: Octagon Books, 1966), pp. 132, 208.

8. *A Memoir of the Life and Writings of the Late William Taylor of Norwich.* ed. J. W. Robberds, 2 vols. (London, 1843), I, 227.

9. Francis Jeffrey, review of Robert Southey, *Thalaba the Destroyer*, *Edinburgh Review*, 1 (1803), 63–82.

3 SIGNIFYING NOTHING: COLERIDGE'S VISIONS OF 1816—ANTI-ALLUSION AND THE POETIC FRAGMENT

1. See for example Marjorie Levinson, *The Romantic Fragment Poem: A Critique of a Form* (Chapel Hill: University of North Carolina Press, 1986).

2. See for example Thomas McFarland, *Romanticism and the Forms of Ruin: Wordsworth, Coleridge, the Modalities of Fragmentation* (Princeton: Princeton University Press, 1981).

3. Marjorie Levinson, *Wordsworth's Great Period Poems* (Cambridge: Cambridge University Press, 1986), pp. 35–38.

4. *Examiner*, September 8, 1816, 571–73.

5. Cf. Frederic Jameson's account of the disguised appearance in texts of a political unconscious: "Terms or nodal points implicit in the ideological system which have, however, remained unrealized in the surface of the text, which have failed to become manifest in the logic of the narrative, and which we can therefore read as what the text represses" (*The Political Unconscious. Narrative as a Socially Symbolic Act* [Ithaca: Cornell University Press, 1981], p. 48).

6. Thomas Moore, Review of *Christabel*, *Edinburgh Review*, 27 (September 1816), 58–67. In *Coleridge: the Critical Heritage*, ed. J. R. de J. Jackson (London: Routledge and Kegan Paul, 1970), p. 235.

7. He prefaced it to a 1795 lecture and in 1811 published it in *The Courier*, August 31, 1811.

8. Review of *The Statesman's Manual*, *Edinburgh Review*, 27 (December 1816), 444–59. In *Coleridge: The Critical Heritage*, p. 264.

4　Positioning *The Missionary*: Poetic Circles and the Development of Colonial Romance

1. On these see David Fairer, *Organising Poetry: The Coleridge Circle, 1790–1798* (Oxford: Oxford University Press, 2009), pp. 99–100, 131–33, 169–70, 241–43.
2. July 22, 1794, CL, I, 94.
3. See Anthea Morrison, "Samuel Taylor Coleridge's Greek Prize Ode on the Slave Trade," in *An Infinite Complexity: Essays in Romanticism*, ed. J. R. Watson (Edinburgh: Edinburgh University Press, 1983), p. 147; Tim May, "Coleridge's Slave Trade Ode and Bowles's 'The African,'" *N&Q*, 54 (December 2007), 504–9.
4. "The African" appears in Bowles, *Monody, Written at Matlock* (London and Bath, 1791).
5. "The American Indian's Song," *Sonnets and Other Poems* (London, 1794), p. 98.
6. *The Poetical Works of William Hayley*, 3 vols. (Dublin, 1785), II, 243.
7. *A Voyage Round the World in the Year 1740, 1, 2, 3, 4; Compiled from Papers and Other Materials of the Right Honourable George Anson* (London, 1748), pp. 68–69.
8. Fairer, *Organising Poetry*, pp. 302–6.
9. *The Morning Post*, June 6, 1799; *The Times*, June 6, 1799, quoted in Joseph W. Donohue, *Dramatic Character in the English Romantic Age* (Princeton: Princeton University Press, 1970), p. 138.
10. II, 104.
11. See *Gentleman's Magazine*, 75.1 (January 1805), 57–59; *Monthly Review*, 51 (November 1806), 325; J. S. Mill's review of *Lettre aux Espagnols-Americains, par un de leurs compatriots*, *Edinburgh Review*, 13 (1809), 277–311.
12. (London, 1807), p. 61.
13. On the liberators in London see *Andres Bello, the London Years*, ed. John Lynch (Richmond, Surrey, UK: The Richmond Publishing Co., 1982).
14. See Karen Racine, *Francisco de Miranda A Transatlantic Life in the Age of Revolution* (Wilmington: University of Delaware Press, 2003), pp. 178–79.
15. Review of "Molina's Account of Chili," *Edinburgh Review*, 14 (1809), 333–53 (p. 336).
16. Giovanni Ignazio Molina, *The Geographical and Natural History of Chili*, 2 vols. (London, 1809).
17. William Lisle Bowles, *A Wiltshire Parson and His Friends. The Correspondence of W. L. Bowles*, ed. Garland Greever (London: Constable, 1926), p. 142.
18. *The Spirit of Discovery; or, the Conquest of Ocean* (London, 1804), p. xi.

19. *The Annual Review for 1805*, 4 (1806), 568–73.
20. Bowles, *Wiltshire Parson*, p. 149.
21. Ibid., p. 143.
22. See Robert Harvey, *Liberators: South America's Savage Wars of Freedom 1810–30* (London: Constable and Robinson, 2002), p. 339.
23. In her introduction to *Madoc*, vol. II of *Robert Southey: Poetical Works 1793–1811*, gen. ed. Lynda Pratt (London: Pickering and Chatto, 2004), p. xxix.
24. Cited in ibid.
25. *Edinburgh Review*, 7 (1805), 10, cited in ibid., p. xxix.
26. Eclogue 3, "Humphrey and William," SPW, V, 73. Cf. Bowles's "The American Indian's Song," *Sonnets and Other Poems*, pp. 97–98.
27. January 1816, quoted in *Wiltshire Parson*, p. 152.
28. Private communication, November 2005.
29. See C. J. Bayly, *Imperial Meridian: The British Empire and the World 1780–1830* (London and New York: Longman, 1989), p. 140 for a discussion of the rise of missionary societies at this point.
30. "As a poet, the author of *The Missionary* may compete with the foremost of his contemporaries. . . . that a poet's *last* poem should be his best, is his highest praise": Byron's *Observations upon "Observations" A Second Letter to John Murray, Esq. on the Rev. W. L. Bowles's Strictures on the Life and Writings of Pope* in *The Works of Lord Byron. Letters and Journals*, ed. Rowland E. Prothero, 6 vols. (London, 1898–1901), V, 584.
31. For Bowles hoping Byron would add lines to this effect, see his letter of April 4, 1813, *Wiltshire Parson*, p. 143.
32. Quoted in John Lynch, *The Spanish American Revolutions 1808–1826*, 2nd ed. (New York and London: W. W. Norton, 1987), p. 155.
33. See Stephen E. Lewis, "Myth and the History of Chile's Araucanians," *Radical History Review*, 58 (1994), 112–41 (pp. 137ff.).

5 THE PRODUCTION OF A POET: ROBERT BLOOMFIELD, HIS PATRONS, AND HIS PUBLISHERS

1. From Bloomfield's enthusiastic letter to his brother George, April 19, 1801 (letter 52 of BL), cf. letter 94, September 2, 1802, wherein Bloomfield endorses Wordsworth's aim, in the Preface to *Lyrical Ballads*, of writing in "the language of men."
2. Byron, *English Bards and Scotch Reviewers*, note to lines 765–94. ByPW, I, 253–54.
3. Capel Lofft, *Laura; or, an Anthology of Sonnets*, 5 vols. (London, 1814), sonnet 506. Lofft's last line alludes to the fourth sonnet of Robinson's "Sappho and Phaon" sequence, lines 13–14: "Let pity waft my spirit to the blest / To mock the barb'rous triumphs of despair!"

4. *Laura*, sonnets 251, 252, 151.
5. *The Farmer's Boy*, ed. Peter Cochran (e-book), pp. 22–23; http://petercochran.files.wordpress.com/2011/08/robert-bloomfield-the-farmers-boy.pdf.
6. *The Seasons*, ed. James Sambrook (Oxford: Oxford University Press, 1981), "Summer," lines 432–36; 444–47.
7. *The Vanity of Human Wishes*, lines 1–2. *The Poems of Samuel Johnson*, ed. D. Nichol Smith and E. L. McAdam Jr., 2nd ed. (Oxford: Oxford University Press, 1974).
8. Milton, "L'Allegro," line 134.
9. I cite the text from its first publication in my article "To 'crown with glory the romantick scene': Robert Bloomfield's 'To Immagination' and the Discourse of Romanticism," *Romanticism*, 15.2 (2009), 181–200.
10. See the Wesleys' "Angels, Attend, 'Tis God Commands," lines 1–5, "Angels, attend, 'tis God commands / And make me now your care; / Hover around, and in your hands / My soul securely bear. // With outstretch'd wings my temples shade"; and "Which of the Petty Kings of Earth," lines 45–48, "And when our spirits we resign, / On outstretch'd wings they bear, / And lodge us in the arms Divine, / And leave for ever there." See *the Poetical Works of John and Charles Wesley*, 13 vols. (London, 1868–1872), I ("Angels, Attend"); XIII ("Which of the Petty Kings"). Lofft would emend "outstretch'd" to the less physical adjective "aetherial."
11. (London, 1742), "Night I. On Life, Death, and Immortality," lines 93–102.
12. Mark Akenside, *The Pleasures of Imagination* (London, 1744), Book II, 660–66.
13. Robert Bloomfield to Edward Brayley, April 13, 1804, BL 120.
14. *Anti-Jacobin Review*, 11 (1802), 394–97. See "Contextual Materials," in BL.
15. Mary Lloyd Baker, née Sharp (1778–1812), her cousin Catherine Sharp (1770–1843), her aunt (Elizabeth Prowse, née Sharp) of Wicken Park, Northamptonshire.
16. Cf. Tim Burke, "Colonial Spaces and National Identities in *The Banks of Wye*: Bloomfield and the Wye after Wordsworth," in *Robert Bloomfield: Lyric, Class, and the Romantic Canon*, ed. Simon White, John Goodridge, and Bridget Keegan (Lewisburg, PA: Bucknell University Press, 2006), pp. 89–112. See John Goodridge, "'That Deathless Wish of Climbing Higher': Robert Bloomfield on the Sugar Loaf," in *Wales and the Romantic Imagination*, ed. Damian Walford Davies and Lynda Pratt (Cardiff: University of Wales Press, 2007), pp. 161–79; Simon White, "Rethinking the History of the Wye: Robert Bloomfield's *The Banks of Wye*," *Literature and History*, 16.1 (2007), 46–58.
17. MS Journal: *Banks of Wye*.

18. MS Journal: *Banks of Wye*.
19. *Gray and Collins: Poetical Works*, ed. Roger Lonsdale (Oxford: Oxford University Press, 1977). All quotations from Gray's poems are taken from this edition.
20. "Grongar Hill" in *Poems by John Dyer* (London, 1761), p. 13.
21. Oliver Goldsmith, *The Deserted Village* (London, 1770), p. 23, lines 427–28.
22. Financial aid had come in the form of a small annuity from local aristocrat the third Duke of Grafton. After his death in 1811, the fourth Duke paid it irregularly.
23. Henry Hunt: a radical campaigner for reform of parliament and of the franchise.
24. The Rt. Rev. Richard Watson (1737–1816) was a clergyman and academic, who served as the Bishop of Llandaff from 1782 to 1816. The Rt. Rev. Beilby Porteous, Bishop of London was a notable preacher, a supporter of the Evangelical movement and the antislavery campaign, an opponent of Paine and revolutionary radicalism.
25. John Horne Tooke (1736–1812), a campaigner for parliamentary reform who was arrested and charged with treason in 1794 when, in alliance with the London Corresponding Society, he attempted to organize a radical convention. Thomas Hardy (1752–1832), like Bloomfield a London shoemaker, was a campaigner for parliamentary reform and the extension of the franchise. As an organizer of the London Corresponding Society he, like Horne Tooke, was tried for treason in 1794.
26. *May Day with the Muses* (London, 1822). All quotations from *May Day* are from this edition.

6   IAMB YET WHAT IAMB: ALLUSION AND DELUSION IN JOHN CLARE'S ASYLUM POEMS

1. G. J. De Wilde, quoted in Jonathan Bate, *John Clare: A Biography* (London and New York: Picador, 2003), p. 474.
2. "Clare had a great knack of personating those in whom he was particularly interested. He almost considered himself to represent the idiosyncracy of them of whom he spake, as I was Lord Byron, or I was the Marquis of Exeter, etc": Clare's fellow inmate at Northampton Asylum, William Jerom, quoted in Bate, *John Clare: A Biography*, p. 476.
3. For an incisive discussion of Clare's assumption of identities in the asylum as a means of surviving institutionalization, see Roger Sales, *John Clare: A Literary Life* (Basingstoke, UK and New York: Palgrave Macmillan, 2002), p. 144.
4. John Goodridge, *John Clare, Poetry and Community* (Cambridge: Cambridge University Press, 2012), Chapter 1: "Clare, Chatterton and Becoming a Poet."

5. Clare to Thomas Pringle, March 1832, quoted in Bate, *John Clare: A Biography*, p. 416.

6. Here I pursue a point made by Margaret Russett, who argues that "the act of writing commits him to ventriloquy or impersonation" in paragraph 10 of her article "'Wedding Gowns or Money from the Mint': Clare's Borrowed Inheritance," in *Romanticism and the Law. Romantic Circles Praxis*. http://www.rc.umd.edu/praxis/law/russett/mruss.htm. Accessed January 21, 2012.

7. In *The Life and Posthumous Writings of William Cowper*, ed. William Hayley, 3 vols. (London, 1803–1804), III.

8. *Adelphi* (London, 1816).

9. In *Poems by William Cowper*, 3 vols. (London, 1811), III, lxvii.

10. *Aikin's Select Works of the British Poets with Biographical and Critical Prefaces by Dr. Aikin* (London, 1820), p. 723.

11. The poem is included in *Select Works of the British Poets*, p. 794. Clare's copy is in the Clare Collection in the Northampton Public Library. Clare owned Cowper's *Works* (London, 1814), from the Walker's British Classics Series—autographed "John Clare 1819," *Poems* (London, 1815); *Poems* (London, 1818)—presented by Lord Radstock in February 1820—*Poems* (London, 1824).

12. Clare took Cowper's poems in his pocket when he went fishing and fondly remembered "tame hares and Johnny Gilpin." *John Clare by Himself*, ed. Eric Robinson and David Powell (Ashington, UK and Manchester: Mid-NAG and Carcanet, 1996), pp. 134–35.

13. Verse of which only a Knight Transcript survives. In *The Later Poems of John Clare, 1837–1864*, ed. Eric Robinson and David Powell, 2 vols. (Oxford: Oxford University Press, 1984), II, 871.

14. *John Clare by Himself*, pp. 42–43.

15. Taylor's introduction is reproduced in Mark Storey (ed.), *Clare: The Critical Heritage* (London and Boston: Routledge and Kegan Paul, 1973), p. 138.

16. From a letter to Taylor, October 1831, *The Letters of John Clare*, ed. Mark Storey (Oxford: Oxford University Press, 1985), p. 551.

17. The poem is dated late 1830 by the editors of the Oxford edition of Clare's poetry. See *John Clare Poems of the Middle Period*, vol. III, ed. Eric Robinson, David Powell, P. M. S. Dawson (Oxford: Oxford University Press, 1998), p. 440.

18. From a letter of July 12, 1820, *The Letters of John Clare*, pp. 86–87.

19. Sonnet 16, "To the Lord General Cromwell," line 14. Cf. *Paradise Lost*, X, 990–91.

20. In "'Sages and Patriots That Being Dead Do Yet Speak to Us': Readings of the English Revolution in the Late Eighteenth Century," *Prose Studies*, 14 (1991), 205–30.

21. The passage was first published in *The Unpublished and Uncollected Poems of William Cowper*, ed. Thomas Wright (London, 1900). My transcription from the manuscript, by permission of the trustees of

the Cowper and Newton Museum, may be compared with that in Cowper, III, 83.

22. Lynn Pearce, "John Clare's 'Child Harold': A Polyphonic Reading," *Criticism*, 31 (1989), 139–57.

23. *The Notebooks of S. T. Coleridge*, ed. Kathleen Coburn, 5 vols. (London and Princeton: Princeton University Press, 1957–2002).

24. Henceforth referred to as N MS 19.

25. Here, I take my impetus from Pearce, who argues that the several voices personated in the Child Harold notebook produce a dialogue or argument, in which Clare takes up different class positions: "The 'powerful' voices of the Byronic aristocrat, the biblical and the ballad-singer are continually challenged by the 'powerless': the peasant exile, the languishing courtly lover," in "John Clare's 'Child Harold,'" 152.

26. Knight to Joseph Stenson, March 3, 1846, in "John Clare: Some Unpublished Documents of the Asylum Period," *Northamptonshire Past and Present*, 3 (1964), 192.

27. Pearce ("John Clare's 'Child Harold,'" 146) sees the songs and ballads of the Childe Harold manuscript as disrupting, with a traditional, folk voice, Clare's "high culture" Byronic voice. In Notebook 19, the effect is not so much disruption as alignment of a conventional love lyric vocabulary of nature—flowers and nosegays—with the more intense and individual vision of a health-giving nature present in the Cowperian persona.

28. *The Task*, II, 1–4. In Cowper, II, 139. The phrase derives from Jeremiah 9.2.

29. *Later Poems*, I, 161.

30. N MS 19, p. 46; *Later Poems*, I, 187.

31. To Patty Clare, July 19, 1848; *The Letters of John Clare*, p. 657.

32. Bate, *John Clare: A Biography*, p. 416.

33. N MS 19, p. 68.

34. *Later Poems*, I, 200.

35. N MS 19, pp. 15–16 "Opening of the Seals Rev. Chapter 6th"; *Later Poems*, I, 151.

36. N MS 19, pp. 16–17; *Later Poems*, I, 168.

37. See *Don Juan*, Canto III, stanza 103; ByPW, V, 197–98.

38. N MS 19, p. 130; *Later Poems*, p. 208.

39. N MS 19, pp. 129–27; *The Letters of John Clare*, p. 661.

40. N MS 19 p. 30; *Later Poems*, I, 174.

41. Philip W. Martin, "Authorial Identity and the Critical Act: John Clare and Lord Byron," *Questioning Romanticism*, ed. John Beer (Baltimore: Johns Hopkins University Press, 1995), pp. 71–91; Anne Barton, "John Clare Reads Lord Byron," *Romanticism*, 2.2. (1996), 127–48; Simon Kövesi, "Masculinity, Misogyny and the Marketplace: Clare's 'Don Juan a Poem,'" in *John Clare: New Approaches*, ed. John Goodridge and Simon Kövesi (Helpston, UK: John Clare Society, 2001), pp. 187–201.

42. N MS 19, pp. 22–24 (first draft) and pp. 30–32 (fair copy: reproduced here); *Later Poems*, I, 175.

43. N MS 19, p. 6; *Later Poems*, I, 165.

44. N MS 19, pp. 6–7; *Later Poems*, I, 165.

45. N MS 19, pp. 88–86; *Later Poems*, I, 230.

7 ROMANTICISM LITE: TALKING, WALKING, AND NAME-DROPPING IN THE COCKNEY ESSAY

1. On the Romantic-era cultivation of an intimate persona for a mass readership, see Tom Mole, *Byron's Romantic Celebrity: Industrial Culture and the Hermeneutic of Intimacy* (Basingstoke, UK and New York: Palgrave Macmillan, 2007).

2. See Jonathan Bate, *John Clare: A Biography* (London and New York: Picador, 2003); John Goodridge, *John Clare, Poetry and Community* (Cambridge: Cambridge University Press, 2012).

3. See Anne D. Wallace, *Walking, Literature, and English Culture: The Origins and Uses of Peripatetic in the Nineteenth Century* (Oxford: Oxford University Press, 1993); Robin Jarvis, *Romantic Writing and Pedestrianism* (Basingstoke, UK: Macmillan, 1997); Celeste Langan, *Romantic Vagrancy: Wordsworth and the Simulation of Freedom* (Cambridge: Cambridge University Press, 1995).

4. Bloomfield quotes the last line of "Autumn" from his own *The Farmer's Boy* (London, 1800).

5. Text from Robert Bloomfield, *Selected Poems*, ed. John Goodridge, rev. ed. (Nottingham, UK: Trent Editions, 2007).

6. *HMS Thunderer*, a 74-gun ship of the line of the Royal Navy.

7. On Cockneyism in the essay and in verse see Jeffrey N. Cox, *Poetry and Politics in the Cockney School: Keats, Shelley, Hunt and Their Circle* (Cambridge: Cambridge University Press, 1999); Elizabeth Jones, "Keats in the Suburbs," *Keats-Shelley Journal*, 45 (1996), 23–43; Gregory Dart, "The Cockney Moment," *The Cambridge Quarterly*, 32.3 (2003), 203–23; Nicholas Roe, *Fiery Heart: The First Life of Leigh Hunt* (London: Pimlico, 2005).

8. Reviewers belittled Bloomfield for using the slangy, colloquial language of lower-class Londoners: "The author's humour is generally very poor; and the language of it too coarse even for his honesty of style of poetry," *The Eclectic Review*, 7 (December 1811), 1103–20. The author "wears much too great an air of familiarity with the reader, not unfrequently, as we shall see, degenerating into vulgarity," *The Critical Review*, 1 (April 1812), 375–79.

9. "A Rustic Walk and Dinner," *The Monthly Magazine*, 96 (July 1842), 233–40, 343–46.

10. On this see Jarvis, *Romantic Writing and Pedestrianism*, p. 215: "The poem ends in a benign, well-fed torpor of love and tolerance—the sort of easy-going goodwill that Hunt has communicated

throughout. To the end, the poem exudes 'Cockney' wit, charm and swagger, a kind of adult delinquency in language and behaviour."

11. "On Londoners and Country People," *The Complete Works of William Hazlitt*, ed. P. P. Howe, 21 vols. (London: Dent, 1930–1934), XII, 66–77.

12. Hazlitt praised the inn as a welcoming haven for the solitary walker in "On Going a Journey," *The Complete Works of William Hazlitt*, VIII, 181–88.

13. *Blackwood's Magazine*, 5 (November 1820), 208.

14. *The Letters of Charles and Mary Anne Lamb*, ed. Edwin W. Marrs (Ithaca: Cornell University Press, 1976), II, 177.

15. "The Superannuated Man," first published in *The London Magazine* (May 1825), *The Works of Charles Lamb*, ed. Thomas Hutchinson (Oxford: Oxford University Press, 1924), pp. 712–19.

16. A London brewer.

17. Thomas Hood, from *Hood's Own* (1827) in Edmund Blunden, *Charles Lamb: His Life Recorded by His Contemporaries* (London: Leonard & Virginia Woolf at the Hogarth Press, 1934), p. 164.

18. P. G. Patmore, *My Friends and Acquaintances*, 3 vols. (London, 1854), I, 29–40.

19. Ibid.

8 ALLUSIONS OF GRANDEUR: PROPHETIC AUTHORITY AND THE ROMANTIC CITY

1. *Critical Dissertation on the Eighteenth Chapter of Isaiah* (1799). Quoted in W. H. Oliver, *Prophets and Millennialists: The Uses of Biblical Prophecy in England from the 1790s to the 1840s* (Auckland: Auckland University Press, 1978), p. 52.

2. G. S. Faber, "Letters to the Author Convention," quoted in Oliver, *Prophets and Millennialists*, p. 61.

3. See Robert Hole, *Pulpits, Politics and Public England, 1760–1832* (Cambridge: Cambridge University Press, 1989); W. H. Oliver, *Prophets and Millennialists*; J. F. C. Harrison, *The Second Coming: Popular Millenarianism 1780–1850* (New Brunswick, NJ: Rutgers University Press, 1979).

4. See Jack Fruchtman, "The Apocalyptic Politics of Richard Price and Joseph Priestley," *Transactions of the American Philosophical Society*, 73/4 (1983), 1–121.

5. Richard Price, *A Discourse on the Love of our Country* (London, 1790), pp. 49–50.

6. Priestley was also attacked by Burke; the critique helped precipitate a number of alarmist attacks that presented prophecy as part of an international revolutionary conspiracy. See John Robison, *Proofs of a Conspiracy against all the Religions and Governments of Europe, Carried on in the Secret Meetings of Free-Masons, Illuminati and*

Reading Societies, etc., Collected from Good Authorities (Edinburgh, 1797); W. H. Reid, *The Rise and Dissolution of the Infidel Societies in this Metropolis* (London, 1800).

7. Burke, *Reflections on the Revolution in France* (London, 1790), p. 99.

8. Ibid., p. 100.

9. Thus, for example, Burke compared Price to the seventeenth-century regicide preacher Hugh Peters, who had also invoked the *nunc dimittis* and had ridden in triumph through London before the captive King Charles I.

10. See E. P. Thompson, *The Making of the English Working Class* (London: Gollancz, 1963). The culture of the artisan classes in London, though not the urban experience of London as such, is considered in the account of millenarian radicalism given by Iain McCalman, *Radical Underworld: Prophets, Revolutionaries and Pornographers in London, 1795–1840* (Cambridge: Cambridge University Press, 1988). See also Jon Mee, *Dangerous Enthusiasm: William Blake and the Culture of Radicalism in the 1790s* (Oxford: Oxford University Press, 1992); David Worrall, *Radical Culture: Discourse, Resistance and Surveillance, 1790–1820* (Hemel Hempstead: Harvester-Wheatsheaf, 1992).

11. A term applied to him in *The Evangelical Magazine* (February 1794), 82–83.

12. Lines 4–7; from Lee's *Songs from the Rock* (1795). Quoted in Jon Mee, "'The Doom of Tyrants': William Blake, Richard 'Citizen' Lee, and the Millenarian Public Sphere," in *Blake, Politics and History*, ed. Jackie DiSalvo, G. A. Rosso, and Christopher Z. Hobson (New York: Garland, 1998), pp. 97–114.

13. On the prevalence of allusions that connected George III with Nebuchadnezzar, see Mee, "The Doom of Tyrants," 110–11. On biblical prophecy bolstering radicals' imagination so as to let them overcome the psychological hold that legitimacy has established, see John Barrell, *Imagining the King's Death: Figurative Treason, Fantasies of Regicide 1793–1796* (Oxford: Oxford University Press, 2000).

14. Quoted in Mee, *Dangerous Enthusiasm*, p. 64.

15. From stanzas 2 to 4 of Spence's 1794 "Jubilee Hymn," quoted in Michael Scrivener, *Seditious Allegories: John Thelwall and Jacobin Writing* (University Park: Pennsylvania State University Press, 2001), pp. 103–5. The biblical allusions are to Isaiah 14 in which the trees celebrate the fact they will no longer be cut down to build tyrants' palaces.

16. As revealed by David Worrall, "William Bryan, Another Anti-Swedenborg Visionary Engraver of 1789," *Blake: An Illustrated Quarterly*, 34 (2000), 14–22.

17. Southey details their prophesying in *Letters from England: Translated from the Spanish by Don Manuel Alvarez Espriella* (1807), ed. Jack Simmons (London: Cresset Press, 1951), p. 422.

18. *A Revealed Knowledge of the Prophecies and the Times* (London, 1795), pp. 1, 47–48.

19. Mudie, *Babylon the Great: A Dissection and Demonstration of Men and Things in the British Capital*, 2 vols. (Philadelphia, 1825), II, 293 (labyrinth), I, 49 (insignificance).

20. Brothers, *A Description of Jerusalem* (London, 1801), p. 40.

21. Barrell, *Imagining the King's Death*.

22. (September 1825), 75.

23. Gregory Dart considers Martin's painting and improvement schemes in the context of London in "On Great and Little Things: Cockney Art in the 1820s," *Romanticism*, 14.2 (2008), 149–67.

24. Ian Balfour, *The Rhetoric of Romantic Prophecy* (Stanford, CA: Stanford University Press, 2002), p. 263.

25. Thomas Carlyle, *A Carlyle Reader*, ed. G. B. Tennyson (Cambridge: Cambridge University Press, 1984), p. 460.

26. John Scott's Prospectus to *The London Magazine*, 1 (January–June 1820), iv, alluding to the sonnet "Composed upon Westminster Bridge" in which Wordsworth portrays the city at dawn, unclogged by people or pollution, as the height of beauty—a portrayal very different from that made in *The Prelude* (an as-then still unpublished text that De Quincey knew and Scott did not).

27. *Autobiographical Sketches*, chapter VII "The Nation of London," in DeQ, XIX, 112.

28. My text is that of the 1821 *London Magazine* publication.

29. On the involuntary nature of De Quincey's dreams as a critical deconstruction of Coleridge's idealism, see Nigel Leask, *British Romantic Writers and the East: Anxieties of Empire* (Cambridge: Cambridge University Press, 1992), p. 223.

30. *Excursion*, II, 869–86. See the perceptive reading by Joshua Wilner, "The Stewed Muse of Prose: Wordsworth, De Quincey, Baudelaire," in *Feeding on Infinity: Readings in the Romantic Rhetoric of Internalisation* (Baltimore: Johns Hopkins University Press, 2000), pp. 68–77.

31. On Lowth's and Michaelis's redefinition of prophecy and inspiration see Stephen Prickett, *Words and* The Word: *Language, Poetics and Biblical Interpretation* (Cambridge: Cambridge University Press, 1986), Chapter 3.

32. On De Quincey's new definition, dividing literature from other kinds of writing on the basis of its ability to communicate power, see Jonathan Bate, "The Literature of Power: Coleridge and De Quincey," *Coleridge's Visionary Languages: Essays in Honour of J. B. Beer*, ed. Tim Fulford and Morton D. Paley (Cambridge: D. S. Brewer, 1993), pp. 137–50.

33. De Quincey's phrase is derived from Wordsworth's 1815 characterization of the poet (quoted in Bate, "The Literature of Power," p. 145).

34. Baudelaire adapted the city seen in the clouds into his *Petits poems en prose*, having translated *Confessions of an English Opium Eater*. On this, see Wilner, "The Stewed Muse." On De Quincey as the constructor of the Romanticism he knows in perverse form see Margaret Russett, *De Quincey's Romanticism: Canonical Minority and the Forms of Transmission* (Cambridge: Cambridge University Press, 1997), p. 189; on his inauguration of modernity see Alina Clej, *A Genealogy of the Modern Self: Thomas De Quincey and the Intoxication of Writing* (Basingstoke, UK: Palgrave Macmillan, 2001), p. 160.

35. Mudie, *Babylon the Great*, I, 77.

36. A tendency enshrined and perpetuated by Francis Turner Palgrave's anthology *A Golden Treasury of English Songs and Lyrics* (1861–1891), the enormous influence of which lasted into the second half of the twentieth century.

37. James Thomson's 1874 poem *City of Dreadful Night* found no redemption in London, configuring it as a benighted city of the lost:

O melancholy Brothers, dark, dark, dark!
O battling in black floods without an ark!
   O spectral wanderers of unholy Night!
My soul hath bled for you these sunless years,
With bitter blood-drops running down like tears:
   Oh dark, dark, dark, withdrawn from joy and light.

(lines 710–15), *The Poetical Works*,
ed. Bertram Dobell, 2 vols.
(London, 1895), I.

INDEX

Aikin, John
  Aikin's Select Works of the British Poets, 168
Akenside, Mark, 131
  The Pleasures of Imagination, 141
alienation, 4, 18, 39, 57, 60, 131–2, 140, 142–3, 174, 185, 191–3, 213, 220, 222–3, 224–5, 229–32. *See also* colonization of the self
allusion
  and coterie language, 1, 6–10, 17, 23–4, 30, 40–2, 52, 58, 61, 63, 100, 116–17, 148, 165–6, 189–90
  fundamental feature of Romantic poetry, 7, 78
  as hallmark of coterie style, 1, 9, 33, 46–7, 57, 68, 163
  in laboring-class poetry, 14–16, 131–2, 140, 142
  literalization of allusion, 18, 178, 217, 220, 221–2, 225–6
  as mark of friendship, 9, 15, 17, 24, 40–2, 50, 63, 73–4, 82, 100–1, 132, 144, 146–7, 150, 190, 199, 202, 204–5
  politicized allusion, 12–13, 23–4, 31–2, 47–50, 95, 215–17, 221
    reactionary allusions, 28, 30–1, 33, 34, 43, 47
    use by radicals, 8–9, 18, 24, 32–3
  and self-definition, 11, 19, 63, 68, 74, 77–8, 94, 139–40, 186

as substitute for literary community, 16–17, 160, 162–3, 167, 174, 186
types of allusion, 6–9
  allegory, 12, 74–5, 92–3, 99, 104–7, 109, 113, 116, 126, 231
  anti-allusion, 12, 79–81, 89, 95–6
  Biblical allusion, 18, 32–3, 47–8, 92, 106, 178–82, 185–6, 214–30 (*see also* prophecy)
  borrowing, 6–9, 11, 12–13, 16, 19, 41, 42, 45–6, 49, 54, 58–9, 68–9, 71, 72, 74, 94, 100, 102–3, 116–17, 148, 162, 185, 214, 228, 230, 232
  echo, 7, 9, 13, 16, 32–3, 42, 47, 48–9, 54, 61, 95, 100, 116–17, 121, 140, 148, 152, 155–6, 160–1, 165, 167, 179, 221, 232
  imitation, 9, 36, 100–1, 117, 138–9, 165, 166, 167, 174
  impersonation, 165–6, 167, 174, 179
  innuendo, 24, 30–1, 33, 47
  irony, 42, 48–50, 152, 176, 207
  name-dropping, 17, 135, 189–90, 198–9, 201–2, 204–5, 207–8, 209 (*see also* gossip)
  parody, 10–11, 34–5, 42–3, 47–8, 50–1, 52, 64
  puns, 202
  self-borrowing, 92, 94

Anderson, Benedict, 26
Annual Anthology, The, 10, 25, 40, 44–52, 54–5, 58, 61, 63, 73
Anson, George, 103
Anti-Jacobin Review, 45, 52
antislavery poems, 24–5, 55–60, 101–2, 123, 126
Ariosto, Ludovico, 58–9
Astley, Philip, 106
Athenaeum, The, 207
Augustanism, 15, 132, 139–42, 154
authenticity, 109, 133
authorial personae, 4, 165, 167, 174

Barlow, Joel
   Vision of Columbus, 140
Barrell, John, 221
Barton, Anne, 182
Bate, Henry, 28–9
Bate, Jonathan, 16, 177, 230
Bate, Mary, 28–9
Baudelaire, Charles, 231
Beaumont, Francis, 205
Beddoes, Thomas, 75
Blackwood's Edinburgh Magazine, 1, 2
Blake, William, 18, 25, 186, 229, 231
   Europe a Prophecy, 219
   Jerusalem, 221–2, 223
   Marriage of Heaven and Hell, The, 218
   Songs of Innocence and Experience, "London," 192, 220
Bligh, William, 123
Bloom, Harold, 72
Bloomfield, George, 134, 192, 194–5
Bloomfield, Robert, 3, 6, 8, 13–18, 131–63, 167, 192–7, 200, 205–7, 211
   Banks of Wye, The, 6, 14, 144–57
   Farmer's Boy, The, 14, 132–40, 142, 157, 192–3

May Day with the Muses, 159–63
   "Ode to Immagination," 15, 139–42
   Rural Tales, 14, 132, 142–3, 157
Bolivar, Simon, 110, 114
Bonaparte, Joseph, 110
Bonaparte, Napoleon, 85, 88, 104, 106, 109, 110, 113
Boo, Lee, 101
Bowles, William Lisle, 3, 8, 9, 12–13, 40, 41, 43, 99–103, 108–9, 112–26
   "African, The," 101–2
   "American Indian's Song, The," 102
   Missionary, The, 13, 99–100, 112–24
   Spirit of Discovery, The, 112–13, 115
"Bristol sound," the, 5, 9–10, 23–5, 42–5, 47, 63, 100
Brothers, Richard, 219–22, 226, 229
Bryan, William, 219, 221, 229
Burke, Edmund, 221, 222
   Reflections on the Revolution in France, 216–17
Burke, William, 110
Burns, Robert, 37, 167, 175
Bushell, Sally, 6
Butler, Marilyn, 9
Butler, Samuel, 15, 132, 152
   Hudibras, 146, 147–8
Byron, Lord, 4, 12, 13, 16, 89, 90, 91, 99–100, 113, 120, 125, 135, 157
   Age of Bronze, The, 123
   Childe Harold's Pilgrimage, 182
   "Darkness," 177, 183–6
   Don Juan, 165, 180, 182
   Giaour, The, 99
   Island, The, 123–4
   John Clare's impersonation of, 165, 167, 174–5, 178, 182–5

Carlyle, Thomas, 223
celebrity, 4, 17, 25, 26, 28–30, 90,
    138–9, 190, 198–9, 209
Charles II, 161
Chatterton, Thomas, 10, 39, 40,
    51, 64, 166
Churchill, John, 1st Duke of
    Marlborough, 50
Clare, Charles, 174
Clare, John, 3, 6, 8, 13–14,
    16–17, 134, 143, 165–86,
    191, 214
    Asylum notebooks, 16–17, 167,
        173–86
    "Child Harold," 182
    "Don Juan," 182
    "Fallen Elm, The," 169–73
    "Favourite Place, A," 182
    Midsummer Cushion, The, 167
    "Song Last Day," 182–4
    Village Minstrel, The, 169
    "Wreck of the Emelie, The,"
        185–6
Clare, Martha, 181
Clarkson, Thomas, 34
Clive, Robert, 214
Cobbett, William, 159
Cochran, Peter, 136
Coleridge, Samuel Taylor, 2–7,
    9–13, 17–18, 23–5, 32–61,
    63–78, 79–97, 100–1, 107,
    108, 112–13, 123, 135, 157,
    167, 175, 189–90, 204–5,
    213, 215, 222–3, 230
    "Apotheosis; or, the Snow-drop,"
        38, 45
    Biographia Literaria, 189
    "Christabel," 11, 12, 75–8, 80,
        90, 93, 96
    Christabel: Kubla Khan, A
        Vision; The Pains of Sleep,
        80–2, 89–91, 92, 93, 94
    "Composed While Climbing
        the Left Ascent of Brockley
        Coomb, in the County of
        Somerset," 41

Conversation poems, 13, 36,
    64, 190 (see also individual
    poems)
"Dejection: An Ode," 12, 71, 82
"Destiny of Nations, The," 38
Fall of Robespierre, The, 66
"Fears in Solitude," 24, 58, 104
"Fire, Famine and Slaughter," 10,
    47–50
"Foster Mother's Tale, The," 102–3
"France: an Ode," 35, 88–9, 104
Friend, The, 4, 6, 34, 189
"Frost at Midnight," 16
"Greek Ode," 101
"Kubla Khan," 11, 12, 44, 65–6,
    68–75, 77–8, 80, 90, 93–4,
    112, 222
Lay Sermon, 81, 91–7
"Lewti," 46
"Lines Written in a Concert
    Room," 73
"Mohammed," 11, 65–8, 70–2,
    75, 77
"Monody on the Death of
    Chatterton," 44
Nehemiah Higginbottom son-
    nets, 42–3
Notebooks, 17, 81, 83–5, 88,
    95–6, 174, 186
"Ode to the Rain," 93
"On the Christening of a Friend's
    Child," 42
"Pains of Sleep, The," 11–12,
    80–3, 86–91, 94–5, 97
Piccolomini, The, 73
Poems (1797), 36, 40–2
"Raven, The," 50
"Reflections on a Place of
    Retirement," 25
"Religious Musings," 42, 215
"Rime of the Ancyent Marinere,"
    45–6, 49, 52–5, 112
Sibylline Leaves, 190
"Songs of the Pixies," 42, 44
Sonnets from Various Authors, 6,
    40, 100–1

Coleridge, Samuel
    Taylor—*Continued*
    Statesman's Manual, The, 96–7,
        223
    "Stranger Minstrel, A," 60–1
    "This Lime-Tree Bower My
        Prison," 10, 15, 46, 64, 211
    "To a Young Ass," 43
    "To a Young Lady with a Poem
        on the French Revolution,"
        101
    "To an Unfortunate Woman,
        Whom I Knew in the
        Days of Her Innocence:
        Composed at the Theatre,"
        36–7, 52
    "To C. Lloyd, on his Proposing
        to Domesticate with the
        Author," 41
    "To Simplicity," 42
    "Vision of the Maid of Orleans, a
        Fragment," 37–8
    Watchman, The, 32, 39–40
Coleridge, Sarah, 82–3
Collins, William, 140
colonial romance, 12–13, 99–100,
        115–16. *See also* Bowles, *The
        Missionary*
colonialism, 4, 8, 26, 34, 50,
        55–60, 126–7, 214
colonization of the self, 191,
        193–4, 205–7, 210. *See also*
        alienation
Combe, William
    *The Tour of Doctor Syntax, in
        Search of the Picturesque*, 148
commodification, 4, 7–10, 12–13,
        14, 17–19, 23–9, 33–5, 39,
        42, 44, 45, 50–1, 55–60,
        94, 123, 126, 135–6, 206,
        211, 213, 220, 224, 227,
        230–1
Conan Doyle, Sir Arthur, 231
confession, 3, 7, 11–12, 49, 57,
        79–81, 89, 91, 96, 97, 173,
        184, 186, 213. *See also* De

Quincey, *Confessions of an
        English Opium Eater*
Conrad, Joseph, 231
conversation, 6, 13, 32, 40, 64,
        68, 72, 74, 77, 84–5, 132,
        146, 152–3, 157, 190, 194,
        198–208. *See also* speech
Cooper, Astley, 144
Cooper, Robert Bransby, 144–5
Cortes, Hernan, 104
coteries
    Bristol coterie, 5, 8–10, 11, 13,
        23–5, 39–61, 63, 64, 78,
        82–3, 100, 108, 109, 166,
        211
    Cockney coteries, 1, 3, 13–14,
        16, 17–19, 90, 166–7,
        189–91, 197–211, 213,
        223–4, 225, 229, 230, 231–2
    Della Cruscans, 30, 33, 36, 42
        (*see also* poets of sensibility)
    gang, 2
    "Jacobin crew," 5, 12, 33, 43,
        47–50, 61, 80 (*see also* Bristol
        coterie)
    laboring-class writers, 2, 3,
        13–17, 131–86 (*see also*
        "rural tribe")
    Lake poets, 2–3, 5, 11–12, 13,
        17, 18–19, 54, 78, 80, 132,
        166, 211, 213, 225, 227–9,
        231
    poets of sensibility, 30, 38, 100,
        108, 135–6 (*see also* Della
        Cruscans)
    "rural tribe," 1, 3 (*see also*
        laboring-class writers)
    sect, 1, 2, 5
    tribe, 1, 2–3, 43
    West Country coterie, 3, 10–11,
        13, 14, 17, 39, 132, 166,
        211 (*see also* Bristol coterie;
        Wordsworth circle)
    Wordsworth circle, 2–3, 6, 60,
        82, 108, 142 (*see also* Lake
        poets; West Country coterie)

Cottle, Joseph, 10, 24–5, 39, 40, 52, 61
"Markoff: a Siberian Eclogue," 73
Courier, The, 89
Cowper, William, 7, 9, 16, 35, 101, 126, 133, 138, 162–3, 165, 166, 167–9
"Castaway, The," 185–6
John Clare's impersonation of, 174–8, 182, 185
Task, 26–7, 29, 137, 161, 165, 167, 168, 175, 177–8, 182
"Yardley Oak," 161, 168, 169–73, 178
Cox, Jeffrey, 3
Crabb Robinson, Henry, 32
Crabbe, George, 2–3
The Village, 1
Cross, Ashley, 6, 44, 45
Cunningham, Allan, 207
Curran, Stuart, 9

Dart, Gregory, 3
Darwin, Erasmus, 15, 132, 140
The Botanic Garden, 140
Davy, Humphry, 6, 10, 40
De Quincey, Thomas, 3, 18–19, 97, 166, 213, 223–32
Confessions of an English Opium Eater, 18, 97, 223–31
degeneration of print culture, 4, 26–8, 89–90, 106–8
Della Cruscans, 30, 33, 36, 42
D'Herbelot, Barthélemy
Bibliothèque Orientale, 65
Dialect, 2, 7, 23, 24, 43, 136
Dickens, Charles
Great Expectations, 194
Dickinson, Emily, 186
Dobbs, Francis, 226
Drayton, Michael, 205
dreams and dreamworks, 12, 68, 70, 71–2, 74–5, 80, 82, 83, 87–9, 90, 94, 97, 221–2, 224–30, 231. *See also* nightmares; visions

Dryden, John, 142
Dyer, John, 15, 132, 133, 146, 153, 157
"Grongar Hill," 148, 154

early Romanticism, 9, 25, 38, 42, 58
Edinburgh Review, The, 1, 90, 91
Eliot, T. S., 2, 231
Ercilla, Don Alonso de
La Araucana, 103
Erickson, Lee, 4
Ezell, Margaret, 5

Faber, G. S., 215
Fairer, David, 9, 121
Fellowes, John, 32
feminist perspectives, 25, 30–1, 33–4, 37–9, 56–7, 117
Ferdinand VII, 110, 113
Fletcher, John, 205
Flower, Benjamin, 87, 106, 107
Foxites, 134, 135
Franta, Andrew, 4
Freud, Sigmund, 88
Fricker, Edith May, 82–3
Fricker, Mary, 82–3
Fricker, Sarah, 82–3

Gamer, Michael, 28
George III, 218, 219, 221
Georgic poetry, 133, 136–7, 139, 192
Gerrald, Joseph, 86
Gifford, William, 31, 34
Beauties of the Anti-Jacobin, The, 34
Gillray, James
"The New Morality," 43
Gilpin, William, 14, 132, 148, 151, 152, 160
Godwin, William, 33, 44
Goldsmith, Oliver
The Deserted Village, 155
Goodridge, John, 166
Gordon, Lord George, 214

gossip, 4, 17, 26–7, 90, 190–1, 199, 205, 209. *See also* name-dropping
Grafton, 3rd Duke of, 138
Gray, Thomas, 14, 50, 151, 157
"Elegy Written in a Country Churchyard," 150–1
"Ode on the Spring," 151–2
Green, J. H., 74

Hardy, Thomas, 13, 159
Hayes, Charlotte, 26
Hayley, William, 100, 103, 104, 108, 126, 168
Life and Posthumous Writings of William Cowper, The, 167
Hazlitt, William, 166, 190, 202–3, 207, 225
Liber Amoris, 97
"On Going a Journey," 203–5
"On Londoners and Country People," 203
Homer, 201, 202
Hood, Thomas, 3, 207–8, 209
Hood, Thomas (bookseller), 145
Horace, 201
Horne Tooke, John, 159
Horsley, Samuel, 215
Hunt, Henry, 159, 160
Hunt, Leigh, 1, 3, 17, 166, 190, 197, 204, 205, 207, 230
"Rustic Walk, A," 197–202
Hutchinson, Sara, 41, 74, 82, 83

imagination, 3, 16, 31–2, 68, 70–2, 126, 131–2, 139–42, 150, 153, 157, 177, 186, 191, 194, 199, 202–3, 213, 215, 220, 221–32
imagined communities, 16, 126–7, 131–2, 160–3, 165–6, 167, 186, 194, 230
Inskip, Thomas, 147
Irving, Edward, 229

James, Felicity, 9
Jeffrey, Francis, 1, 2, 78, 116
Johnson, John
"Sketch of the Life of Cowper," 168
Johnson, Samuel, 139, 155–6
Jones, William
"The Seven Fountains, an Eastern Allegory," 69–70

Kafka, Franz
The Castle, 206
Keats, John, 166, 167, 190, 197, 205
Klancher, Jon, 4
Knight, William, 6, 16, 174–5
Kövesi, Simon, 182
Kucich, Greg, 3

Ladies Monthly Museum, The, 135
Lamb, Charles, 2, 3, 9, 11, 18, 39, 40–3, 46, 61, 64, 100, 166, 190, 202, 205–11, 213, 224, 225
"Defect of Imagination in Modern Artists, The," 207, 208
"Superannuated Man, The," 206, 208
Landor, Walter Savage
Gebir, The, 73
landscape poetry, 15, 41, 132–3, 138
Las Casas, Bartolome de, 118
Lautaro, 103, 111–12, 115–21
Leask, Nigel, 8
Lee, Richard, 221
"Babylon's Fall," 217–18
King Killing, 218
Levinson, Marjorie, 81, 108
literary partnerships, 2–3, 6, 9–12, 14, 16–17, 25, 28–9, 30, 36–8, 40–1, 44, 51–2, 63–78, 82–3, 113, 143–5, 157, 166–7, 174, 186, 225. *See also* coteries

Lloyd, Charles, 2, 3, 9, 11, 39–43, 61, 64–5, 100
  "Lines addressed to S. T. Coleridge," 40–1
Lloyd Baker, Mary, 143–9, 157, 158
Lloyd Baker, Thomas John, 144–6, 158–62
Locke, John, 111
Lockhart, J. G., 1
Lofft, Capel, 14, 134–8, 141–3, 144, 149–50, 157
  Laura: or, An Anthology of Sonnets, 134
London Magazine, The, 13, 16, 18, 166–7, 189–91, 209, 213, 223–4, 225
Lovell, Robert, 10, 40, 82
Lowth, Robert, 226

MacGregor, Rob Roy, 84
MacPherson, James
  Ossian, 112
magazine essays, 3, 17–18, 189–91, 197–202, 203–9, 211, 213, 225, 231–2
Majeed, Javed, 8
Makdisi, Saree, 8
Margarot, Maurice, 86
Marlowe, Christopher, 205
Martin, John
  Belshazzar's Feast, 222–3
  The Fall of Babylon, 222–3
Martin, Philip, 182
Marx, Karl, 23
McGann, Jerome J., 108
Mee, Jon, 218
Melville, Herman
  Bartleby, the Scrivener, 206
mercantilism, 23, 25, 56, 217
Merry, Robert, 30, 33
Michaelis, Johann, 226
Mill, John Stuart, 110–11
Milton, John, 69, 155, 171, 189, 224, 229, 230–1
  Paradise Lost, 47, 231
Miranda, Francisco de, 110–11, 114

Mitford, Mary Russell, 123
Molina, Juan Ignacio
  History of Chile, 111–12, 115, 117
Montesquieu, 111
Monthly Magazine, The, 42, 45, 73, 197, 200
More, Hannah, 24, 39, 57
Morning Herald, The, 28–9
Morning Post, The, 35–9, 43–5, 47, 52, 54, 55, 58, 60, 103, 106–7
Morton, Timothy, 34
Mudie, Robert, 220, 232
Murray, John, 113

native peoples, 8, 9, 55–60, 101–27
Newlyn, Lucy, 5
newspapers, 2, 4, 17, 25, 26–9, 30, 44, 45, 54, 107–8, 166, 191, 194
Niebuhr, Carsten, 72
nightmares, 81–3, 86–91, 94. *See also* dreams; visions

Odoricus, Beatus, 72
O'Higgins, Bernando, 114, 123–5

Paine, Thomas, 32, 158
Painites, 219
Paley, Morton D., 221
Park, Thomas, 149
Patmore, Eliza, 210
Patmore, P. G., 3, 208–10
patronage, 1, 4, 14–16, 39, 131–6, 141–4, 147, 149, 150, 157, 158–60, 171
Pearce, Lynne, 174
"peasant poets," 3, 15, 131, 134, 138–42, 166
pedestrianism, 18, 153, 197, 202–6, 210–11. *See also* rambling
picturesque, the, 14, 132, 136, 144, 151, 156
Pitt, William, 34, 47–8
Pizarro, Francisco, 104

Poe, Edgar Allan, 231
Poole, Thomas, 61
Pope, Alexander, 15, 132
   The Dunciad, 190
Porteous, Beilby, 159
Pratt, Lynda, 9, 116
Price, Richard, 215–16, 221, 222
Price, Uvedale, 132
Priestley, Joseph, 214–15
Prince of Wales, 33
prophecy, 16, 17, 18–19, 67–8, 166,
     174, 175, 179–82, 213–27,
     229–30, 231–2
Purchas, Samuel, 72
   Purchas His Pilgrimage, 74

Quarterly Review, The, 122

Radstock, Lord, 143
rambling, 17–18, 190–1, 194,
     196–203, 205, 208, 210–11,
     231–2. *See also* pedestrianism
Randall, Jack, 162
Recitation, 1–2, 6, 69, 89, 107–8,
     112–13, 159–62
Rickman, Thomas Clio, 219
Rippingille, Edward, 166
Robertson, William, 111
Robinson, Mary, 3, 5–6, 8, 9–10,
     17, 25, 28–39, 42, 43–6, 47,
     51–61, 100, 108, 135
   Angelina, 34
   "Anselmo, the Hermit of the
     Alps," 45
   "Elegy Written in a London
     Church Yard, An," 50–1
   "Haunted Beach, The," 10, 44–7,
     50–5
   "Jasper," 44–5
   "Lascar, The," 55, 57–60
   *Letter to the Women of England,
     A*, 33–4
   Lyrical Tales, 10, 36, 54–5, 60
   "Negro Girl, The," 55–7
   "Ode, Inscribed to the Infant
     Son of S. T. Coleridge," 60

   "Ode to the Snow Drop," 37–8,
     45
   "Sappho and Phaon," 37
   "Storm, The," 55
   Walsingham, 33, 36, 52
Robinson, Terry, 28
Rogers, Samuel, 112, 149
   Pleasures of Memory, The, 149
   Voyage of Columbus, 113
Romantic Orientalism, 8, 11, 63,
     65–75, 77–8, 99
ruralism, 3, 13, 18, 106–7, 111–12,
     133, 143–4, 159–62, 190,
     194, 196, 208, 211, 213,
     214, 225, 226–8, 230,
     231–2

Said, Edward, 8, 71–2, 75
Sale, George, 65
San Martín, Jose de, 110, 114, 123
Schelling, Friedrich Wilhelm
     Joseph, 74, 189
Schlegel, August Wilhelm, 74
Schneider, Elizabeth, 73
Scott, John, 207
Scott, Walter, 6, 12, 90, 134, 157
   Lay of the Last Minstrel, The, 96
   Vision of Don Roderick, The, 99
Scrivener, Michael, 219
Seward, Anna, 116, 135
Shakespeare, William, 48, 137, 165,
     199, 202, 205, 230–1
   Hamlet, 137
   King Lear, 231
   Macbeth, 47
   Much Ado about Nothing, 31
   Troilus and Criseyede, 202
Sharp, Granville, 143
Sharp family, 143–50, 157, 159
Shelley, Percy Bysshe, 164, 198–9
Sheridan, Richard Brinsley, 126
   Pizzaro, 104–7
Sherive, C. H.
   "On leaving Bristol Wells," 51
Smith, Charlotte, 43, 135
Southcott, Joanna, 221–3

Southey, Edith May, 82–3
Southey, Margaret, 85
Southey, Robert, 1, 2–3, 4–7, 8, 9,
    10–13, 24–5, 32, 34–45,
    49–61, 63–78, 80, 82–3,
    85–6, 90, 100–9, 111–13,
    125, 126, 157, 160, 163,
    166, 167, 191
  Annual Anthology, The, 10, 25,
    40, 44–52, 54, 55, 58, 61,
    63, 73
  "Battle of Blenheim, The," 10,
    48–50
  "Botany Bay Eclogues," 117,
    119–20
  Fall of Robespierre, The, 66
  "History," 58
  "Humphrey and William,"
    119–20
  "Huron's Address to the Dead,
    The," 103
  "Jasper," 44
  Joan of Arc, 66
  "John, Samuel and Richard," 117
  Madoc, 13, 100, 115–17, 121–3
  "Mary, Maid of the Inn," 64
  "Mohammed," 11, 65–8, 70–2,
    75, 77
  National Songs, 13, 103–9,
    116–17, 126
  "Old Chikkasah to his
    Grandson," 103
  "Poor Mary," 117
  "Sailor who Had Served in the
    Slave Trade," 52–4, 55
  "Song of the Araucans During
    a Thunder Storm," 103,
    105–8, 117
  Tale of Paraguay, 123
  Thalaba the Destroyer, 1, 13, 65,
    67–78
speech, 23–4, 93–6, 102, 104, 108,
    126, 136, 166, 169–73, 178,
    186, 198–9, 204–5. See also
    conversation; gossip
speech communities, 2, 168, 171

Spence, Thomas
  "Jubilee Hymn," 218–19
Spenser, Edmund, 69, 75, 76
Stevenson, Robert Louis, 231
Stillinger, Jack, 5
Stuart, Daniel, 35, 44
Swedenborgians, 214

Tacitus, 103
Taylor, John, 16, 17, 143, 167, 169,
    174
Taylor, William, 73
Terry, Garnett, 218–19
Thelwall, John, 24, 32
Theocritus, 201
Thompson, E. P., 32
Thomson, James, 133
  Seasons, The, 136
  "Summer," 136
tourism, 6, 11, 15, 132–3, 144–6,
    147–8, 150–3, 156–7, 194
Treason trials, 23–4, 31–2, 159,
    219, 221

Valdivia, Pedro Gutiérrez de, 103,
    112–13, 115
Verdugo, José Miguel Carrera, 114
Vernor, Thomas, 145
Virgil, 58–9, 151
visions, 12, 16, 18, 32, 66, 80,
    88, 90–1, 92–4, 97, 99,
    178–82, 215, 220–32. See
    also dreams; nightmares;
    prophecy

Wadström, Carl Bernhard, 219
Wakefield, Gilbert, 87, 106, 107
Walton, Isaac, 207, 208
Watson, Richard, 159
Wedgwood family, 39
Wellesley, Arthur, 110
Wesley brothers, 140–1
Weston, Joseph, 147
Wilberforce, William, 122
Williams, Helena Maria, 100, 108
Wolfson, Susan, 5

Wollstonecraft, Mary, 33–4, 35, 39, 43, 56
Wordsworth, Dorothy, 5, 6, 11, 82, 83, 84, 86–7, 108, 152, 199
Wordsworth, Mary, 82
Wordsworth, William, 2–3, 4, 5–6, 9, 10, 11–12, 18–19, 46–7, 54, 57–8, 60, 63, 64–5, 71, 73, 74, 78, 79–90, 100, 107, 111, 121, 133, 163, 166, 167, 170, 191, 194, 207, 213, 214, 225–31
    "Complaint of the Forsaken Indian Woman, The," 55, 108
    "Ellen Irwin, or, the Braes of Kirtle," 160
    Excursion, The, 125–7, 189, 225–8, 229
    "Female Vagrant," 57
    "Goody Blake and Harry Gill," 160
    "Last of the Flock," 85
    Lyrical Ballads, 6, 10, 13, 25, 54, 60, 108, 132–3, 137, 153, 160, 168 (*see also individual poems*)
    "Mad Mother," 119
    "Ode: Intimations of Immortality," 12
    Poems in Two Volumes, 6
    Preface to *Lyrical Ballads*, 2, 16, 25, 133, 160, 196
    Prelude, The, 17, 26, 58, 194, 220, 225, 226
    "Ruth," 57
    Salisbury Plain poems, 139
    "Solitude of Binnorie," 54
    "Song at the Feast of Brougham Castle," 160
    "Thorn, The," 160
    "Tintern Abbey," 14–15, 59, 81, 133, 139, 142, 150, 152–3, 157, 199
    "Yew Trees," 161
Wright, John, 219
Wroe, John, 222

Yearsley, Ann, 24, 39, 57
York, Prince Frederick, Duke of, 50
Young, Edward, 140
    Night Thoughts, 141

Lightning Source UK Ltd.
Milton Keynes UK
UKOW06n1632040915

258019UK00006BB/50/P